M000290052

THE SOUTHERN FOREST

THE
SOUTHERN
FOREST

A Chronicle

LAURENCE C. WALKER

University of Texas Press, Austin

Copyright © 1991 by the University of Texas Press
All rights reserved
Printed in the United States of America

First edition, 1991

Requests for permission to reproduce material from this work should be sent to Permissions, University of Texas Press, Box 7819, Austin, TX 78713-7819.

∞ The paper used in this publication meets the minimum requirements of American National Standard for Information Sciences—Permanence of Paper for Printed Library Materials, ANSI Z39.48-1984.

Library of Congress Cataloging-in-Publication Data

Walker, Laurence C., (date)
    The southern forest : a chronicle / Laurence C. Walker. — 1st ed.
      p.   cm.
    Includes bibliographical references and index.
    ISBN 0-292-77648-9 (alk. paper)
    1. Forests and forestry—Southern States—History.   2. Foresters—Southern States—History.   3. Logging—Southern States—History.   4. Forest products industry—Southern States—History.   5. Forest ecology—Southern States.   6. Shipbuilding—Southern States—History.   I. Title.
SD144.A15W35   1991
634.9'0975—dc20   91-14285
                                                  CIP

Jacket photo © 1990 by Jess Alford

To Anne,
who promised to live
in the woods—
even in a firetower—
and who has shared
my life
in the southern forest

Contents

Photographs and Drawings

Maps

Preface

ORE THAN forty years of practicing forestry in the South provided a lot of experiences that I wanted to pass along. Others encouraged me to do so. Before I came to work in and to study the southern woods, explorers, pioneers, and lumbermen had quite literally left their marks on the region. Understanding the significance of those blazes in the forest appeared to me to be essential to appropriately manage the woodlands today and to suggest trends for the future husbanding of these renewable natural resources.

The experiences of one person's career, of course, tell but a little of what has occurred during that period. It is but a sample; and as foresters deal daily with sampling theory, I am well aware of the limitations. So it is that I am indebted to hundreds of fellow foresters, wood-using industrialists, academic colleagues, and former students who, over the years, have contributed to my grasp of Dixie's lands and people. We have labored together in the woods, at the laboratory bench, in the statistical analysis room, and around the seminar table. Always the interest of these friends has been altruistic, always to prepare for the laborers who must follow, always to provide wood and wooded landscapes for future citizens of the South to utilize or to enjoy. I shall forever be grateful to these fellow sojourners—the contributions of many of them no doubt unknown to themselves—who have guided me along the way. I recall their words, their example, and their occasional disagreements with me that have enlivened my career as a professional forester.

My career has brought no regrets, spanning as it has the dramatic rise of the forestry profession immediately following the Second World War to the present reduction in the roster of foresters. The decline, so prevalent as I write, relates to the difficulties now experienced in the timber industry for which many serve as journeymen and to budget trimming by governments that employ many more.

Chapters 1 through 5 deal principally with history, but it is not "pure" history. The author's personal experiences and his own interpretation and speculation about the significance of events occurring in particular periods have been intentionally woven into the text's fabric. The final chapter, 6, is not solely a collection of the writer's predictions. Many ideas came about through participating in foresters' never-ending informal group discussions, listening to formal presentations, and reading contemporary material as well as from gut feelings. Thus, these lines are not *the* story of the southern forest; they are *one* story that I hope will be helpful to readers within and outside of the forestry profession.

Some colleagues deserve especial mention for a list of reasons too long to elaborate: John E. Johnson, Ivan J. Nicholas, Ab Smith, Thomas Croker, and Dr. William Campbell, all of the U.S. Forest Service; Professor Donald P. White, Dean Hardy Shirley, and the late Dean Svend O. Heiberg of the New York State College of Forestry; Professor Harold J. Lutz and Professor David M. Smith of Yale University; and Donald Young of the Texas Forest Service. I express my appreciation too to my fellow faculty members over the years at Stephen F. Austin State University (SFASU) for encouraging me to tell this story.

Chapters of this volume have been critiqued by Bruce Miles, Dr. Hans van Buijtenen, Edwin Barron, and Donald Young, all of the Texas Forest Service; James Webster of the Kirby Lumber Company; Ron Hufford, Texas Forestry Association; Roger Dennington, U.S. Forest Service; and Macky McClung, Kathryn Duncan, James Meeker, James Mitchell, and Stephen Rockwood, graduate students at SFASU. Dr. Robert Maxwell, my colleague and late Regents' Professor of History and Adjunct Professor of Forest History at SFASU, reviewed the entire manuscript. Although these others assisted me, please fault me alone for any errors.

I thank Jamie Taylor, Michele Allen, Melinda Escude, Sheila Wilhite, and Stacy Shaw, typists who patiently and pleasantly transcribed the scribbles of an arthritic hand. Dr. Kent T. Adair, my successor as dean of the School of Forestry at Stephen F. Austin State University, encouraged this endeavor. And to Beth W. Allen, editor extraordinary, my grateful thanks for patient attention to detail.

L.C.W.
Nacogdoches, Texas

THE SOUTHERN FOREST

CHAPTER 1

The Explorers' Forest

REAT FORESTS of large loblolly pines, laced with fingers of hardwood trees astride the rivers, faced the hardy English subjects as they stepped from settlers' boats. The shores of Jamestown, Charleston, and Savannah, cities later to be hewn from those forests, are the sites of these debarkations. The years were 1607, 1608, and 1733, respectively. Exploration of the southern forest at these coastal vantage points then began. The pine trees, unnamed when first observed by European explorers, shortly thereafter would be called *loblolly*—from English dialect meaning a thick gruel—*pines*. The tall timbers were so named because the ground from which they emerged appeared as murky as the thick gruel fed the pioneering travelers on the wooden vessels of the sea.

Exploration Precedes Exploitation

The Reverend Francis Higginson, in 1630, glimpsed the southern forest and its potential to supply the needs of society. In it he found "foure sorts of oke, . . . ash, elme, willow, birch, beech, saxafras, juniper, cipres, cedar, spruce, pine, [and] firre" that would "yield an abundance of turpentine."[1]

Earlier, sometime around 1513, Juan Ponce de León trooped his explorers over the ridges and through the bottomlands of these

---

Note: Currently used common and scientific names for trees of the southern forest are listed in Appendix B. Scientific names are given in the text only if necessary for clarity or relevance to the narrative.

Virgin longleaf pine in Deep East Texas. These extraordinary stands perhaps measured one hundred thousand board feet per acre. (Courtesy Steen Library Archives, Stephen F. Austin State University, Nacogdoches, Tex.)

Coastal Plain forests. They sought the Fountain of Youth and, more probably, new lands not yet controlled by the sons of Columbus and his Spanish financiers. Through the slash pine forests of *La Florida's* flatwoods, Ponce de León staked out land for the Spanish throne. The center of the territory's peninsula in the geologic past had been formed by the deposition of coarse sediments washed from the north. Now sand pine covered the land in dense, even-aged stands of slender stems. Those Iberian sojourners drank of Florida's abundant water as it seeped into springs well-filtered by the zone's silicate sands. But would "the water thereof being drank . . . mak[e] owld men yonge agayne"?[2] Ponce de León and his sailors never reported finding the fountain that could truly restore one's youth.

　　Game and other wildlife were abundant in these woods. Deer were considered the bison of the Southeastern forest, though John Lawson, a naturalist of the period reported the presence of buffaloes and elks. Before long, the conquistadors' horses and cattle would roam free to establish feral herds.

　　Red-cockaded woodpeckers—now listed by the U.S. Fish and Wildlife Service as a threatened species—made their homes in hollows of living pines, provided the trees had a soft interior caused by red heartrot. It often is said the red-cockaded woodpecker is the only woodpecker to carve its nests in living trees, though flickers may nest in living boles. These southern forests were habitat, too, for other now-threatened or extinct species. Families of ivory-billed woodpeckers claimed territory. The largest of North American woodpeckers, the ivory-billed woodpecker is probably now extinct except for the possible survival of a few pairs in the mountains of Cuba. In the explorers' forest, where civilized humans had never intruded, the required half million–acre unbroken tracts of pines and hardwoods provided adequate habitat and food for the ivory-bills' far-ranging ventures. Here, too, "turkies" abounded, and Cabeza de Vaca noted among the wild beasts "an Animal with a pocket in its belly."[3]

De Soto's Ventures

　　Then came Hernando de Soto. With six hundred men in about 1539, he set about charting the lands, and thus the forests, of the New World for Spain. His exploring party covered a territory that now makes up six southern states. Those explorers no doubt observed the vast longleaf pine forests of the lower Gulf Coastal Plain. The use of these timbers for ship masts would engage a seaman's fancy. The ceaseless wind in the crowns, sounding like waves breaking on a distant shore, may have reminded him of this use.

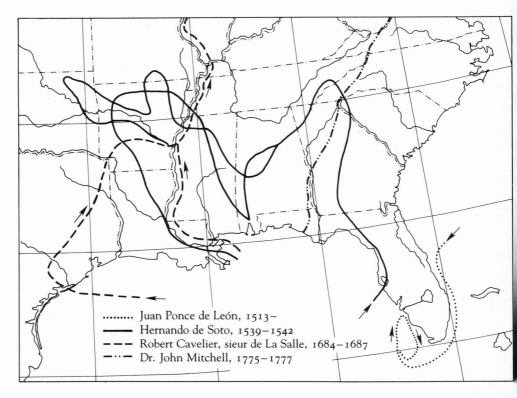

Map 1. Likely approximate routes of the explorers through the present southern United States. Adapted from J. L. Clark, ed., Denoyer-Geppert Co. map series (Chicago, 1936); *The World Book Encyclopedia* (Field Enterprises, 1959); and Edmund Berkeley and Dorothy Berkeley, *Dr. John Mitchell* (Chapel Hill: University of North Carolina Press, 1974).

Lightning-caused fires and burning by the American Indian had occurred in these woods. As we shall see, fires prepare seedbeds to receive seed for germination; they control seedling disease, limit the extent of brush that competes for soil moisture and nutrients, and release seed-producing trees from their competitors. Ecological relationships are especially obvious for this species.

But fire in the days of de Soto's ventures would also play a role in maintaining habitat for many kinds of wildlife. Quail, turkeys, and white-tailed deer, especially of value to people for food, foraged and browsed among the stems in stands burned at various periods. The amount of overstory and understory depend on the time lapsed since the woods were last burned. As the birds depended upon insects and the white-tails upon succulent woody browse for food, fires affected the abundance of both during various periods. De Soto also noted no limit to the fish as he trooped from swamp to swamp. And cabbage from the low palmetto on the islands provided food.[4]

While writers about natural resources in the present environmental age often dwell upon the Indians' so-called balanced ecological system, at least one noted historian of the region entered a partial dissent: "The southeastern Indians were . . . evolving complex cultures, . . . not part of a balanced self-maintaining system. Like the whites and blacks of a later day, they pressed against the land's resources and reshaped its forms in lines with their own desires."[5] The same historian reports that in the early 1600s, sailors smelled smoke as they sought docking sites off Virginia's shore, and that one wrote, "The land was smelt before it was seen."[6]

Spruce pine trees (at first glance appearing to be a member of the *Picea* genus in which are cataloged spruce trees, but then quickly noted to be a *Pinus*) were found in the slightly lower and thus damper sites surrounding the higher, drier islands of longleaf pine through which the explorers tramped. The straight and tall stems of the spruce pine, with little taper, would catch their eyes, but not likely would they see them west of the Mississippi River.[7]

En route to the longleaf pines, whose deep tap roots provide support against the ravages of wind in the open, parklike forests, de Soto encountered the squatty, but rugged live oaks. Perhaps he noted, as others later did, that these trees with broad buttresses could provide tough timber for warships. In time, the broadleaf evergreen was so used, and even before Florida was declared a state, forests of live oaks were set aside for that purpose in United States' Reserves. There, experiments, initiated in 1817, were to assure the permanence of trees that could be used for battle boats and for the fleets of commerce. Reserves were later established, in 1820 and 1827, by Congress in Alabama and Louisiana. Lumber for the U.S. frigate *Constitution,* the Boston-built ship nicknamed "Old Ironsides," famous for its ability to repel the shots that cannonaded broadside, came from the live oaks of the southern forest. Rot-resistant eastern redcedars from Georgia helped form its superstructure, and caulking of oakum from longleaf pine resin sealed its pores and cracks. But we do not know if de Soto cared about or evaluated the commercial potential of the many species of trees in these woods. Though de Soto brought Europeans to these shores, it was an English father and son whose early scientific expeditions sought to calculate not their economic potential but their plant and animal wealth.

Botanists for the Crown

William Bartram, exploring chronicler, was the son of Crown Botanist John Bartram of Philadelphia. In the year 1773, the younger Bartram departed by horse from Charleston, exchanged his mount for a canoe, and then plodded on foot, alone and with others, to tally the vegetation of the New World. One must not neglect the doxology with which his book begins its description of "this world, as a glorious apartment of the boundless palace of the Sovereign Creator," exhibiting "a more glorious display of the Almighty Hand." Those phrases attest to the Quaker's faith, which seems to have imparted to him a unique appreciation of the plant kingdom of the southern forest.[8]

After departing the southeastern oceanside city, Bartram encountered in the Coastal Plain an infertile sandy soil, except where seashells had been carried by Indians to lime the soil. Where "dissolved vegetables," the organic matter, were mixed in the fine white sand, the soil served "as a nursery bed to hatch . . . the infant plant." The subsoil was the color of ashes—"cinerous," he called it, and "tenacious." This grayish, highly reduced subsoil of sticky structure gave rise, according to his account, to a "vast growth of timber."[9]

Trees that attracted the naturalist's attention on the Coastal Plain included loblolly pine, the tall timbers in the gruel. Pitch and broom pines were also in abundance. These were most likely what we now popularly call slash pine and longleaf pine, though the latter is also referred to in Bartram's *Travels* as "long-leaved" pine. Bartram's *Pinus lutea* and *P. squarrosa* also give modern taxonomists some difficulty. Perhaps the first is slash pine or, as Sargent suggests, longleaf pine.[10] (In analyzing the explorers' forest, problems with nomenclature are to be expected. Even today's trained and experienced observers may have difficulty establishing identities of some species of trees because of variations in appearance. These could be due to hybridization, variation in site quality, density of the stand, and age of the trees.) Along with the pines were plains of dwarf prickly fan-leaved palmetto and "lawns" of grass. Groves of magnolia and clumps of water oak, considered evergreen by Bartram (he elsewhere refers to the "evergreen" live oak), were interspersed with the forests of pines and other hardwoods.

Among the lesser vegetation singled out in the explorer's eighteenth-century trek is a lupine, which was then called *Lupinus villosus*. Its pale green leaves contrast with its flowers of celestial blue or milk white, the flower petals gleaming against the shrubby backdrop in the sandy highlands. This "lady lupin," as Bartram called it, is still seen along the post road southeast of Waynesville, Georgia, about where it is believed Bartram mapped it. Why the ancients believed that the lupine legume, with its nitrogen-fixing capacity, destroys soil is a mystery. But they did so suppose, as evidenced by the name they gave the plant. *Lupine* is from *lupus,* or wolf, the destroyer.

The farmer-Quaker Bartram team of father and son had earlier trekked inland in the South in 1765. In a palmetto-lined swamp they discovered a small tree resembling a bay, its gold-centered white flower catching the eye, first by John, the older of the botanical geniuses, and then by William. In honor of their friend and supporter, Benjamin Franklin, they called it *Franklinia alatamaha.*[11]

The species is not misspelled. Early maps show the present Altamaha River, for which one may suppose the species of the plant is named, spelled with the additional *a.* The river forms the south boundary of McIntosh County, the locale of the last observations of the tree, in 1803.[12] Last, that is, until the late G. Norman Bishop, a dendrology professor at the University of Georgia's School of Forestry, found the tree in the 1950s. Lost again except in cultivation, this member of the Theaceae family is one of ninety possibly extinct wilderness plants in the lower forty-eight continental United States. It may turn up again, as did the round-leaf birch, originally discovered in Virginia, only to be promptly forgotten until "small populations" were again found in Old Dominion in 1975.[13]

Although another seven plants of the southern forest are believed to be extinct, to my knowledge no other tree is in this category. Those listed as currently endangered or threatened, numbering in the hundreds, were probably never abundant.[14]

Along the Altamaha, too, the Bartrams found tupelo and named it *Nyssa sylvatica.*[15] Perhaps no tree in the South spells autumn as colorfully as this "gum," with its variations in orange and crimson hues against a backdrop of black water.

Working the soil were pocket gophers of the genus *Geomys*. Bartram, I believe mistakenly, attributed the "little mounds or hillocks of fresh earth thrown up in great numbers in the night" to a large land tortoise, rather than to the nocturnal rodent. There *is* a gopher tortoise, but not the maker of these "dens or caverns dug in sandhills." Yet the observer was at the time probably the first in the New World to refer to the genus *Geomys*, the rodent he described as "the ground rat." Larger mammals seen by the Pennsylvanian were "roebuck" and "tyger," along with wolves, raccoons, foxes, hares, and wildcats. The "roebuck" is of course the white-tailed deer and the "tyger," not so obviously, is the panther. Bear, of the black variety, were abundant, providing explorers with both meat and fur clothing.[16]

Birds recorded by these temporary sojourners included the wild pigeon. This is the now-extinct passenger pigeon. It must have been ubiquitous. And the social nighthawk's shrill cries must have kept the lone travelers on edge while trying to rest on their pallets in the Indian-inhabited woods.

Other Participants in the Ventures

Financed by Lord Petre and others of the Old Country, John and William carried out their own instructions, directions they gave to John Tradescant, another early plant collector. Specimens were to be laid between leaves in a book. These were sometimes sent abroad for scientific naming with Latin binomials by another father-and-son team, the world-famous Linnaeuses of Sweden.

While the Bartrams' principal assignment in the deep coastal south was to bring the plants of the area to their home in Philadelphia to grow in gardens for beauty and for medicines, William Bartram also put pen and brush to paper.[17] Among his paintings are an "alegator," the so-called seadragon of the St. John's River in northeastern Florida; a great golden speckled bream of fresh-water drainages along the Atlantic seaboard; an unnamed hummingbird on the North Carolina coast; a coachwhip snake found in eastern Florida; and pitcher plants nearby.[18]

Near present-day Pensacola, Bartram found the hooded pitcher plant. Alas, it seems to be no longer in that vicinity. Venus's-flytrap, another insectivorous plant, however, is still found—as it was then—in the wet pine barrens of coastal Carolina. *Ilex vomitoria*, the yaupon shrub, was recorded in east Georgia, perhaps near, or on, the Fall Line of deep sand hills. Not there now, it is supposed that Indians had introduced the plant to a small locale, cultivating it for medicinal purposes.[19]

Along the streams grew river birch, its bark appearing like poorly glued paper torn from an old wall; the thin-crowned water tupelo; and ironwood that looks as though its bark is a thin skin stretched over muscular arms. Mistletoe clung to the branches of many smooth-barked trees while fermenting wild black cherry fruit attracted a multitude of insects. Tenuous grapevines provided fruit in season for weary sojourners, as did many other plants of the southern forest.[20]

Observant exploring travelers spotted petrified trees near the Carolina coast. They did not identify the species. In the 1950s, my students and I observed a log partially submerged in a mucky bottomland of the Savannah River, north of Augusta, Georgia. The section of bole was silicaceous, like the sand of the seashore, and could be cut only with diamond-toothed gravestone-shaping tools. The twelve-inch-diameter "tree" was a palm, retrieved beyond the natural range in which such tree-like monocots grow today. How far back in geologic time would explorers have needed to trek these woods to find the palm tree living in this vicinity? One may only speculate.

The Lowland Trek

Coastal Swamps

We now must backtrack in time, visiting some swamps along the way. The Dismal, near the Virginia-North Carolina coast; the Okefenokee, made famous by Stephen Foster's "Sewanee River" (*Suwannee* is the correct spelling); and the Everglades of Florida's tip all received attention by the explorers. All are near sea level, as low as three feet in elevation, and bordering a tidal marsh. Dominant in each of the forests of these gigantic sloughs, in the order named above, are Atlantic white-cedar, its occurrence depending upon the microrelief of the swamps for seed germination and seedling survival; southern baldcypress, whose skirt flares and whose roots have appendages that rise above the water; and the subtropical forest of mangrove that forms dense tangles of aerial roots.

Bartram, in his travels of the Revolutionary War period, skirted the swamps, unable to penetrate their interior. His observation at the periphery and the comments of his later editors provide some insight into the forests of those times and climes. Of the Okefenokee Swamp, on what is now the eastern border of the Georgia and Florida boundary, the botanist understood its name to be derived from a Hitchiti dialect of the Muskhogean tongue and to mean "trembling water."[21] This, of course, would be an unlikely description for the natural impoundment of a shal-

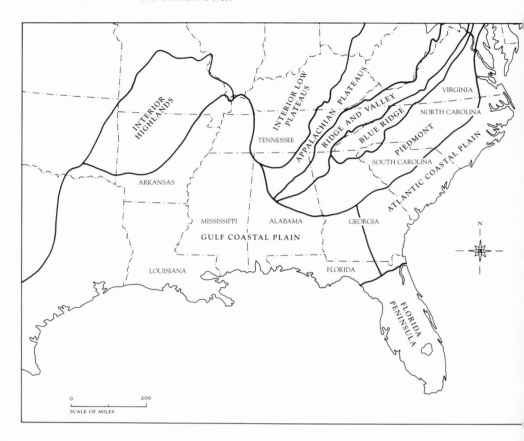

Map 2. Physical divisions of the southeastern United States. Adapted from National Atlas sheet 59, Geological Survey, U.S. Department of the Interior, 1969.

low, slow-moving water course. More correctly it means trembling earth and probably stems from a Creek Nation description of the place: Ikanfinoka. Indeed the land there does tremble. Jump up and down, and several rods away large baldcypress trees may shake as if blown by a moderate wind.

A few European inhabitants already subsisted in these southern woods when Bartram explored the land. With assistance from them and from the indigenous people, he saw and recorded that a third of the lower Coastal Plain of the Atlantic side of the South is swamp. The rivers from the plain flowed salty near the confluence with the ocean, he noted, because of the influence of the tides. The upper soil of the swamps was black, soapy, and rich. Sometimes Bartram found a "stiff mud," two to three feet deep, resting on calcareous fossils of white marl. Lime sinks, now as then, were often encountered. On the higher knolls of this boggy ground were found, and described as beautiful, the clumps of azaleas, the canes of *Arundo gigantea*, the woody vines of *Bignonia*, and species of the *Smilax* vine we now call greenbriar. Bartram was justified in lumping together the many species of *Smilax*, for classifying the greenbriars calls for patience unyielding.[22]

The *Bignonia* vine that he found climbing tall trees and exhibiting a showy flower is in the trumpet-creeper family. This species we now call cross vine. Cutting through the woody stem reveals a cross. *Arundo*, no longer listed in the botanical manuals, is an ancient name for a giant reed now cultivated as a long-leaved ornamental in the South that tends to escape northward.[23] But, if Bartram was an explorer botanist and the years are the mid-1770s, how did a large perennial grass that Gray states was introduced from the Mediterranean region already become so well entrenched on the high knolls within the swamps of the southeastern coast? It is a question for historical ecologists to ponder.

Other forests, perhaps missed by the first explorers of the continent's treasures, were the pond pines of the wet-site pocosins in North Carolina. Or perhaps the chain of swamps (of which Bartram wrote) that extend into the Carolinas included the pocosins. These wet sites—the word *pocosin* is Indian for "swamp on a hill"—along the coast almost always appear from the air as elliptical bays roughly lying in a southwesterly and northeasterly direction. Some believe they developed from showers of meteorites, blasting out the earth as though they were giant bombs dropped from military aircraft. Subsequently filled with organic debris, these pocosins serve as habitat for the short-lived pond pine tree dependent upon fire for its regeneration. Pond pine cones containing viable seed remain closed and clinging to the tree, resin sealing the scales, for perhaps a decade or two. In time, the pocosin dries out. Fires then race at

nature's randomly selected intervals across the swamp of tinderlike material. The rising heat melts the resin in the cones high in the trees so that
shortly the scales unfold to release the winged seed.

Marshes, too, were encountered along the coasts of both the
Atlantic Ocean and the Gulf of Mexico. These morasses, populated with
reptiles and with malaria-transmitting mosquitoes, along with other
pesky insects, were often obstacles to further exploration of the forests
thereabouts.

To Florida

Bartram ventured into the Florida peninsula from his base
camp at Charleston. Florida was initially the name only for the area surrounding the inlet at St. Augustine.[24] Soon, however, the explorers appropriated the name Florida for the appendage to the mainland. Flora was
the Roman goddess of flowers. The showy hibiscus in the marshes, yellow
cactuslike prickly pear on drier sands, and the yellow and red fruit of the
mayapple were reason enough for the descriptive title given to the lands
of the south-pointing finger.

The name was probably given the area by its discoverer, Ponce
de León, in 1513. One writer attributed the title to the timing of that
event: "They named it La Florida, because it had a very pretty view of
many and cool woodlands . . . in the time of the Flowery Festival."[25] The
Feast of Flowers occurred shortly after Easter in that year. Here, as further
northward, coastal forests into which explorers roamed were dark and
labyrinthine. Great live oaks, as much as eighteen feet in girth, twenty
feet to the lowermost branches, and fifty "paces" from base to crown periphery, overtopped sweet bay and holly trees. The latter were often mistaken for English holly, now grown in plantations for Yule decorations.[26]

Rivers of Florida

Long mosses, now called Spanish or black moss, appearing as
fifteen- to twenty-foot streamers waving in the wind, clung to the
branches of the oaks, the southern baldcypress, and other species. Strong
winds of hurricane force, often occurring in this clime, tore off the strands
and mounded them in piles upon the ground. Bartram called this
Tillandsia moss a parasite. It is, however, an epiphyte, a nonparasitic
plant growing on another plant but deriving its nutrients and moisture
from the air. Spanish moss is a member of the pineapple family and is
found almost exclusively in tropical and subtropical climates. Early reports noted that deer ate the moss. When dried and with the exterior

coating removed, threads of the Spanish moss were woven into ropes and, perhaps even in that period, used to stuff furniture.[27] An exhausted explorer would appreciate a mattress of the spongy, soft fiber.

The name *Tillandsia*, implying disdain of the species for water, was Linnaeus's error, according to Gray. Tilland, by another name, was a seventeenth-century professor in Turkey. In his youth, he became so seasick on a trip in the Gulf of Bothnia that he returned to his Scandinavian home in Stockholm by walking more than one thousand miles around the water's edge. From that time on, he would be called Tilland, meaning "by land" in the Swedish tongue. This title was subsequently given to species that dislike water. Thus, the genus into which Spanish moss is classified got its name.[28]

Interspersed among the live oaks were orange trees, palms, laurels, groves of myrtles, and southern baldcypresses. Bartram found the Indians extracting oil from the oak acorns for food and also eating the meat in them. Of the baldcypress trees, he noted how their trunks narrow as they rise from water two to three feet deep. The buttressed stem reminded him of the architect's pilaster, the column supporting a ceiling or roof. Perhaps it is an error or perhaps the water was extraordinarily deep during the botanist's visit, but he found the knees, described as cones, but four to six inches high. The orange trees he observed already had been established as groves from introductions by the Spanish.[29]

Along the river courses, such as the St. Mary's in Florida, the magnolia tree reached upward to one hundred feet, its trunk erect, the column "beautiful," and the wood, though not a hard hardwood, somewhat harder than that of poplar (perhaps yellow-poplar or cottonwood). Grapevines, with mainstems twelve inches in diameter, produced "ill-tasting" fruit that hung from massive branches. In this forest too was a tree we now call Hercules'-club. Bartram described it as a beautiful spreading tree and the source of food for the turtledove.[30] The spiny (thus *Hercules'* club), small tree exhibits peculiar pyramid-shaped growths of corky fiber protruding an inch from its bole. Because Indians and pioneers chewed on its smooth gray bark as a remedy for a toothache, dendrology books today may call it "the toothache tree." Back from the rivers and interspersed within the deciduous forests are the salt plains. These apparently were skirted by the roaming agents of crown and empire. Sedges, rush grasses, and other saline-loving plants broke the monotony of these morasses.

Unvaried landscapes on the drier sites free of salt were also broken by dense growth of Adam's needle. The pointed fronds of this member of the *Yucca* genus were so thick that "a rat or bird could scarcely pass" among them. Those who followed the explorers blamed them for its

A remnant of a virgin stand of slash pine in South Florida. The trees were used locally for shanties through the 1940s. (Photograph of Corkscrew Swamp Sanctuary by Max Hunn. From National Audubon Society.)

presence, naming it "Spanish bayonet." Bartram called the royal palmetto a tree because of its size, yet he recognized it as an herb crowned with a beautiful chaplet of daggerlike leaves.[31] More accurately, as Gray reminds, the showy flowers rise to four or more feet above the leaves on a tall stalk. More widely dispersed than the tree palmetto is the saw-palmetto. Hugging the ground in the coastal forest, this knee- to head-high shrub is a dispassionate stabber. Barefoot workers in days gone by received their share of wounds to their feet and legs, sometimes encountering infection that led to blood poisoning.[32]

Explorers did not need to remain long in Florida, especially in the barrier islands, to recognize the continual alteration of coastal lands by strong winds. Hurricanes redrew the contours even while conquistadors sought riches. Subtropical vegetation, like mangrove woodlands, were periodically devastated, bird rookeries destroyed, and pines among the dry debris set afire. While many such storms occurred along both the Gulf and Atlantic shores, explorers found them less severe than in the lower peninsula of Florida and still less damaging along the Atlantic than the Gulf coast.

Encounters with Reptiles

The animal life of the Florida peninsula fascinated exploring travelers. Bartram recounts an exciting skirmish with alligators. The story of his intrusion into the habitat of the reptiles is best told in his own words.

> The verges and islets of the lagoon were elegantly embellished with flowering plants and shrubs; the laughing coots with wings half spread were tripping over the little coves, and hiding themselves in the tufts of grass; young broods of the painted summer teal, skimming the still surface of the waters, and following the watchful parent unconscious of danger, were frequently surprised by the voracious trout; and he, in turn, as often by the subtle greedy alligator. Behold him rushing forth from the flags and reeds. His enormous body swells. His plaited tail brandished high, floats upon the lake. Clouds of smoke issue from his dilated nostrils. The earth trembles with his thunder. When immediately from the opposite coast of the lagoon, emerges from the deep his rival champion. They suddenly dart upon each other. The boiling surface of the lake marks their rapid course, and a terrific conflict commences. They now sink to the bottom folded together in horrid wreaths. The water becomes thick and discoloured. Again they rise, their jaws clap together, re-echoing through the deep surrounding forests. Again they sink, when the contest ends at the muddy bottom of the lake, and the vanquished makes a hazardous escape, hiding himself in the muddy turbulent waters and sedge on a distant shore. The proud victor exulting returns to the place of action. The shores and forests resound his dreadful roar, together with the triumphing shouts of the plaited tribes around, witnesses of the horrid combat.[33]

Seminoles who called Bartram Puc-Puggy, meaning flower hunter, prevailed upon him to kill a rattlesnake in their village. This was possibly a test of the white man's will. The reptile was almost as large as the ten-foot eight-inch-diameter snake reported by the explorer on another occasion. (I have seen eastern diamondback rattlesnakes exceeding this size on islands off the Georgia coast.) Mammals sighted in the region by the traveler were bears, deer with "white flag erect" (Bartram is careful to tell us this is its tail), foxes of a small red species that move swiftly, and a great black fox squirrel that measured two feet from nose to tail. The white-tails were in some areas scarce. Raccoons and opossums were abundant, but the "muskcat" was not to be seen within a hundred miles of the coast.[34]

What was this "muskcat"? Helpfully, Bartram placed it in the genus *Castor*, where we now classify the beaver. He may have been referring to the muskrat, an aquatic rodent. Its habitat, however, is in more northerly climes, and the muskrat is classified in the genus *Ondatra*.

As for birds, Bartram's frequent reports of the "mock-bird," the whippoorwill, coot, and water hen suggest their prevalence in the Florida peninsula, at least in the season of his travel. Wild turkey cocks were heard saluting each other from perches atop the baldcypress trees, and pelicans pranced without caution.[35]

Insects of the woods worthy of mention in the botanist's chronicles included the common gray caterpillar, with which he was familiar in Pennsylvania. In the South, tree leaves were stripped and the branches laid bare by the larvae of the colorful butterfly.

Mayflies were called "ephemera" because of the short span of time spent in adulthood. The Greek word implies lasting but a day. Bartram appropriately observed—for the five-plus billion people on the earth today as well as for the less than one billion of his time—that the numbers of the insect hatching each year were greater than the figure for the whole human race.[36]

The Inward Trek

To the Fall Line

Leaving the coast by paved road, today one readily notes the terraces that mark the earlier shorelines of the southeastern Coastal Plain. That Bartram was able to do this as he traveled Indian trails and journeyed cross-country indicates that he was especially observant. The first "step" he noted to be about fifty miles wide, comprising high pine

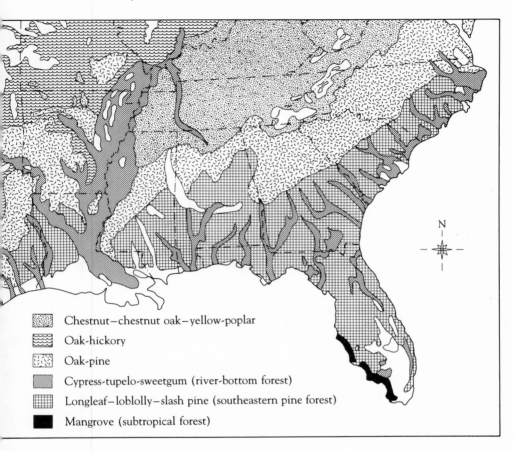

Chestnut – chestnut oak – yellow-poplar

Oak-hickory

Oak-pine

Cypress-tupelo-sweetgum (river-bottom forest)

Longleaf – loblolly – slash pine (southeastern pine forest)

Mangrove (subtropical forest)

Map 3. Major forest types of the southeastern United States.

forests on loose sandy soil. Oaks of many species and shapes accompanied the dense stands of sweetgum. Here, too, were found the sycamore, its limbs appearing to Bartram like the arms of an oriental dancer. While he omitted the rolling wire grass (*Poa*) country, he noted the step some two hundred to three hundred feet above sea level, which I judge to be just below the Fall Line Sandhills. In this "flight," as he called each change in elevation, was a vast plain with extensive savannas. Here he found the earth covered with grass, the trees principally longleaf pine, and an "infinite variety of herbs." Were it not for the sparkling ponds of water and the clumps of magnolia of which he wrote, one might envision this zone as the Fall Line Sandhills.[37]

Explorers followed a long-used Indian trail along the Fall Line Sandhills from points that now position modern cities. Proceeding southward, Richmond, Raleigh, Durham, Columbia, Augusta, Macon, and Columbus mark the path. At the Chattahoochee River, the Fall Line bends northwestward to pass through present-day Montgomery, Alabama. The streams on this route that needed to be forded could be readily crossed on the rocky cataracts that gave the narrow belt its name: Fall Line. Along the path in the Georgia zone, journals maintained by travelers recorded the presence of the oak-leaved hydrangea. That shrub has now spread to the Northeast from the South by introduction and cultivation. In its native habitat the species is presently scarce, perhaps because of overgrazing by cattle in the forests for a century and a half.

In time, Sidney Lanier and other poets would memorialize the Chattahoochee as a river that flows to the sea. Perhaps the rocks along the shore were observed by exploring parties as they crossed the stream on the Fall Line near today's Columbus, Georgia. The name Chattahoochee is not for the Uche or Yuchi tribe, as an early writer believed, but rather stands for those sculptured rocks. Bartram found along such a river course a "white buckeye," a shrub spreading from runners.[38] I cannot determine its present name.

To the Piedmont Province

We return to de Soto's adventures, to what is now the Piedmont Province, supposedly named for the Piedmont of the European continent that lies north of the Mediterranean Sea. This foot-of-the-mountains of the Appalachian chain supported forests of a diversity of broadleaf hardwoods and conifers, the likes of which had long been harvested in the continent de Soto had left behind. Soils were deep, rich in organic matter, gently rolling, and not greatly encumbered with stones that so often slow the plowman. Had he sent home such reports, as others

Dense stands of high-quality white oaks and hickories. These trees, found along fertile river courses, provided tough timbers for construction and wood for fine furniture in pioneer times. Walnut was sometimes relegated to the lowly estate of serving as dresser drawer bottoms, the defect-free solid oak boards exposed for the appreciative eye on tops, sides, and fronts. (Courtesy Forest History Collection, Steen Library Archives, Stephen F. Austin State University, Nacogdoches, Tex.)

soon did, farmer migration from the North and perhaps from Europe would have been greatly encouraged. The march to the hills to break new ground would have occurred at an earlier time.

Among those who later did report the agricultural benefits of the soil of the region was William Bartram. The cataracts of Augusta attest to the Fall Line in his book, *The Travels of William Bartram*. Just above the rapids are the rich rocky hills of the Piedmont. Here were found rhododendrons and an "odoriferous" pancratium, the latter charted on little rocky islets of the streams.[39]

In the fertile Piedmont were stands of black oak and sweetgum. Indians used the bark of the black oak for a yellow dye. The sweetgum's trunks were said to appear like superb columns, rising forty to fifty feet to the first limbs and being eight to eleven feet in diameter at a height of five feet above the ground. Its large buttresses were attributed to nature's support, or jamb, construction, the tree at its base being appreciably larger in girth than at five feet above the ground.[40]

Early explorers found these rolling fertile hills covered with a deep rich dark "mould" resting on reddish brown clay formed in place from native underlying rocks. The soil was not washed in by erosive forces from lands higher in elevation. Soil moisture in the Piedmont was readily replenished by "rivulets coursing about the fragrant hills," and the coolness and purity of those waters invigorated "the air of this otherwise hot and sultry climate." Here were the deciduous hardwoods, like honey locust, beech, and walnut, the last reported in the rich vales along with tuliptree—often called yellow-poplar—and ash.[41]

Bartram observed salt licks in the Piedmont, calling them "buffalo" licks. One such was still visible and visited by cattle as late as 1934. Perhaps the natives were pulling Bartram's leg when they claimed the licks were used by buffalo; perhaps not, for evidence supports the contention that bison ranged the openings in the forests of the East. Bartram believed the lick was caused by impregnation of the soil "with saline vapours arising from fossile salts deep in the earth."[42]

To the Mountains

Explorers, in time, searched out the mysteries of the mountains northwest of the Piedmont that Indians called the Appalachians. There forests of spruce and fir and hemlock, all climaxing in ecological succession and therefore in mixtures of all ages, send out a fragrance of terpenes as their resins exude from the foliage of small needles. Those sections of the mountain chain called the Smokies and the Blue Ridge attest to the haze of natural air pollution attributed to the oils secreted by

these conifers. With but little imagination, one may appreciate the pleasure the aroma brought to weary and dirty explorers as they proceeded
onward and upward toward the summits.

Sometimes mixed with the conifers, but more often apart from
them, the forests of broadleaf mesophytes lent a pleasing landscape even
to exhausted explorers. These broadleaf stands of perhaps three-score
species of trees that require moist but well-drained sites are probably the
most ecologically complex in all the world. Foresters call them *mesophytes*
(*meso*—meaning middle, with regard to moisture—and *phyte*—meaning
plant). An equal number of shrubs and a ground cover of multitudinous
herbs add to the profusion.

These herbs were the reason for excursions like the younger
Bartram's. Sent by the British king to discover supplies for the royal medicine cabinet, he collected and named many of the plants of the Southern
Appalachian forests. Bartram sometimes alluded to this rugged land as
the Cherokee Mountains and even the "Alegany" Mountains—the northern extension of which was familiar to him from his haunts in Penn's
Woods.[43]

Among the herbs observed by the Quaker as he traversed the
Great Ridge, a near synonym for the Appalachian chain, was the psychic-
nut. That name was given to the Indian olive by the white men who
noted how the natives carried its seed on the hunt as a good luck charm.
Here, the herbalist found a yet unnamed species of *Caryophyllata*. Possibly
it was a rose. Losing his footing on the rocky land, he stumbled, tearing
the plant's roots from the ground. Of these broken radicals, he said they
"filled the air with animating scents of cloves and spicy perfumes."[44]

Together the Bartrams noted the abundance of mountain laurel in the Southern Appalachian Mountains. They gave it the Latin binomial *Kalmia latifolia*. Describing this "wild azalea" (there is another),
named for a Finnish friend, they said that when seeing it "suddenly [in]
view from dark shades" (of the dense shadowy broadleaf overstory), they
were "alarmed with the apprehension of the hills being set on fire."[45]
Others would call such hills "pink beds," possibly an allusion to the color
of the granite underlying the earth, rather than to the ericaceous shrub.

Closely related botanically to the pond pines of the Carolina
coast already mentioned are the forests of pitch pines. They are, however,
geographically separated by a wide zone that includes much of the Coastal
Plain and the Piedmont Province. Possibly de Soto's soldiers hiked under
these serotinous trees in crossing the rugged ridge of the Southern Appalachian Mountains. Like pond pines, pitch pines depend on fire for
opening their cones. They often grow in narrow bands on the ridges of
the hilltops, an array of mesic broadleaf trees appearing just below the

crest on the sides of the slopes. Holocaust fires, running up the slopes to meet at the summit, melt the resin that seals the seeds within the cones. As the ground cools, the seeds fall and germinate to form a new stand of pines that once again appears like a Paul Bunyan scalp lock.

Fascinating to the inquisitive explorer in the Appalachians must have been the dramatic change in climate with an ascent along the cascading creeks of but several hundred feet in elevation. The traveler progresses from the hot, sultry valley floor covered with yellow-poplars and pines to a near boreal forest of hemlock and northern hardwoods (beech and maple) in a short vertical distance. In an enchanting scene, Bartram describes how his soul was "delighted wondrously" in finding magnolia trees with leaves nearly two feet long and their flowers white and fragrant. We now call this tree a big-leaf magnolia, or *Magnolia macrophylla.*[46]

Nowhere on the continent, except possibly on the west side of the summits of the Olympic and the Sierra Nevada mountains, is water so plentiful and so pure as in the Southern Appalachians. Snowmelt and rainfall give rise to many springs that feed the streams and rivers that finally collect in the Mississippi River through the Tennessee and Ohio rivers. Other creeks flow eastward from the subcontinental divide to fill the rivers that flow into the Atlantic Ocean. The deep mull soils, created by the mixing of decaying organic matter and mineral soil, serve like sponges to absorb and retain water. Precipitation then slowly percolates into streams. Explorers would have likely noted this source of thirst-quenching liquid as they traipsed the rugged landscape.

Bears, panthers (Bartram's "tygers"), wolves, and wildcats then were common in the mountain forests of the South. William and John Bartram noted these and other large animals of the wild as they traversed the ranges. In the uplands as well as in the bottomlands of broadleaf trees, squirrels were abundant, hiding acorns and hickory nuts in caches that often were forgotten. From these concealed storage bins, seedlings sprouted in dense clumps.

Large eastern redcedars occurred in vast pure stands in the geologic bowl of dissolved limestone rock in what is now called the Nashville Basin of Tennessee. These trees (really junipers), here as elsewhere, exhibit their calcium-loving character; and, too, they stand as symbols of the Temple in Jerusalem, the timbers of which were hewn from giant stems in the Lebanese mountains to the north. (*Cedrus libani*, however, is a true cedar and not a juniper.) A town called Lebanon is rooted nearby in Tennessee's limestone dish.

An exploratory trek through the tablelike lands of broadleaf trees and Virginia pines of the Cumberland Plateau of Tennessee must

Virgin stand of red spruce trees. Overtopping a bed of ferns, as well as the under-story of seedlings and saplings, these overmature trees were found high in the South-ern Appalachian Mountains. (Courtesy U.S. Forest Service.)

wait for later adventurers into the Appalachian Mountains. The pioneers would harvest there the stands of small-boled trees, which were sometimes called scrub pines.

All was not esthetically sylvan for the adventuring explorer. Grasslands, characterized by the crescent-shaped blacklands of northern Alabama and the fingerlike protrusions that extend from Oklahoma to Texas, were encountered. In these locales, one may justifiably conjecture, grass was as high as the belly of a twenty-hand horse, for the soils have a high pH, usually on the sweet side of the scale.

Westward Exploration

To the Land of the Father of Waters

Not many years lapsed before discovery of the waterways of Alabama and the Mississippi country and the myriad of tree species, mostly deciduous, that tie together the land of the great drainage basin. Mostly to the west of the Mississippi River and in the rich alluvial bottomlands, adventurers discovered the highest-quality sites in the temperate-zone world for the growth of deciduous hardwood species. They likened the fertility of the land to the rich annual overflow of the Nile in Egypt, and so gave names like Cairo, Memphis, and Alexandria to the communities established on the edge of the Mississippi Delta. In time, the long-staple cotton fiber cropped from these slate-colored clays would rival that of the high-quality strands produced for world markets by the Egyptians. De Soto eventually found the Mississippi, a river "almost halfe a league broad; . . . the water alwaies muddie; [with] many trees and timber, which the force of the water and streame brought downe."[47]

Above the Delta, immediately to the east, are the Bluff Hills of silty soils blown by the prevailing westerlies in times past from the Mississippi River's overflow bottom. Geologists guess at the period when drought was accompanied by Dust Bowl winds that lifted these fine sediments from a once-soggy site to form giant mounds on the leeward edge. Those loess deposits are so fertile that in these soils sassafras—usually a weed tree of scrub size—grows to twenty inches in diameter in as many years. If trees grow so well, so too would cotton. It was not long until sojourners reported the value of the bluffs for agriculture: the deep and erosive silt deposits were homesteaded as easy lands for cultivation. Later we will learn of the tragedy of these staked claims, tragedy that would eventually take its toll upon the land but which would be delayed because the explorers either ignored, neglected, or bypassed the fertile bluffs.

Dense stands of black willow seed in on sandy "new land" that forms along the sides of southern rivers. Through old stands like this pioneering settlers paused in their travels to boil the bark from the tree for its purgative and vermin-destroying powers. The lightweight logs provided timber at the water's edge for small boats. The soft wood was readily whittled and woven into baskets.

De Soto, we believe, made it to the hills the Indians called Ouachita in what is now central Arkansas and eastern Oklahoma. In his time, mostly deciduous hardwoods covered the slopes, with fingers of shortleaf pine invading where fire had ravaged the land in the not-too-distant past. At the southern edge, loblolly pines, the same species occurring at Jamestown on the Atlantic coast on sites considered a miry mess, here are found on higher, drier lands. In the Arkansas border of the southern region, de Soto found the Tulas Indians living on buffalo. He reported them to be far more primitive than the gatherers and cultivators of the southeastern corner of the continent.[48]

Entering the Ozarks

A long time later, Anglo explorers entered the forests of the Ozarks in what is today northern Arkansas and southern Missouri. There they found stands of pure white oak. So too would be discovered—on the limestone-derived soils of the Ozark Mountains—forests of pure eastern redcedar. Geographers call these coniferous forests "glades." While mixed with deciduous trees on ridgetops, slopes, and flatlands of various degrees of alkalinity and acidity, it is on the rocky, alkaline lands that the redcedars are found with little competing vegetation.

Many more years would pass until someone would pay note to the western extremity of the southern forest. Oklahoma's shortleaf pines in the Ouachita Mountains were in Arkansas territory and the pineries of East Texas's redlands and yellow sands were controlled first by the Spanish and then by Mexicans. These Lone Star forests, consisting mostly of three species of yellow pines and a score of useful hardwoods, were visited by the de Soto expedition in about 1540 and 1541. Indeed, the name of Caddo Lake, the South's largest natural lake, was shown as Tsoto, in honor of the explorer, on early maps of East Texas.[49]

Robert Cavelier, sieur de La Salle, and his followers more than a century later, in 1687, were probably the next to intrude on the lands of the Indian tribal Kadohodacho (meaning "real chief"), from whence the name we now ascribe to the earthquake-caused lake was likely derived. Not until 1813 when a smuggler and horse thief used an Indian trail into Arkansas territory was there further white penetration into the swamp country of northeast Texas. As late as 1820 the area remained firmly Caddo (a corruption of Kadohodacho) and in Indian hands.[50]

Texas's eminent forest historian and his colleague tell of the virgin tracts of the eastern pineries of that state: "The towering pine forest was almost overpowering. Travelers often described the magnificent pines [probably longleaf] soaring 100 to 150 feet in the air with bases 4 or 5 feet in diameter. The forest floor under the great longleaf trees was clean, and the forest was . . . parklike. . . . The combination of sandy soil and wood fires had eliminated most competing growth. . . . Majestic trunks pointing skyward, often 50 or 60 feet to the lowest limb, were a spectacular sight."[51]

To the west of the East Texas pineries is the transition to the Post Oak Belt attributed solely to rainfall. (Some mappers of this zone consider it a part of the Central Hardwood Forest, rather than a forest of the South, for it is contiguous to the vast expanse of broad-leaved trees that were once interspersed with the grasses and forbs that covered the prairies to the north. If the Post Oak Belt is a finger, the prairie of the Central States is the palm of the hand.)

Still farther west are two other fingers, these of scrub oaks, called by early transients the East and West Cross Timbers. They remain so-called. In the extreme southwest corner of the region are the islands of Bastrop pine, a race of drought-hardy loblolly pine dramatic in contrast in site and structure to the tall, wide-girthed stems described in the opening lines of this chapter. The Lost Pines, as they are often called because they are far away from similar stands, are short, with much taper, and produce cones considerably smaller than those of the typical loblolly pine.

Indian Influences

Native American Encounters

Even by Bartram's time, long-deserted Indian settlements were overgrown with forests. So too were the native Americans' ancient cultivated fields. Indians cleared the land, usually along stream terraces, for nomadic homes, ritual grounds, and burial places. The Indians' practice of moving on to better sites for cultivation was a great convenience for the whites who would later intrude. Heavily timbered areas interspersed with savannas of hundreds of acres covered by grass as high as a man's shoulders and spotted with soggy bogs of organic soil were improbable planting sites for the settlers whose tools were yet crude. Open lands left by Indians sufficed for awhile. The aborigine also cut trails for travel.

Persimmon, honey locust, Chicasaw plum, black walnut, and shellbark hickory may have all been tended in the native Americans' orchard. Pre-Columbians cultivated persimmons and plums for fruit, locust trees for their vegetable beans, and walnuts and hickories for their edible nuts. The nuts of shellbark hickory, which Bartram placed in the same genus with walnut, were pounded and cast into boiling water. When strained, the oily part of the liquid was retained as "milk of hickory." It is sweet, rich as fresh cream and, we might assume, provided some culinary delight for explorers when it was used in cooking hominy grits and cornbread.[52]

For food, too, Indians ground the elderberry into flour for bread (though leaves, stems, and bark are poisonous). Chinquapin nuts were boiled, and the resulting oil was skimmed from the surface and used in cornbread. The pods of black and honey locust were consumed when other vegetables were scarce (but the natives knew the inner bark to be poisonous), and wild black cherry bark, when boiled, produced a satisfying tea.[53]

American Indians had probably long used products of the woods for medicinal purposes. Yaupon, an emetic whose powers are reflected in the species name *vomitoria*, was imbibed in purification rites. A solution from white oak bark was used to treat burns, sores, and hemorrhoids; another from witch hazel remedied muscular ailments; and a drink produced from the roots and leaves of eastern redcedar encouraged the curing of coughs.[54]

For fish bait, the hornworm larvae of a moth, always accompanying catalpa in damp woods, was, and is, a favorite. (Bamboo—locally called "river cane"—should be interplanted with catalpa; thence the fishing worms and fishing poles are side-by-side!) For fish hooks, the spikes of the hawthorn would do. For dye, the bark of the root of Osage-orange was useful; for ritual incense, the needles of eastern redcedar; and for woven baskets, the bark of young shoots of eastern redbud.[55]

Possession by Adverse Claim

Indian use of the products of the southern woods did much to alter the forests of the land they inhabited. Possession was by adverse claim, just as surely as it was for the white men—and brown men and some black men—who would follow, for anthropologists usually consider the earliest native Americans migrants who crossed from the Orient on a bridge of land over what is now the Bering Sea. Thousands of years lapsed before groups like the Cherokees were well-established in the southern forest.

These eastern-migrating cousins of Mongoloids likely first arrived in the South about 8000 B.C. in what is now the Texas Llano Estacado, or "staked plain," at that time a green savanna with wooded valleys. The Woodland Indian tradition is believed to have taken form along the Mississippi River, perhaps about 1000 B.C. Those that migrated more southerly toward the Texas Gulf Coast remained quite primitive, roaming the lands naked even to the time of Cabeza de Vaca's (1528–36) chronicles. Not hunters, gatherers, or cultivators, they staved off their children's starvation by nursing them until they were twelve years old.[56]

The American Indians' principal produce in the South was corn, *Zea mays* that probably originated in the Tehuacan Valley of present-day Mexico. This most-efficient of all cereals in converting nutrients and sunlight into starch and sugar served not only the aborigine; without corn the whites would have starved. Unlike the northern cultivators, southern Indians had not learned to plant a fish with the kernels, so cornfields cleared of trees within the forest were soon abandoned in a kind of shifting cultivation economy. This slash-and-burn agriculture affected the pattern of forest types and timber stand ages noted by the explorers. Riverbottom gardens were more enduring.

The Indians knew to interplant beans with the corn, the leguminous pod plant that would provide nitrogen for the corn. In the diet, the beans were also essential, for corn eaten alone produces the vitamin niacin in a chemical form that resists digestion.

Corn, the Indian staple so responsible for pre-Columbian land transition, has been aptly called humanity's most remarkable plant-breeding achievement. How it arrived at its present state would be a remarkable tale. The kernels do not scatter; they must be separated from the cob for planting. Otherwise, under natural conditions, a fallen ear would result in untold numbers of new plants, each competing with one another to the likely demise of all.

The cultivated plots of the mound-building Indians in the South also produced squash and tobacco. White men adopted the latter, making it an important export product which in time would take a heavy toll of the region's soil. Less damaging to the ecosystem was the life-style of the gatherers, those Indians who collected nuts, fruits, and seeds (including ragweed). Among these were the forest-dwelling Choctaws of the Mississippian tribes.

American Indians burned the woods regularly. Evidence suggests that tribes that long ago had settled in the East, as well as the more recent intruders from the Continental West, set fire to the forests. They likely followed the practices of the Shoshoni, Paiute, and other seed-gathering tribes that remained in the West. Some foresters now call the pre-Columbian settlers pyromaniacs. Flint stones sparked the tinder to clear the understory. Low-lying vegetation hid deer, camouflaged enemies, and obstructed travel: it needed to be removed. The overstory, one

Still a mystery to ecologists are the causes of the treeless, dome-shaped summits of the Southern Appalachian Mountains. In the foreground the "bald" is seen to be covered with grasses and heatherlike vegetation. The deep soils have no chemicals known to be toxic to trees. Though above four thousand feet, the bare areas are below tree line, for nature draws no such boundary in the eastern forests.

may suppose, was often destroyed with it; for conflagrations inevitably occurred in such perennial ignitions and consequently resulted in dramatic changes in forest cover types. Variations in species composition found by the explorers were directly related to such activities. The rare occurrence of dry-lightning strikes, a cause for fires in the western United States, rules out the prevalence of naturally caused fires in most of the South. In this region, lightning is almost inevitably accompanied by rain. Though trees may literally explode by the electrical discharge, rain prevents the grass and duff on the forest floor from igniting.

A Dynamic Forest

Tree Size and Stand Volume

Except in recently regenerated forests, following fire or other clearings made by the aborigines, the southern forest found by the explorers was fairly open and often parklike in its appearance. Growth was slow on the already large and over-mature stems that made up the forest. Perhaps five trees to the acre, averaging five feet in diameter, 175 feet tall, and three hundred years old, stood where today's foresters anticipate sixty stems per acre, averaging perhaps fourteen inches in diameter and one hundred feet in height at an age of fifty years. Cabeza de Vaca's chronicles of his travels from Florida to Texas from 1528 to 1536 noted the open woods with large trees.

Volumes differed: twenty thousand board feet in an acre of explorer's old growth contrasts to ten thousand board feet in the forester's managed woods. Another distinction is often overlooked: rate of growth. The old-growth forest visited by armored knights and their sailing colleagues was physiologically overmature, and net growth rate was virtually zero. The site was fully occupied; the soil, its nutrients, and its water were unable to sustain any further cellulose production. Only as trees succumbed to lightning strikes, disease infection, insect infestation, or flame could growth on residual stems be accelerated. Without these intrusions by nature or by Indians, old forests lived on in a stagnated condition. (Gross growth and production of cellulose continues as long as a tree lives. Net growth of the stand of trees depends upon volume growth of all of the stems exceeding the volume lost to fires, insects, diseases, and tree-tossing storms.)

These climax and subclimax forests thus were at their zenith when the explorers arrived. Leaving nature alone, keeping humans and axes out of the woods, and trusting fire and storm cooperated, they would be perpetuated ad infinitum. For vegetative cover to continue without noticeable change "world without end" is a fair definition of ecologically climax vegetation.

Marion Clawson, in discussing America's forests in the long sweep of history, notes how the rate of growth for every stand of trees retained in its primeval state eventually culminates. At some time, depending upon site characteristics and species, stand volumes arrive at their maximum. Beyond that and eventually, with the certainty of mortality for all living things, the stand deteriorates and perhaps entirely disintegrates.[57]

Standing in the long shadow of history, one must assume the

fascination of the explorers with these forests, the wildlife in them, and the waters that flowed through them. Could they not also have been intrigued, even then, with the possibilities of harvest and exploitation, having been born and bred in lands where forest depletion, if not timber famine, was already apparent. Later Europeans, as we shall see, would capitalize on these green treasures to enhance their economies and creature comforts.

No Wild Monotony

The southern forest, to the early explorer, was diverse and variable in species, rate of growth, age, and size. It could not have been a "wild *monotony*" (italics mine), which is one historian's description. Indeed, it was a land of immensity that filled those rugged men with awe, as the chronicler also suggests.[58]

But the southern woodlands were not always landscapes for poetic description. The forests were found in all stages of development, from seedlings with infant cotyledon leaves to Methuselah-age monarchs. The forests of the South were, and shall be, dynamic and ever changing, always new and always old.

In these pages, I have attempted to suggest from a limited available bibliography what we know and what we surmise the explorers observed as they intruded upon, and proceeded across, the southern forest. Those adventurers, often the agents of European crowns, traipsed upon soils of various mixtures of sand, silt, clay, and organic matter— ranging from the sand hills of old coastlines to the peaty surfaces of the lowest of the lowlands. These men, bent on discovery, journeyed through some twenty distinctly different physiographic zones, describing the mountains, foothills, bluffs, valleys, rivers, and swamps. They blazed trails through about sixty categories of forest vegetation that foresters call "cover types." Encounters with Native Americans enabled the explorers to appreciate the animal and plant life, as well as the trees of the forest, encountered along the way.

I believe the reader will be fascinated as I describe in more detail in the chapters that follow the nature of these woodlands, how the pioneers altered them, their use and abuse by often well-intentioned exploiters, their restoration by people and Providence, and their future when managed by foresters or set aside for posterity.

CHAPTER 2

The Pioneers' Forest

XPLORERS OF the New World, in their journeys inland and their experiences with the continental aborigines, had little effect upon the forests. Some, like John and William Bartram, cataloged plants found in the woods that could be used for medicinal purposes. In doing this, they prepared the way for low-grade exploitation. For the most part, however, the forests in the early 1800s were as they had been seen by Ponce de León, de Soto, La Salle, and their inquisitive associates.

For the pioneers, the story is different. Settling along the Atlantic coast to establish centers of commerce, like Savannah and Charleston, they began to clear the land of timber to produce corn and tobacco. Because the plow's wooden moldboard and share were inadequate for bringing nutrients stored in the subsoil to the surface, crop failures resulted. Wheat, too, was planted, only to fail in the acidic virgin soil formed from water-laid deposits of sand and clay. The soil would eventually support cotton, seeds for the white fiber being brought in 1621 from the Mediterranean region. The cotton industry would in time become king, ruling and controlling all aspects of both business and culture. King Cotton played a role in exploitation and consumption of the region's wood as land was cleared for its cultivation.

Unlike the cut-out-and-get-out practices of timber exploiters in the Northeast and the Lake States that began in earnest in about 1660[1] and 1860, respectively, removal of the forests of the South followed another pattern. Here movement of men, mules, and machinery related to agricultural pursuits rather than to the demand for the abundant supply of timbers with which to build the cities of the nation.

The lumber barons, sometimes justifiably condemned for their greedy abuse of the forests in the Northeast and the Lake States, were not responsible for initial timber harvesting in the South. Here it was the farmer or a small group of rugged individuals who would penetrate the wilderness curtain. Tools were crude, the work was hard, and the risks high. Indians, offended by the whites' intrusion, were often unfriendly and harassing. Neither the antebellum southern plantation owner nor the "ignorant woods-dwelling cracker" (as one historian called the commoner white) had any sense of conservation.[2] Writers seem to have ignored the forest in stories of the region's early economy.

Even before breaking new ground for crop production, the pioneers had to remove the trees. The forest was a barrier to progress. The best lands were the earliest converted. Their quality would be judged by the height and girth of the deciduous broadleaf trees found on them. Only those trees needed for use locally on the farm were likely to be harvested by pioneering homesteaders. The rest lay waste.

Soil Destruction

Because using crude axes and saws for timber removal was slow and physically exhausting, tree trunks were simply girdled—bark and trunk were cut in a ring to stop nutrient and water translocation—and left to die. Subsequent burning of the deadened snags was readily accomplished and, although those farmers probably did not realize it, the ash of the wood, bark, and foliage provided readily available nutrients for food and fiber crops. Nutrient cations, especially the positively charged atoms of potassium and calcium, stimulated growth of the cotton crop for a few years. It did not take long for cotton production to use up these nutrients. Then the farm family moved on—usually inland—to clear the woods again and to break new ground. Exhaustion was slower in the soils derived from beds of marls exposed along some rivers. The soils were worn out more rapidly where gravel, often containing hard chert and flint minerals, outcropped as components of the surface soil.

Soil Deterioration

Why was the land so soon worn out nutritionally and the elemental deficiencies so dramatically evident? The answer lies in the rapid oxidation of organic matter in the red and yellow podzolic soils found in southern coastal climes (these are now called "ultisols" in the new international classification developed by the U.S. Department of Agriculture Soil Survey Staff). Organic matter from fallen leaves and trees and dying brush and vines had accumulated over the ages. Especially in climax oak and hickory forests, earthworms, millipedes, and macrofauna like moles drag parts of the fallen material into the soil. The amount of organic matter, made up of dead vegetable matter and animals, thus increases. It is this organic matter along with the minute particles of soil, both holding nutrients to their surfaces by what soil chemists call "cation adsorption," that tell the fertility story.

Fine soils, like clays and to a lesser degree silts, and organic matter—the latter working like a sponge—provide a large surface area on which positively charged nutrient particles are held by the negatively charged anions of soil and decaying vegetable matter. When these soils are exposed to the sun by removing the overstory and then further exposed by turning the ground with the plow, loss of the organic matter results. In warm southern climes, this "burning" occurs rapidly. Oxidation in such soils is as complete as if the soils were placed in a muffle furnace and the thermostat set at 500°C. Natural oxidation may require a few years instead of the minutes it takes in the oven to eliminate the once-living material. Without organic matter and with the mineral soil particles already saturated with nutrient ions, these newly released chemical atoms leach downward and laterally through the soils, eventually percolate into streams, and then flow on and add salts to the ocean.

More advanced weathering of the clay fraction of southern soils in the region's warm, moist climate, in contrast to those of the cooler northern forests, results in the disappearance of primary weatherable minerals. Secondary clay minerals of low cation exchange capacity then accumulate. Plant nutrient reserves thus tend to diminish in these soils.

Nitrogen Loss

Nitrogen, not a mineral cation, was also lost in the times of the pioneers by destruction of organic matter and the forest that temporarily stored it. Nature's nitrogen tank is the atmosphere, releasing perhaps six pounds per acre per year of the gaseous element in lightning strikes in regions of moist temperate climate. Electrical charges convert the atmospheric gas to nitrate and ammonia forms, both compounds readily washed to the ground by rain and subsequently made available to plants.

When an overstory of forest is removed, even if the soil is not disturbed by logging or plowing, the amount of nitrogen leached to streams is appreciably increased. In a disturbed site, such as one planted with cotton, this essential plant nutrient disappears rapidly. That which is not utilized by plants nor lost through drainage into streams may be returned to the atmosphere for recycling: not much is available for next year's cotton patch. Within a few months all nitrogen is dissipated.

Organic matter in poorly drained forest soils, apart from the peat and muck swamps, may be as much as 6 percent in the surface four inches. It abruptly drops to about 1 percent a half-foot below the ground surface. As the ratio of organic matter to nitrogen is usually a constant of about 20:1, one readily notes the sensitive balance of this important nutrient element to any land disturbance that depletes the organic matter.

While additional nitrogen exists in the atmosphere, this abundant gas cannot by used by plants. Bacteria living in nodules on the roots of leguminous and certain other plants, with an assist from enzymes in other microbes, convert elemental nitrogen in the atmosphere to ammonia and nitrate forms available to plants. Among the leguminous trees in the southern forests with this ability are the locusts and Kentucky coffee bean. Lesser nitrogen-fixing vegetation, like the lupines, vetches, and the Spanish-introduced alfalfa, effectively supplied the nutrient element. An important tree that is not a legume but also has the ability to fix atmospheric nitrogen is smooth alder, a medium-sized shrub found along the streams of the lower coast.

Depletion of the soil's nutrient elements, especially nitrogen, soon terminated the effort to grow tobacco, rice, corn, cotton, and other crops on any particular piece of ground in the pioneers' forest.

Emigration for a Hardy People

Pioneer observations of the southern forest were often recorded by clergymen. Being among the most literate of travelers and having a curiosity that aroused an interest in education, men of the cloth were often impatient when forced by circumstances to remain stationary. A permanent hitching post was not for the circuit rider. For example, the Rev. John Banister, who arrived in Virginia in 1678, was so attracted by the bluebell of the Old Dominion state that he sent seeds to England. There the herbaceous plant is an escape today.[3]

Promotion

The ecological significance of the soil upon the vegetation it supports is not a new concept. As early as 1775, promotional pieces appeared in Europe to encourage migration. One such article penned by "an American" was published in London in the interest of British colony migration. It dealt with points by which the immigrant could be a "judge of

the soil . . . through all these central colonies." The colonial journalist
continued:

> The trees which are the spontaneous product of the land should in
> general be first attended to; if they abound with fine tall red hicko-
> ries, white oaks, chestnut oaks, scarlet oaks, tulip trees, black
> locusts, walnuts, locust, mulberry trees, etc., they may be pro-
> nounced good, and the value will usually be in proportion to the
> size and straitness of those trees; pine, live oaks, laurels, bays,
> liquid amber and water oaks are, among others, signs of bad land;
> and in general that soil will be best which is free from underwood:
> nor should the planter take a few trees of any sort as a guide, but as
> predominancy of them in whole woods. This rule of judging must
> be united with that of the appearance of the soil when dug into,
> particularly color and depth . . . as . . . in America the sands are
> generally white and dry, and produce little besides pines.[4]

There is an analogy here of which the promotion-minded author of 1775 probably was unaware. We know that people migrate. Much
has been written in the histories about this, but is it not also true that
"trees, like people, sometimes migrate to soils which they particularly
cherish?"[5]

During the period, attempts were made to produce silk.
Mulberry trees "in prettie groves" were cultivated for the purpose, but the
silkworms were eaten by rats.[6]

There were other topographic, cultural, and political per-
suaders and dissuaders of settlement and development of the pioneers' forest, a land sometimes referred to as a realtor's Eden. The lay of the land—
mountains and swamps and prairies and rock-free soils—discouraged or
encouraged migration. So, too, cultural obstacles and enticements, such
as fear of the law, the hardships that accompany people far from civilization, or the desire to be alone, further impeded or beckoned movement
inland or westward. Among the human impediments were Indians, including the land-clearing Cherokees under the leadership of Sequoya.
The chief, a man of many talents, is the one for whom the botanical genera *Sequoia* and *Sequoiadendron* were named (in the latter dendrologists
sometimes now catalog the bigtree and in the former the redwood of California). He requested from the Colony of South Carolina protection from
the French who were penetrating the headwaters of the Tennessee River.
The government obliged, built a cantonment of wood at Fort Lowden in
Tennessee, bivouacked militia at the fort, and hauled cannons by pack
mules from a supply depot near Augusta, Georgia. Perhaps the Indians
also found some of the white-man's firewater, for they later had a change

of heart. In the struggle that followed, most of the garrison's guns were surrendered and the troops massacred by Sequoya's warriors. Though the chief invented a Cherokee alphabet so perfectly phonetic that every tribal member could read and write with a few years' practice, his braves resisted indoctrination with civilization's methods. Hence, fear precluded continued development of an Anglo settlement in the woods near the fort at Tellico, Tennessee, and migration proceeded elsewhere.

Trappers and Traders

Among the early self-invited visitors to the often junglelike wilderness just inland from the coast were hunters, trappers, and traders. This vanguard to the region lived, as did the Indians, off the land as a nomadic people. Some were misfits from society, but more often the misfits followed the trails blazed earlier by "stalwart old iconoclasts," who were "unconvinced by axe and gibbet that all virtue was the Past's."[7] The uncouth too often destroyed favorable relationships that those who preceded them had developed with the Indians. Some were drifters who, with their wives and children, squatted on another's land. They cleared it of forest, built shacks for short-term habitation, and after a season or two moved farther into the wilderness.

Behind them came the families of those with titles to land yet unseen. Some would call these people substantial citizens. For the most part, they came to stay. Eventually their kind spread out across the Coastal Plain and into the Mexican state of Texas. A few found their way up the Mississippi River and through western Tennessee; others trudged up the Arkansas River to the outposts of that territory and its western sector, later to become the Indian lands of Oklahoma.

Times of hesitation along the way were not infrequent. The vast Mississippi Delta, with its rich, but flood-prone soils, enticed some to stay for a while. So too the fertile bluffs of wind-blown silts in western Tennessee and Mississippi encouraged the laying down of roots by an otherwise restless people.

Texas Settlement Grants

The closed border on the Sabine River, entering point for settlers into Mexican Texas, impeded traffic considerably. Migrants moving west into the pine-hardwood forests there needed "papers," membership in a settlement grant like that which Stephen F. Austin had negotiated with the Mexican government. Entry also required a willingness to be baptized into the Roman Catholic Church by a priest who would oblige at the river's edge. Often the new Texans recanted upon returning to the United States, and local alcaldes were quite lenient upon discovery of Protestant worship in secrecy in the homes of Anglo pioneers.

In Texas, too, lies the Big Thicket, a moist jungle of a myriad of hardwood species with a few loblolly pines piercing the sky through the broad-leaved overstory of shorter trees. Today the Big Thicket is as much a product of the imagination and wishful thinking as it is a geographical area. But for those who crossed the river at Orange, traipsed through the swamp at Blue Elbow, and hiked over the strand of open parklike longleaf pine forest, the briars and "ty-vine" they encountered served as natural fences for the exclusion of men.

Descriptions of the area by early missionaries to the Spanish forts brought fear to the minds of those about to step into the reptile-infested wilderness. Only after the thicket's conquest and the carving out of small farms by isolated squatters around 1840 did the possibility of its habitation become more than imagination and wishful thinking.

Many inhabitants of southern forests lacked interest in cutting the woods and for good reason. The forest was a convenient hiding place for draft dodgers and deserters during the nation's various wars. This was especially so in the Big Thicket of Deep East Texas for the Civil War. Folktales of such exploits in this wilderness have been handed down to this day.

Even before the struggle to keep the Union together, however, whites and Indians were hiding from each other in deep woods. No doubt this was the situation in the 1830s when southeastern Indian tribes were rounded up for the escorted march to Oklahoma territory, now called "The Trail of Tears." This era is a good general starting time for discussing the southern pioneers' forest.

Legislation Hastens Exploitation

Government Encouragement to Use the Forest

Acts of government were intended to encourage settlement in, and subsequent exploitation of, the southern forest in the days of the pioneers. Most notable among these acts was the establishment of the head-right system that provided fifty acres to an immigrant or to one who brought in another from abroad for tobacco farming. That was in 1617 and 1618. Not until 1748 did the right to hold land in fee simple encourage plantation development. Other acts in the times of British control dealt with fire prevention and naval stores trade, but it was the United

States government that later greatly influenced migratory pursuits in the South. Federal legislation had dramatic effects well before the Civil War and continued to play a large role in the use of the region's forest even after World War II.

To accommodate westward expansion, the public domain was opened to purchasers; preemption claimants; homesteaders; and builders of railroads, wagon roads, and canals. Beginning in 1820, surveyed public domain lands were available at auction, provided the bid price exceeded $1.25 per acre. Individuals could become owners of quarter-sections, or 160 acres, of government land under the Pre-emption Act of 1841 and the Homestead Act of 1862. Under the first legislative authority, the settler paid $1.25 per acre for the land on which he would settle and build a house and farm. The 1862 legislation, though not greatly utilized in the South, permitted free distribution, title passing only after living on the land or cultivating it for five years. These latter restrictions were obviously designed to overcome the fraudulent claims made under the Pre-emption Act, specifically the filing of a claim and the assertion of residence by those who had not actually squatted on the land staked in the claim.

Transportation entrepreneurs under other congressional acts were awarded considerable acreages of government land. Usually they received every other section (one square mile) for a distance of six miles on both sides of a proposed right-of-way wherever the swath would cross the public domain. Thus, vast amounts of forested public land were transferred to private ownerships.

A Homestead Act for the South

All southern states were not privy to these federal give-away programs. The original thirteen states (in the South, Virginia, North Carolina, South Carolina, and Georgia) had surrendered their unclaimed lands to the United States of America in order to become states of the new union. Extensions of the original states (such as West Virginia, Kentucky, and Tennessee) also contained no public domain lands available for settlement under congressional acts. Nor was Texas to benefit from the distributions, for in the treaty by which it obtained its statehood, all lands owned by the republic, now freed from Mexico, within the bounds of the new state were to remain in the possession of the state for subsequent disposal. Thus, Florida, Alabama, Mississippi, Louisiana, Arkansas, Missouri, and Oklahoma contained public lands that were available for entry under these laws. However, the general economic, political, and cultural climate at various times stalled the movement west, delaying homesteading or development of these lands belonging to the federal government by citizens of the East.

To overcome reluctance to possess lands in the region, Congress enacted the Southern Homestead Act, specifically to encourage poor whites and freed slaves to own farms of either 80 or 160 acres, the price of which was $5.00—for the farm, not for an acre. Most timberland at the time was selling for $1.25 an acre, though some went for as little as $.125 an acre shortly before the Civil War. In a ten-year period, beginning in 1866, 47 million acres in the aforementioned public domain states were opened to entry, yet less than forty thousand entries were recorded, taking up perhaps 10 percent of the available acreage.

Abuse of Public Domain Grants

If individuals were uninterested in being claimants to the public domain, northern entrepreneurs were not. For the next ten years, following 1866, government land was sold to speculators of the financial institutions of the country who responded to advertisements boldly proclaiming a "timber colony for absentee owners." Still, land and its stumpage were available and crying for consumption, ushering in the period of the fraudulent dummy entryman. People or groups would apply for a southern homestead, pay the required five dollars for the "farm," cut the timber, sell the logs to a mill, and then give up the homestead right by simply not living and husbanding the one-quarter– or one-eighth–section grant for the required time.[8]

Laws of the land soon enabled, and some would say encouraged, illegal access to the choicest timber in the South. In Louisiana, for example, the U.S. government seized one hundred thousand logs cut for shipment to the West Indies by the "lumber king of the world." One might suppose this to be southern baldcypress, butt logs of which often contained five hundred board feet. If so, the theft totalled some fifty million feet. At even a dollar a thousand, the take of $50,000 in those days possibly would be comparable to a million-dollar swindle today. This was not an isolated case. Elsewhere in the South, the vast acreage of the public domain, with inadequate security, was subject to timber trespass, as illegal entry to steal stumpage is called.[9]

The Timber and Stone Act of 1878 also was abused in the region, especially after it was amended to extend immunities, specifically in the South, for timber trespass on the public domain. Under its provision, agricultural pursuits were not required in order to allow transfer of these public lands to private ownership. Abuse resulting in soil erosion and watershed destruction finally led to its repeal, but not until 1955.

One more example should suffice: In the Mississippi River bottoms, especially in Louisiana, the public domain was available for canal construction. Builders were encouraged by the checkerboard pattern of grants on public domain lands procured, in this case, in the Louisiana Purchase of 1803. This trade of a thirty-six–square–mile tract for a mile of canal was a fair deal for the time, provided the canal was built. Too often, apparently, the timber was cut and the boat route project then abandoned.

Entry onto lands not owned by the pioneers was often condoned for the harvest of timber, wildlife hunting, livestock grazing, and even cultivation. Persuading settlers to alter their habits became necessary. This was not an easy task, for many southerners of whatever descent—Scotch-Irish, English, French, French-Canadian, Spanish, African, or American Indian—had by this time arrived at the philosophy that the woods, whether owned fee simple by an industrial enterprise, worked by a neighbor, or held by government, was a common available for all to utilize.

Settling the Coastal Plain

A Britisher's Account

Plant succession or vegetative ecological migration was evident to Sir Charles Lyell,[10] the Britisher, in his travels through the pioneers' farms and forests in the 1840s. However, he likely would have changed the reasoning for his observations had he returned to the area a few decades later. By then, he would see that oaks came in following the harvest of pines which he earlier had attributed to the caching of acorns by the jay, the feathered rook, and squirrel. Oaks do follow pines in the absence of fire, whether the conifers are harvested or not. Broad-leaved trees also arise from mast cached by rodents and birds. But the prolific regeneration of a multitude of hardwood species in the pioneers' pineries is due mainly to the sprouting of long-dormant buds in roots of broad-leaved trees just beneath the surface of the ground. When the ground is exposed to light by the harvest of the overstory, the light heats the soil, causing adventitious buds to expand and burst into new shoots. The new trees form a coppice.

Live oaks in coastal North Carolina were classed as two kinds by the geologist Lyell. Perhaps one was what we now catalog as water oak or willow oak, both with persistent leaves that often shed only upon the budding of new foliage in the spring of the year. The real live oak (*Quer-*

cus virginiana) is the tree whose dense wood encouraged its utilization by boat builders.

One live oak tallied had a crown spread of sixty-three feet when only thirty-five inches in diameter and seventy-three feet tall. Its age was but thirty-five years. Another had a nine-foot six-inch girth at one and a half feet above the ground at age forty-two. On these trees, as on stems of other species, the mistletoe parasite obtained its nourishment.[11]

As an aside, Lyell made an interesting observation about lightning-struck trees. He saw a small cloud of steam, appearing as smoke, emanating from a struck bole.[12] Others since have noted this dissipation of intense heat from the moist inner bark of a tree trunk.

Lyell noted the endless pine woods extending from Charleston to Augusta. With the longleaf pines in the area, however, were magnolias, live oaks, hollies, and the dwarf fan palm, or palmetto. In the interspersed wetter sites were fragrant myrtles; canes twenty feet tall; and the southern baldcypress, what he called a lofty "cedar" with angular bends in its top boughs that arch over to form long isles in the swamps.[13]

Bartrams Return South

While the Bartrams explored the forests before the pioneers had arrived, as noted in the previous chapter, they also, on their treks, reported on the forests where pioneers had settled.

William Bartram, for instance, classified soil texture, anticipating a "percolating quality" of sandy soil that would ordinarily "suffer the rain water quickly to drain off." Yet he recognized that soil in the maritime province is moist an inch or two below the surface even after long periods of drought, and that situation may exist where the clay subsoil lies five to ten feet below the surface.[14]

Although only slightly lower in elevation, the river bottoms presented to Bartram a rich, "tenacious" clay. In times of drought, such fine-textured soil is baked several feet deep, causing crops to suffer. In contrast to the coarse sands, "this kind of earth admits more freely of a transpiration of vapours, arising from intestine watery canals to the surface; resulting in better growth." Thus, the contemporary of Benjamin Franklin concluded, subterranean water is moved by capillarity to the surface layers of the soil for use by plants.[15]

Proper names for the southern pines were still in a state of confusion in the days of the pioneers. One is reluctant to be adamant about taxonomic classification. Even William Bartram referred to longleaf pine as "pitch pine," "yellow pine," "broom pine," and "long leaved pine," depending upon the locale of his observations.

Bignonia bracteate, common enough to be noted and named by Bartram as a component of the pioneers' forest, was seen in but two other places outside of Florida. This climbing vine is no longer cataloged in *Gray's Manual of Botany*. It may be extinct.

Bartram's ventures into the Atlantic coastal zone were only slightly behind those of the first settlers once he left the principal cities. In the openings of the pine and hardwood canopy were plantings of corn, rice, cotton, indigo, and peach trees. Wild turkeys from the forests were bred in captivity.

Under girdled trees pioneers in the denser forests grew crops like ribbon-cane sugar or corn. Beneath the leafless dead boles men gathered in holiday fashion to "roll logs," while women held quilting parties nearby.

Canes, tall woody grasses, probably of the *Arundinaria* genus, grew ten to twelve feet tall. They grew in brakes so close together that no man and few animals above the size of rodents could penetrate them. Cane reeds were used for making rafts and harpoons and for fuel and light. Indians used them as hair ornaments and in marriage ceremonies. (As courtship concluded, the groom stuck his reed in the ground outside of the dwelling of the bride-to-be. If she was willing, she placed her cane reed next to his.) The several cane species grew in brakes, in swamps, in meadows and pastures, and in dry sandy hills among beech trees and hollies.[16]

Two decades before the "War between the States," as citizens of logging communities continue to call the Civil War, accounts of the forests were still being reported to interested Europeans. Lyell, for example, describes what he considered the "Pine Barrens" in Virginia and North Carolina. Monotonous stands of longleaf pine and pitch pine (probably now called loblolly pine) grew on the upland sandy soils. He did not classify similiar stands in South Carolina as *barrens*, perhaps because of the mix of broad-leaved trees he recorded in the woodlands of that state.[17]

The Great Florida Freeze

By the time of settler entry into northern Florida, the natural range of the royal palm had apparently become more limited. Bartram reported its prevalence there at the time of the American Revolution. Its subsequent demise is attributed to the disastrous freeze of 1835. Bartram's travelogue editor notes that for ten days the wind blew severely, the thermometer dipped to 7°F, and the St. John's River in Florida was partly frozen. All fruit trees were killed to the ground. One must suppose the ground froze, killing all roots, for the palm tree did not resprout.[18]

The freeze of 1835, so devastating in Florida, was still on the minds of more northerly settlers in 1841. Lyell found its influence at that time in South Carolina, where wine had frozen in bottles and oysters had perished in the estuaries. Later, in 1849, he wrote of how orange trees that had been planted by General Oglethorpe in 1742 were destroyed by the ice of this storm. No doubt the freeze influenced the composition of the forests of the Atlantic coast a century later.[19]

A Poet's Description

Among those not disposed to consider the southern forest monotonous was Georgia's native son and poet laureate. No finer lines illustrate the woodland scene along the southeastern coast than those from Sidney Lanier's "The Marshes of Glynn," written in 1878. For decades, every child of the Peach State memorized its melodic lyrics:

> Glooms of the live-oak, beautiful-braided
>   and woven
> With intricate shades of the vines that
>   myriad-cloven
> Clamber the forks of the multiform
>   boughs . . .

Natural Areas of the Coastal Plain

A few tracts of virgin, or near-virgin, forest remained in the South as of 1963. At that time, I made a study of all of the alleged virgin tracts in the three most southeasterly states.[20] Because these likely approximate the appearance of the pioneers' forest, they are described here. Foresters call these sites "natural areas." In describing stands of timber, one refers to diameters measured at breast height (d.b.h.) and to basal area. D.b.h. is determined four and a half feet above the ground. Basal area, a measure of stand density, is the total area of the tree boles at breast height on an acre.

St. Mark's Refuge

The St. Mark's National Wildlife Refuge on the Gulf Coast in north Florida, contains a natural area on a level site three to five feet above sea level. The soil is alluvial. While only a few scattered old pine trees of the original forest remained in 1963, they averaged but twelve inches d.b.h. and forty feet tall. Stunted growth may have been caused by salt spray or wind on these coastal trees. Cabbage palmetto there averaged fifteen feet in height and eight inches d.b.h. The four hundred acres of slash pine and cabbage palmetto—slash pine forest cover types that then made up the forest—were only about twenty-five years of age. Having a young stand of trees among virgin remnants is attributed to an especially good seed year. Such regenerated woodlands probably were common in the pioneers' forest.

Osceola Forest

The Osceola natural area in the national forest of the same name, near Lake City in northeastern Florida, supports slash pine, long-leaf pine, pond pine, pondcypress, and sweetbay–swamp tupelo–red maple types. The land is level, of alluvial origin, and just a few feet above sea level. The slash pine is the youngest of the forest types represented there, while the pondcypress—if one can be confident of the precision with which the species lays down annual rings—exceeds 250 years.

Blackbeard Island

A Blackbeard Island National Wildlife Refuge stand of slash pine–hardwoods exists on a poor site consisting of low sand ridges with alternating sloughs. Geologically, the refuge off the coast of Georgia is a barrier beach formation. The hundred-year-old pines in the three hundred–acre stand averaged about eighty feet tall and twenty-four inches d.b.h. in 1963. The hardwoods, probably much younger, were about fifty feet tall and fifteen inches d.b.h.

Sapelo Island

Sapelo Island, also off the coast of Georgia, contained two natural areas. One was a twenty-acre live oak stand, certain to exceed two hundred years of age. The other was fifty acres of loblolly pines and a variety of broad-leaved hardwoods with a considerable mix of slash pines which, in 1963, were about one hundred years old. A dozen or more other hardwood species and sawpalmetto occured with the live oaks. Site productivity was only fair, the pines in 1963 averaging about eighty feet in height (for three merchantable logs), and the hardwoods fifty feet. Diameters averaged twenty and twenty-four inches, respectively. One tree measured was 115 feet tall, the maximum pine d.b.h. being about twenty-eight inches. Basal area ranged from fifty to eighty square feet per acre. The soil, derived from Coastal Plain barrier beach sediments, is a deep fine sand.

Hauss Park

At the time of the survey, a longleaf pine natural area occurred on industry land, near Flomaton, in southern Alabama. The forty-acre stand, on soil derived from Coastal Plain sediments, was well preserved in 1963. Its ninety-foot tall trees exceeded twenty inches d.b.h. at two hundred years of age. The site was named Hauss Park in honor of a former president of the company that earlier owned the land who cherished and personally guarded the stand.

A War Memorial

A loblolly pine–shortleaf pine tract within the city limits of Camden, Alabama, had belonged to the owner for seventy years in 1963. When he was a boy, he said, the stand looked as it did in that year. That the last half-inch radius of many trees over three feet d.b.h. had more than twenty-five annual growth rings attests to the reliability of this observation. By extrapolation, we ascertained the age of the timber to be about one hundred forty years. That was approximately the time the area was settled by whites. Indeed, the forest is believed to have been picturesque in the days of the Civil War. Later it honored the participants in that event. The stand, on slightly rolling Coastal Plain sediments, probably matured at about age seventy. In the last seventy years, there had been but one fire, and this occurred fifty years prior to my observations.[21]

In 1963, the stand contained as much as 34,000 board feet per acre of sawtimber, gross scale (without deduction for the prevalent interior red heartrot and butt rot). Trees were more than 125 feet tall and had more than six merchantable sixteen-foot logs. Shortleaf pines averaged five feet shorter than the loblolly pines. Basal area for the conifers approximated seventy square feet per acre, while the understory hardwoods contributed another thirty square feet. As the pines continue to gradually succumb, due to breakage and wind throw, the stand undergoes a transition to the loblolly pine–hardwood type and eventually is expected to be characterized principally by American beech and southern magnolia. Oaks, hickories, and elm were noticeably absent, and pines were not found in the understory in 1963.[22]

Marshall Forest

Another loblolly pine–shortleaf pine forest, about 130 years old, lies in the Valley and Ridge province of northwest Georgia within the city limits of Rome. In 1963, trees averaged twenty inches d.b.h. and were eighty-five to ninety feet tall in the forest, which was then called Edgehill.

Marshall Forest is believed to have originated following a disastrous fire at the time the Cherokee Indians, who occupied the area in great numbers, were forcibly moved to Oklahoma. The woods may have been burned by white soldiers during the roundup or by Indians in retaliation and to confuse the troops. The pines, including a few longleaf and Sonderegger (a hybrid of loblolly and longleaf pines), then seeded-in. Less severe fires occurred until state protection was available in the early 1930s. Hence, most hardwoods (blackjack oak, black oak, northern red oak, hickories, and yellow-poplar, the latter except in the coves) were less than thirty years old in 1963. Severe wind and ice storms occurred in 1950 and 1960, respectively, after which about two hundred board feet per acre of downed timber was salvaged to avoid insect infestation of residual trees. The use of insecticides was prohibited because the forest was regularly used for Audubon Society outings. Loss of the conifers expedites a transition to an oak-hickory forest. The sixty-acre tract included ten acres of virgin yellow-poplar.[23] It is now under the stewardship of the Georgia Nature Conservancy.

Lewis Land

Another longleaf pine natural area was the Lewis tract in the western panhandle of Florida near the Alabama line. This fifty-acre stand of 150-year old trees was on a Coastal Plain site ten to forty-five feet above sea level. Basal area for the pines in 1963 exceeded 150 square feet per acre and tree heights averaged ninety feet. Individual stems exceeded eighteen inches d.b.h. and averaged fifteen inches. Incidentally, a former stand of the same species had evidently occupied the site: a single tree several hundred years old still stood.

Millpond Plantation

On the Millpond Plantation in South Georgia stood a ninety-acre open parklike woodland of longleaf pine over 250 years old (fifty to eighty square feet per acre basal area). Tree heights averaged eighty feet and d.b.h. twenty inches in 1963. About fifty sawlog-size trees per acre remained at the time of the study, but red heartrot probably had culled one-half of the 30,000-board-foot volume. Rotten cores in the interior of the boles of the trees prohibited accurate age determination. One tree thirty-two inches in diameter that had been blown down, for instance, had over 225 annual rings to the decayed center of its stump, which was only nine inches from the bark. Growth of the outer inch of radius required forty years. Longleaf pine is a fire-climax type, and because this stand was periodically burned for wildlife habitat improvement, the forest floor was a "rough" of living and dead grass. By such controlled fire, scrub oaks are kept in check. Some young longleaf pines, still in the grass stage, had germinated from a recent seed crop. [24]

Pioneers Encounter Swamps

Akin to the Coastal Plain on the Eastern seaboard were the swamps of the pioneers' forest. The Dismal in Virginia and North Carolina and the Okefenokee of Georgia and Florida were prime candidates for utilization and for mystery.

The Dismal Swamp

The Dismal Swamp, "one enormous quagmire" to the geologist Charles Lyell, was considered peculiar because it was higher than the surrounding dry land by some twelve feet. This, however, also describes the pocosins that lie to the south in North Carolina. [25]

By the 1840s, timber removal had begun in some of these swamps. Straight canals were cut through the peat to facilitate harvest of the baldcypress, sometimes referred to as cedar, and for the Atlantic white-cedar. Evidence existed that stands of timber had been thinned by fire and that severe storms had toppled trees. Boles of fallen trees of ages past were encountered as the standing trees were felled. While pioneers logged the living, standing timbers, they also salvaged trees that had been blown down. Lyell said the sapwood was less than an inch thick. (He may have referred to that portion of the sapwood that remained; for sapwood of even resistant-to-rot species decays readily, and the heartwood of both the baldcypress and the white-cedar is slow to decompose. On the other hand, old trees have relatively little sapwood.) Ingeniously, the logs were recovered and "sawn into planks while half under water." Further south,

Stands of Atlantic white-cedar grow in Eastern Seaboard swamps characterized by peat soil as deep as forty feet. The fine-grained, light wood once found use in home interiors, and when it was boiled, the pioneers said the "infusion" was good for "stomachic." The species' durability recommended it for telegraph poles in the Civil War years. (Courtesy U.S. Forest Service.)

some time later, the same observer noted baldcypress trees girdled about thirty years before at the edges of rice fields. They still stood, the heart-wood resistant to destructive fungi and insect attacks.[26]

The peat of the swamp, ten to fifteen feet thick and giving a pale brown color to the water, was notably free of mineral matter. (By definition, peat may contain up to 50 percent mineral matter.) Even in this hot climate, inundated organic matter decays slowly, yet the freshly fallen leaves and twigs ferment so rapidly that distinguishing the origin of the surface material is virtually impossible shortly after its accumulation in the water of the swamp. Quickly the newly acquired organic matter is homogenized and incorporated into the deep humus layer.

In the swamps singled out by Sir Charles Lyell were the "pecu-

Southern baldcypress. Buttressed stumps and knees of these trees provide stability against wind in the soft, fibrous, organic soils. This tree, which was named in honor of General Sam Houston, is now under Toledo Bend Reservoir. (Courtesy U.S. Forest Service.)

liar kinds" of evergreen oaks, willows, and white-cedar, along with shrubs nine to eighteen feet tall, ferns, reeds, and mosses. He described the Atlantic white-cedar as having deep taproots, perhaps believing so because of the relative wind resistance of the trees in soggy soils.[27] Rather, the wind resistance of this laterally rooted tree on these sites can be attributed to the normally great density of the stands. Forests of this species are their own windbreak and shelterbelt, fifteen hundred eight-inch trees to the acre not being uncommon.

Wildlife in the Dismal Swamp noted by Lyell included wildcats, wolves, and bears, which were abundant. Bears climbed trees for acorns and gum berries and even broke branches in order to pull the acorns closer.[28]

Land of Trembling Earth

Natural areas in the swamps of the Southeast, as close to a virgin condition as any likely to be found, give some idea of the appearance of much of the timberland of the pioneers' wetland forests. There can be found the great running water swamp in southeastern Georgia, called the Okefenokee, or "land of trembling earth."[29] Within it stands a virgin forest of pondcypress, a variety of southern baldcypress cataloged as *Taxodium distichum* var. *ascendens*. The 15,000-acre stand was over 250 years of age in 1963; however, the trees growing on the level peat deposits, 120 feet above sea level, were only sixty feet tall and about twelve inches in diameter. Another virtually untouched 2,500-acre tract of timber, though just sixty years old, was nearby in the swamp. It consisted of the sweetbay–swamp tupelo–red maple forest cover type. The peat soils of the Okefenokee comprise interwoven organic matter, such as old roots and decaying branches. Noted earlier, Okefenokee in an Indian tongue relates to the mattress-springlike bounce of the land.[30]

Highland Hammock

The Highland Hammock State Park tract on the edge of the Everglades saw grass morass in South Florida in 1963 consisted of sixteen hundred acres of South Florida slash pine and southern baldcypress that ranged in age from fifty to eighty years old, and of two hundred acres of live oak trees from 250 to 500 years of age. This virgin natural area contained baldcypress trees that in 1963 had a diameter of five feet, though most were three to five feet d.b.h. and with short stems, forty to fifty feet tall. These deciduous conifers were accompanied by an understory of sweetgum, red maple, and magnolia. The gently rolling terrain, characterized by alluvial sand resting on a calcareous base, is broken by water courses.

Corkscrew

The Corkscrew Swamp Sanctuary, owned by the National Audubon Society, also is in the Everglades of southern Florida, near Immokalee. In addition to a unique hundred-year-old stand of South Florida slash pine, the tract contained in 1963 over three thousand acres of pondcypress and six hundred acres of southern baldcypress. The baldcypress averaged one hundred feet in height but only four to eight inches in diameter. The baldcypress is fairly open-grown, while the small pondcypress stems notably grow in denser stands.[31]

Settling the Fall Line

From St. Augustine for four hundred miles upstream on the St. John's River; from Savannah upriver to Augusta; and from Charleston to Cape Fear River and then to the Fall Line, John or John and William Bartram together traversed the wooded land. They often roamed sick with malaria to explore forests like those described above. The elder, enslaved by his declining physical condition, wrote that "if I could but spend six months in . . . Mississippi, and Florida, in health, I believe I could find more curiosities than the English, French, and Spaniards have done in six score of years." He would find even more in the sandhills of the Fall Line.[32]

Pioneer Problems

One is struck by the seriousness of soil erosion in the pioneers' woods of the 1840s. Severe deep-gully erosion followed the cutting of the timber. So devastating to the rivers was sedimentation that fish in the Chattahoochee, according to Lyell, were stifled by the mud. The turbidity of the Ocmulgee, Oconee, and Altamaha rivers was also attributed to the harvesting of the forests.[33]

To the pioneers' problems of sediment-filling rivers and the spoil depletion of their coastal farms were added two other dilemmas of major concern. These were the natural lack of clear, clean water and the malarial infection that took a devastating toll on the people in the lower Coastal Plain. Inward migration was mandated. Men and their families moved, often in small boats and rafts, up the rivers that rake the Atlantic coast. Those forced to abandon the black-water country had little to carry and nothing of value to leave behind in their shanties on the edges of the woods in the coastal forests of loblolly pine and moisture-loving hardwoods.

Rowing of boats and cutting trails ceased at the falls, the barrier between the Coastal Plain and the Piedmont Province on most rivers of the southeastern United States. The physiographic zone connecting the rapids on the many channels to the sea would soon be called the Fall Line Sandhills. Soils were sandy, too sterile for sustained crop production, yet they were easily turned with the plow and hence an inducement to settle and farm. The longleaf pines growing sparsely were minimal hindrance to breaking new ground, and the grass beneath, sustained by the abundant sunshine filtering through the conifer canopy, offered the false hope of a harvest of abundance. The grasses were those we now name poverty and bunch, neither requiring much in the way of nutrient elements for sustenance and moisture for hardiness in times of drought. Occupying the land, too, were scrub oaks, like turkey and blackjack. These some now call "phytometers," plant indicators of poor sites for forest trees or farmers' crops.

Bad Air Hastens Migration

Breaking new ground for farms was only incidental to the move inland through the pioneer forests of the lower, middle, and upper Coastal Plain of the Atlantic Seaboard. At the Fall Line, clear, clean water had been found, and in abundance. Development of communities within the oak-hickory climax forest of the Piedmont Province farther inland could wait. The falls provided not only clear water, free of sediment, for cotton manufacture, but here, too, the pioneers found clean water, free of microbes, to satisfy their thirst. The force with which the water moved, in contrast to the lazy meanders of the rivers at their mouths, provided power. Power was needed for textile production and for the sawmills that would in time dominate the economy in the region.

Here water cascades over rocks in the rivers. In this undulating land, water moves rapidly, seldom lies still, and hence there are few ponds suitable for egg laying by the death-dealing mosquito. Malaria had an impact on the use of the forests, and vice versa. Without understanding the relationship of the disease to the anopheles mosquito, discovered in the 1880s as the carrier of the causal agent of the tragic malady, pioneering homesteaders did comprehend the connection of the illness to dampness. Migrants inland settled on dry, airy ridges to avoid the "agur," as ague was colloquially called. And, too, Cowdrey reports that an emigrant's guide to Louisiana published in 1816 suggested that the mosquito, a "meager biting bug" thriving in stagnant pools of water was the culprit. Some attributed the disease to "vegetable putrefaction" in forests, thus lending support to the belief that the affliction was caused by bad air. After all, the name of the disease was derived from the Italian *mala aria*. [34]

Vegetable putrefaction, or organic matter decay, occurred most rapidly where forests were cleared. One was considered relatively safe from malarial infection if confined to dense, cool uncut woods where vegetation rots slowly. Although pools of water occur in the virgin forests of the coastal flats, they were kept cool by the dense, sun-shading foliage of overstory and understory canopies. Partial removal of the canopy and warming of the water encouraged the mosquitoes to breed. When fully clearing the forest and turning the soil, the pools dried up. Thus clear-felling, in contrast to partial harvests, reduced the spread of infection. Malaria was further controlled by soil erosion, puddles for breeding *Anopheles quadrimaculatus* being eliminated as the surface soil washed down to the sea. Higher, drier land, with less organic matter in the soil, typified the Fall Line. Malaria was therefore less prevalent.[35] Yellow fever was a mere episode in contrast to malaria. After 1830, this disease, transmitted by the *Aedes aegypti* vector, was an exclusively southern ailment in the woodlands of the region.[36]

Wood would be needed shortly, for at the Fall Line, taking advantage of the clean air and power from the river rapids, new villages would bud, blossom into towns, and full flower into cities. Principal among them were Georgetown (now a part of Washington, D.C.) on the Potomac, Richmond on the James, Columbia on the Congaree, Augusta on the Savannah, Macon on the Ocmulgee, and Columbus on the Chattahoochee. The last-named river is the only one of these that flows into the Gulf of Mexico.

Cutting Trees at the Foot of the Mountains

The Piedmont

In the Piedmont, the foot-of-the-mountains northwest of the Fall Line Sandhills, stood forests of "glorious" magnolia among the basswood, oaks, elms, maples, and honey locust. Here too were encountered tuliptree, sweetgum, persimmon, and eastern redcedar.[37] The obvious exclusion of the pines in some of William Bartram's tallies suggests a long period, perhaps a hundred years or more, since fire or tornado-force winds had laid bare the soil over vast areas. Exposure of the site to full sunlight is essential for establishing new stands of southern pines. Land-clearing fires and storms provide this exposure.

Understory vegetation of dogwood, rhododendron, and fiery red azalea prevailed. Bartram found the yellow-flowered shrub *Dirca palustris* in the rich, deep, shaded vales between the hills and always on the cooler, north-facing slopes. There it grew larger than in his native woods near Philadelphia. Because its bark was used by Indians for thongs, it earned its common name, rope bark. Some have also called it leatherwood or moose wood.[38]

Ground cover included cowslips, one among them shooting-star, a perennial herb growing in open woods and on moist slopes. The poetic license in the soul of Bartram often emerged, but never more descriptively than in the forests between the Fall Line and the Appalachian formation he called the Cherokees. So he described the "fragrant" calycanthus, an allspice with flowers that when crushed smell like strawberries; "blushing" rhododendron, with its pink blossoms; "delicate" Philadelphus, a mock-orange shrub; "sky-robed" *Delphinium* larkspur, with its dolphin-shaped flower; and "perfumed" *Convallaria*, a perennial lily-of-the-valley blossoming in the woods of the Piedmont hills on rocky soil. Grapes here, in contrast to those he found in Florida, were listed as edible.[39]

To supply the pioneers' needs, the forests of the Piedmont were available. Site quality was so good and thus the quality of the trees so favorable that timber removal in these rolling hills preceded in large measure that of the level, more accessible pine forests in the Coastal Plain. By harvesting the oak and hickory trees with hard wood, the pioneers could break new land for farms and supply food for the Fall Line inhabitants as well as for those who went further inland to cut the trees.

Cultivating Piedmont Land

Soils of the Piedmont, just inland from the Fall Line and generally west to northwestward of the Coastal Plain, were happily noted by the agrarian minded. The deep mull humus layer, noted by the dark color of the organic matter that penetrated deeply into the surface soil, was evidence for the more-learned farmer that he could grow good crops in this zone. In the excitement of the potential, breaking new ground for agriculture likely outran land clearing of timber for domestic use. Still the cultivator little understood the relationship of soil texture to nutrient retention and hence to plant growth and soil conservation.

While the higher elevations of the Piedmont are characterized by hilly topography with rolling ridges, the zone nearer the Fall Line has broad interstream areas of gently rolling hills. Soils the pioneers found were formed from granites, gneisses, schists, and diorites that weather and release in silt and clay particles an abundance of nutrients that enhance the growth of plants. Sometimes base elements, such as calcium and potassium, would be deficient, especially the former because the region lacks limestone, marble, and other calcareous deposits.

Cleared forest lands became first tobacco farms, then cornfields, and finally cotton patches. No crops perhaps are as detrimental to land as these. Clean cultivation, row cropping, and the demand for plant food soon exhausted the supply of available nutrients, to the discouragement of farmers. The erosive nature of silts and clay on the hillsides of the Piedmont, even when some sand in the surface soil justifies its classifica-tion as a loam, soon became apparent.

Erosion was expedited because of down-slope plowing, which produced little gullies in the furrows that would be plowed over in the next cultivation without concern for the soil that washed from the site. With mules having all four legs of the same length and men having two of equal dimensions, plowing on a contour is strenuous, exhausting to both farmer and beast, and hence not likely to be practiced by even the most faithful of the stewards of soil resources. Only after plowing, even on level land and in a loose coarse soil, does one fully understand the remark by Jesus in Holy Writ that "no man, having put his hand to the plow, and looking back is fit for the Kingdom of God." The one who glances back-ward to examine the plow's work is in trouble; the furrows will wander. It's a tough job for tough men and women. Any means to ease the task can be expected to be used, and that includes cultivating in the direction of the slope, rather than on the contour.

The trying nature of the task resulted in the less-affluent seek-ing out the sandy soils for conversion from forest to food, tobacco, and fiber crops. These sites, easier to cultivate than the richer, siltier soils, could be identified by the pure stands of pine growing on them, often with low-grade hardwoods beneath. A single mule, or sometimes the human back alone, would provide the necessary energy for turning these soils. So intense was land conversion to agriculture in the Piedmont that by 1850 it was the only southern region not covered by virgin forest. By the Civil War's end, most of its land would be farmed for cotton, tobacco, and corn.

Hewing Piedmont Hardwoods

Pioneers in the Piedmont Province employed slaves in the back-rending task of hewing logs. With twelve-pound broad axes, the blacks mounted the massive felled timber; and there, with heavy strokes and perfect cadence, shaped the rounded logs into squared beams. The regular beat echoed and reechoed in the deep forest. I have heard it, in the late 1940s, as cross ties were hand hewn from the post oak boles of the woods of East Texas. The hewers, wearing only undershorts and "mission box" shoes, two men to a timber, worked opposite sides of a log. Sweating beads the size of grapes, they rhythmically shaped the ties. The twelve-inch-wide axe heads were razor sharp, easily able to shave a man's legs had the well-directed blows been diverted. Yet, these "tie hackers" seemed not unlike those described by the younger Bartram. He remarked of their behavior as "content and joyful . . . forgetting their bondage,

[who] in chorus sang the virtue and beneficence of their master in songs of their own composition." [40]

Today, only a single stand is represented as a natural area in the Piedmont of Georgia. This is a sixty-five-year-old loblolly pine–shortleaf pine stand in the lower Piedmont on national wildlife refuge land. The site is good: the stems of both species exceeded eighty feet in height at thirty-five years of age on the rolling alluvial soil. The loblolly pines in this 138-acre tract in 1963 averaged thirteen inches d.b.h. and the shortleaf pines eleven inches. [41] In spite of its youth, this forest is not atypical of considerable acreages of the forests at the foot of the Southern Appalachian Mountains at the time of pioneering development. Natural areas need not be old, but simply virgin—never harvested.

Moravian Influence

The Bartrams, in the days of the explorers of the southern forest, were obviously astute observers of nature. They did not appear to be worshippers, but appreciators, of nature. Nor did they seem to be Transcendentalists like the New England naturalist Henry David Thoreau and his friend Ralph Waldo Emerson. Neither Nature nor the God of nature alone was the subject of their worship. John Bartram wrote, "How can we look [at nature] without amazement, or contemplate the Divine Majesty that rules . . . without the most humble adoration." That adoration was expressed in words he carved above a window of his home: " 'Tis God alone, Almighty Lord / The Holy One by me ador'd." [42] Though neither of the Bartrams remained in the South or reared children on its land, the attitude of the people of this section of the country is notably akin to the father's couplet. That, possibly we'll see, affected the way the forests were utilized by the pioneers and those who would follow them.

In the cut-out-and-get-out days of the lumbermen's forest, still decades in the future, Scripture's admonition for humans to have dominion over nature would be justified by those who controlled purse and people. In the times of the foresters' forest, still farther down the road, quoted passages from the Bible would aid in reducing the arson that annually consumed the trees in the region on hundreds of thousands of acres. But in the era of the pioneers, a religious sect also had a local but significant impact on the forests of the Piedmont Province in central North Carolina.

The Moravians, Protestant Christians adhering to the faith as advocated by the fifteenth-century Roman Catholic reformer Jon Hus, first found a home in the New World in Bethlehem, Pennsylvania. These particular followers of the martyred Bohemian Hus had come from a small province in what is now Czechoslovakia. That province, Moravia, gave its name to the band of Christians that became the Moravian Church.

Although their emigration began in 1735, not until five years later had they established the colony in the North and promptly named it for the little town a few miles south of Jerusalem where Jesus was born. With expansion in mind, devout followers of Hus's theology left Bethlehem with the coming of winter to explore a vast tract of land in North Carolina's rolling Piedmont. The church purchased a hundred thousand acres of fertile broadleaf forest from Lord Granville's Crown grant. Cutting of timber began shortly after the first colonists arrived.[43]

A collegium, a sort of aldermanic board, was appointed to supervise the nonspiritual interests of the colony. Its responsibilities included managing the forests. Thus the true father of forestry in North America could rightly be the first forester appointed by the collegium to cruise, or tally, the timber and to measure and mark the trees for harvest.

Foresters in Salem, the new North Carolina village whose Hebrew name is the equivalent of the English word *peace*, selected trees suitable for woodenware, shingles, fence rails, water pipes, sugar tapping, leather-treatment tannin, housing, and fuel. Foresters blazed the bark on the boles of the chosen trees, and in that spot stamped the wood mark. Type maps were drawn that showed species, age classes, stand density, and potential use for the wood of the timber type. By 1828, overcutting caused the collegium to limit families to twenty-three cords of wood annually for heating. Three decades later the land that was until then leased to the settlers became available for individual purchase. With each property owner now the overseer of his own forest, the community forester was no longer needed.

The record shows that in 1797 unusually heavy pine mortality occurred. This area of the Piedmont suffered widespread and serious southern pine beetle infestation in the 1980s, and perhaps that pest, *Dendroctonus frontalis*, could also have caused the death of the trees in the Moravian timberland.

Fire apparently was a serious hindrance to forest management then, as in more recent times, in the vicinity. The report of a discussion in 1792 notes that "it would be well to plant yellow pine seeds [but] we are afraid that bush fires will prevent their coming up." Hunting was permitted on occasion only on condition that the hunter would not build a fire in the woods.

As one historian observed, "Salem [now part of Winston-Salem] survived its perilous infancy in part because of the direction and foresight provided by these early Moravian foresters." Stewardship of the renewable timber resource played an important role in that survival.

Pioneers Move to the Mountains

After agricultural pursuits began to alter the landscape of the Piedmont Province, pioneers entered to claim for settlement the high-land forests of the Southern Appalachian region. Entry and settlement of the mountains required a century. Whatever their reasons for the effort, the migrants to these mountains were people much given to an appreciation for solitude. Many, like the famed Basque herdsmen, can be alone without being lonely. It was their choice not to gather in communities, but rather to scatter among the hills of beech, birch, and maple; to in-habit the coves of hemlock, American chestnut, and yellow-poplar; and to settle just below the red spruce and Fraser fir forests that appear like quivers of giant arrows pointing heavenward at the summit of the range.

At the edge of the wild country, some mountaineers tried sub-sistence farming. The coves of limestone-derived soil, high in calcium and other nutrients and well supplied with water, could produce corn, beans, and a family's staples. The farmed lands of dark-colored, loamy clay soil were in small plots, perhaps an acre in size, extending on either side of a stream for fifty to one hundred feet or so. Sometimes the land would be cleared, here of basswood and there of black walnut, to provide an open grassy area for a milk cow or two.

But if the open land had been the site of a black walnut grove, discouragement followed. This tree exudes from its roots the chemical juglone (the tree is of the genus *Juglans*), a natural herbicide that is ab-sorbed by the roots of other plants to their detriment. Walnut, one might say, is jealous of its territory. The species' scientific genus name is derived from the Latin *Jovis glan*, meaning acorn of Jove. Jove was the Roman god of the sky.

Fertile Soils for Small Farms

At the higher elevations, the soils are derived from gneisses and granites and give rise to acidic, sandy surface horizons. Throughout the mountains, in uplands and in coves, the soils contain a high percent-age of organic matter. Low temperatures and the predominance of broad-leaved species are responsible for this. Broad-leaved foliage, especially that of flowering dogwood, is high in nutrients. Earthworms, attracted to the leaves for the nutrient supply following autumn leaf fall, consume the foliage and pass it out as casts, each the size of a garden pea, on and below the surface of the ground. Earthworm casts, as do other fecal matter, serve significantly in recycling nutrients.

Energetic early Americans journeyed into the Valley and

Poorly formed longleaf pine. Trees of this species in northern Alabama's Chesha Mountain, above two thousand feet in elevation, have poor form. In the absence of repeated fires, Virginia and shortleaf pines take over the site as the longleaf pines pass from the scene. (Courtesy U.S. Forest Service.)

Ridge Province, a part of the Appalachian chain. Here they found the land characterized by gently rolling broad valleys set between steep slopes capped by long, narrow ridges. In these areas once covered by sea, the soft limestone had weathered, leaving ridges composed mostly of dolomite (a magnesium-coated limestone) and of less-easily weathered sandstone and shale. In the valleys of dolomite, pure stands of eastern redcedar, with trees forty inches in diameter and three logs high, provided choice timbers for chests and wardrobes. For these purposes they were cut. Pioneers found rich soils, whose fertility was diminished only by fragments of chert and flint. Except for wear-and-tear on the plowshare, the soils were an inducement to cultivation. Interspersed with such soils are those derived from shale. These are less fertile. Less fertile still are the light, porous soils whose parent material is sandstone. These are often found on high, relatively flat-topped ridges.

On plateaus, like the Cumberland, extending northerly through Tennessee and Kentucky, the pioneers cleared oaks and hickories. Had fire occurred within the past 50 years or so, dense stands of Virginia pine, which many called "scrub pine," would have occupied the site as an initial seral species.

Indian Relationships

Pioneering Anglo settlements in the South—to the west of the Carolinas and Georgia—were restrained by the British prior to the American Revolution. Agreements between Indians and Crown agents held the ambitious to a line formed by the Appalachian chain. Only shortly before the American Revolution had the line been broken when, by 1760, communities had been established to its west. The Creek Confederacy in Georgia was then ceding lands to British subjects. Although Daniel Boone settled in Kentucky in 1775, conclusion of the War for Independence in 1783 encouraged other expansion enthusiasts to locate settlements in mid-Tennessee and central Kentucky. It was not long until—in the early 1800s—Americans had a network of villages and forts in the western Appalachians that were linked with those of the French and Spanish along the river courses of the west Gulf region.

Bartram encountered some forty-three Indian towns of the Cherokee nation in his travels through the mountainous territory. Indians influenced Anglos' land use once the newcomers were in the forest. These Native Americans taught the whites how to grow corn in fields of freshly broken ground as extensive as two or three miles on a side. Even before the Crown lost its control over the colonies, such crops of corn were cultivated, free of weeds and eighteen inches high.[44]

To be used later by miners were the deposits of minerals like mica and lead earlier recognized by explorers. "Lights for windows" and "lanthorns," wrote Bartram of the wafer-thin strips of isinglass peeled from the layered mineral called "muscovite."[45] Such improvements in the standard of living also would affect forest use.

Trees in the South not yet reported by botanical collectors were encountered by the pioneers in the mountains. Towering over others were eastern white pine and eastern hemlock, which Bartram called hemlock spruce but classified as a pine. He also called one tree *Pinus sylvestris*, today the scientific name of scotch, or Scot's pine, a New World introduction from Europe that would have been an unlikely find in those days. Perhaps Bartram saw table-mountain pine on the ridges and thought it to be the European species.[46]

Magnolia Mountain, the locale of which seems uncertain, displayed its flowering trees and shrubs, exhibiting, according to Bartram, a "high degree of perfection." Among the plants was the perfume-emanating rhododendron, six to seven feet tall, with many stems arising from the root. These shrubs persist among the maples. black walnut, white walnut (usually now called "butternut"), an assortment of hickories and oaks, and lesser trees like dogwood and mulberry. *Stewartia*—the mountain camellia with showy white flowers—was also much in view. Crawling across the ground was partridgeberry, bearing an edible, but rather tasteless, fruit that persists through the winter months to provide sustenance for wildlife. Linnaeus named it *Mitchella*, not for the University of North Carolina explorer for whom Mt. Mitchell is named but for Dr. John Mitchell, a Virginia botanical correspondent of the Swedish taxonomist.[47]

Mitchell's Mountain

In this context Elisha Mitchell, the one for whom the peak is named, deserves mention. The Southern Appalachians were the classroom, the laboratory, and the library for his students. To the Reverend Mitchell, these hills and valleys, along with the Holy Bible, served as God's revelation. Professor of theology, geology, botany, mathematics, surveying, and, one might suppose, other subjects in the fledgling academy now known as the University of North Carolina, he led his young collegians on exploratory field trips in the spruce and fir forests of the high mountain. On one such trip, the Presbyterian cleric and naturalist tragically fell to his death from a precipice. His students buried him near the summit. The mountain, taller than any other peak east of the Rockies in North America, forever stands as his memorial.

To the west of the ridge the pioneers looked for better farmland. Like players in a chess game they jumped the forests to capture the fertile limestone valley of the Nashville basin and the Kentucky bluegrass prairies. They felled the eastern redcedars in the former and cleared the hardwoods in the latter. Other settlers would turn back later to the timberlands passed over, there to claim the economic prizes.

Enter a Landscaper

Frederick Law Olmsted, another early reporter of the woodland scene, trekked to the cove-site homes of the Highlanders of Tennessee. There the designer of New York's Central Park and Asheville's Biltmore Estate found corn, rye, oats, grass, and tobacco cultivated by pioneering settlers in the clearings. The soils, of "rich dark vegetable deposit" and of high infiltration capacity, produced twenty to thirty bushels of corn per acre. Even when farmers cultivated steep slopes, erosion did not form gullies, he wrote. Meadows occurred on level land in the valleys where the timber had been felled and the brush cut to ground level. Too wet for cultivation, the site was captured by grass. Sprouts that followed the felling of the deciduous trees and shrubs were cut annually in August for two to three years. Finally the thick cover of grass led the traveling landscape architect to describe the locale as a natural meadow.[48]

Bee Branch in the Mountains

A fascinating forested tract is the Bee Branch in the Bankhead National Forest of northern Alabama, reclassified in the 1980s by the U.S. Forest Service from a Scenic Area to Wilderness in order to assure its perpetuation in an undisturbed condition. Most of the trees in this truly primeval woodland exceed two hundred years of age, and many, no doubt, are over three hundred years old. As of 1963, a ten-inch hemlock, a late comer, was more than one hundred years old, and a beech with a twenty-two–inch d.b.h. had ninety annual growth rings in its outer 5.5 inches.

The stand, in the moist bottom of a fairly inaccessible gorge, is believed typical of the virgin Southern Appalachian forest. The soil in the limestone bowl, separated from the plateau above by hundred-foot sheer cliffs, is characterized by a well-developed mull humus, though horizon differentiation below the rocky, shallow surface layer is rather indistinct.

Chestnut snags, so often seen as remnants of the recent botanical past in such forests, are not present among the old-growth trees in the gorge. *Endothia parasitica*, causal agent for the blight that once killed millions of high-quality American chestnut trees, played no role in disrupting ecological succession here. The species did not occur in Bee Branch.[49]

The 128 acres at Bee Branch are relatively level, but very rocky, and lie eight hundred to nine hundred feet above sea level. The yellow-poplar trees averaged about ninety feet tall and twenty-four inches d.b.h. when tallied in 1963. Hemlocks were about the same height and eighteen inches d.b.h. A 150-foot-tall yellow-poplar measured 6.6 feet d.b.h. and eighty-five feet to the first limb. Basal area for the stand approximated seventy square feet per acre in 1963.

In contrast, the shortleaf pine–Virginia pine stand on the drier plateau adjacent to the gorge is on friable soil with a well-developed deep loamy surface soil and silty clay subsoil underlying a humus of undecomposed organic matter. The plateau has been frequently and severely burned, judging from the charcoal particles found more than a foot below the surface of the ground. The hardwood and hardwood-hemlock cover types in the moist gorge, in contrast, have been well protected from fire and, by virtue of their location and composition, from lightning and biotic disaster.

The plateau surrounding the natural area also appears to be virtually untouched. White oaks among the conifers exceed one hundred years of age, but large trees are lacking, probably because of fire and the relatively poor site. Here, the pine type is giving way to southern red oak.

Settling the Deep South

South to the Gulf

Turning southward into Alabama, pioneers encountered the black soil that rested on deep beds of white limestone, now classified as Selma chalk. The formation gave rise to the Black Belt, a natural prairie. Travel through this zone was unobstructed, grass replacing brushy vegetation. Migrants, however, were exposed to the ever-watchful eyes of aborigines as the former encroached upon Indian lands.

Further to the west and south along the rivers, pioneers encountered clumps of hydrangea shrubs and the conspicuous whitish-green flower of *Silphinium*. From the latter, a gummy gunk, rich in terpenes, was brewed. When chewed, the turpentine fragrance sweetened the breath.[50]

Of especial fascination for the pioneers were the grapevines that do not hang from trees but, rather, creep from one low shrub to another. They noted, too, the "unalterable" groves of dogwood. Of the latter, Bartram wrote of a stand nine to ten miles across, of trees twelve feet tall, yet with limbs interlocking. Forty years after Bartram's description of a dogwood flat in the northwest of Alabama's present Butler County, a forest was described as a pine flat under which dogwoods had grown in a dense stand. The brown loam soil, according to this appraisal, had, apparently after the Bartrams' trek, produced an "undergrowth of dogwood" with pines in the overstory. The dense-fibered dogwood stems were gone.[51] Perhaps fire, necessary for the successful establishment of longleaf pine, killed them. A fire shortly before pine seed dispersal could have been responsible for the seeding-in of the pine among the stems of dogwood. That fire or another could kill the dogwood trees. If two fires had occurred, they could have differed in intensity. A cool one, perhaps ignited in the winter and running swiftly with the wind shortly after rain, would prepare the pine seedbed. And one of intense heat, likely in the summer months and during drought, would destroy the hardwoods.

Water Route to the Gulf

As the Gulf of Mobile is approached overland from the northeast, one today expects longleaf, slash, sand, and spruce pines to at least be mentioned in the chronicles of travelers into the pioneers' forest. Bartram fails to do so but, instead, lists the variety of broadleaf trees, including the American chestnut, now absent from the area. I suppose he missed the uplands, on which the pines predominate, as he traveled the water courses en route to the coast.[52]

Bartram hiked through the canebrakes, noting the *Arundo gigantea* to be so great in size that a single joint (the section between the nodes along the stem) held a quart of water.[53] Such voluminous examples are no longer encountered, though Charles Lyell in 1849 measured total heights of some specimens at thirty feet.[54] In 1897, Peter Hamilton, another recorder of pioneering encounters, listed a forty-seven–foot specimen.[55]

An uneven-aged stand of conifers in Alabama attracts our attention. It consists of a tree twenty-nine inches in diameter at a three-foot stump height when 120 years old, one that is twenty-seven inches at 260 years, and another forty-eight inches at 320 years. Heights Lyell listed ranged from 70 to 120 feet. One has difficulty determining what these trees were. Lyell called them fir, but none by that name is found beneath the upper reaches of the Southern Appalachian Mountains in the South. Placed in association with longleaf pine in the sojourner's narrative, I think this describes a stand of eastern redcedar[56] in a limestone sink of the area. The trees Lyell called fir were possibly those today called spruce pine.

The rich bottoms along the Gulf Coast are the habitat for southern baldcypress and a tree the younger Bartram described as similar to the white-cedar of the Atlantic coastal swamps of New Jersey (and which also occurs in dense stands in the Dismal Swamp of Virginia). While limited stands of Atlantic white-cedar persist in South Alabama,

A near-virgin stand of willow oak much like those the pioneers found in the delta of the Mississippi River. (Courtesy U.S. Forest Service.)

Bartram may have been observing the pondcypress variety of baldcypress, especially known for its ascending habit, and mistaken it for white-cedar, which was found in dense stands east of his Philadelphia home. Usually confined to shallow ponds and stream swamps, *Taxodium distichum* var. *ascendens* is smaller in girth and slower in growth than baldcypress.

Sire of Rivers

Along the Mississippi River, the "Sire of Rivers," for that is the meaning of the Indian word, the baldcypress and pondcypress are accompanied by magnolia, tuliptree, sycamore, black walnut, ash, sweetgum, and basswood. (That is, if *Tilea* in Bartram's lexicon is *Tilia* in today's classification scheme.) [57]

To the north of the Mississippi's mouth lie the Bluff Hills. One account tells of a forest of stumps of baldcypress buried to a depth of about one hundred feet in the silty soils and then exposed by erosion. Perhaps the trees were "cut" by hurricane winds a millennium earlier. [58]

The report of Olmsted on his trip into the valley of the lower Mississippi in the mid-1850s tells us something of the man as well as of the place. His intolerance of the people was boorish. While ridiculing the citizens, he wrote of the glory of the magnolia in full blossom, its "magnificent chandeliers of fragrance." Beech, elm, sweetgum, young pines, and other plants already indicated impoverished agriculture, or so he reasoned. In truth, any field once abandoned in this region may likely regenerate to pine or sweetgum, depending only on the availability of a seed source. [59]

From above the crumbling faces of the cliffs that form the bluffs to the east of the Mississippi River near Natchez, Olmsted found a "vast expanse of forest, extending on every hand to a hazy horizon." Elsewhere were thickets of blackjack oaks interspersed with glades of grass only slightly broken by shrubs. [60]

Pioneer explorers observed the waxtree, an evergreen shrub, on sandy edges of swamps. Its seed is covered with wax, a source of tallow for candles. Here too is where *Oenothera* was discovered and called by Bartram the "most pompous and brilliant herbaceous plant yet known to exist." Bartram called this evening primrose *O. grandiflora*. Gray, attributing the name to Aiton, says it is naturalized from Europe. The genus of eighteen species is complex to today's taxonomists, so pardon for error is appropriate. [61]

Trekking the South's Far West

Interior Hills

The famous botanist Thomas Nuttall was among the first to describe the forests of the Ozark and Ouachita mountains in, what he called, "The Arkansa Territory." His first venture was dated 1819. Often he noted the similarity of the ash–elm–walnut–maple–hackberry–coffee bean forest cover type to those in the "northern states" from which he had come by the Ohio and Mississippi rivers. Near the Chicasaw Bluffs he called attention to water hickory and overcup oak, both bottomland species adapted to wet sites.[62]

Nuttall noted stands of pecan hickories along the river banks. An occasional black walnut, sweetgum, blackgum, sycamore, and ash grew among the pecan trees. Here, too, was the cottonwood, largest of the region's trees, and tallying more than six feet in diameter. Its wood was described as similar to that of the tuliptree. (Tuliptree in those times often was called "yellow-poplar"; today that is its name in the lumbering trade.) Here, too, the botanist found mimosa, not the Asian or African species of *Acacia* that have escaped to become naturalized in these woods, but probably the prairie mimosa of the genus *Desmanthus,* found in alluvial soils and adjacent plains. Nearby the streams was the horsetail rush, an *Equisetum* that emerges from the soil and shallow water.[63]

Nuttall called some wetlands "oak swamps" because of the many species of the genus *Quercus* found therein. He listed seven kinds for one slough and another two on the knolls of slightly higher elevation within a swamp.[64] The southern variety of pin oak, which he called swamp oak, would eventually be named *Q. nuttallii* in his honor.

Arkansas territory was also within the range of two honey locusts,[65] neither of which are listed in contemporary botanical manuals. At the upper reaches of the White River, Nuttall recorded the presence of the nettle tree,[66] one we now know more popularly as hackberry or sugarberry. The tree with sweet drupes occurs on sites ranging from damp to dry. Greenbriars here as elsewhere tripped up cross-country travelers, especially where fire had made openings in the woods to let in light for the ubiquitous vine's toehold. And in these uplands occurred the Carolina kidney-bean tree, a native *Wisteria,* that could be woven into ropes. Perhaps the legume Nuttall cataloged was the one that bears his authorship, *W. macrostachya* Nutt.[67] We find it now in swamps and woods of rich soil. Cliffs bordering the rivers were often "decorated with the red cedar, and clusters of ferns." These redcedar stands would give way to cedar prairies of luxuriant grass, with a tree here and there, in which herds of fleeting deer would browse and graze.

An "Orange" and a "Lime"

In the forest was bow wood, the name attributed to the use of the hard, tough wood for archery bows; therefore, it is locally called, especially in Texas, bois d' arc or wood-of-the-bow. Elsewhere, the tree is called Osage-orange in appreciation for an Indian tribe of Missouri and the tree's orange-size fruit. The fruit is, however, neither sweet nor orange in color. Its milky juice is bitter, and the color of this orange is green. And the orange is called an apple when harvested for dye.

A few decades later, Osage-orange trees served far beyond the species' natural range in Oklahoma and Texas. Vessels plying the Red and Sabine rivers took on the heavy apples for ballast for the return trip to the Gulf and up the Mississippi River. At ports like St. Louis, these seed-bearing fruit would be unloaded to lighten the ship and then distributed to farmers. Planted in straight rows, the trees that sprouted from the seeds became the fences for the prairie farms of the pioneers.[68]

Nuttall's Ogechee lime of the Arkansas Territory is a strange one. He called it *Nyssa pubescens*, but again I fail to find such a binomial in the literature.[69] The clue may be in the fruit that Nuttall said was utilized for preserves. The tree could be water tupelo, also called cottongum, which has fruit resembling olives. This we know is eaten by birds and mammals.

The exploring botanist told of the use of the bark of the mulberry tree by Indians for cloaks. They allowed the bark to dry in the sun and then beat it until the woody portion parted and fell away. They bleached the remainder and spun it into thread.[70]

As Nuttall roamed westward up the rivers of the territory toward their headwaters, the lush growth of large trees played out. Even on alluvial soil that was similar to the rich river bottoms of Ohio, he noted that the trees were comparatively small. Here, he pointedly stated, was no *Liriodendron*, the tuliptree.[71]

Backwoodsmen Give Way to Planters

With the arrival of the first white settlers into East Texas in the 1820s, the Caddo Indians began their westward movement. This left the virgin forest for use by the intruding backwoodsmen, who were mostly from Georgia and Alabama. It was also a time, shortly after statehood, when the Caddo found it expedient to sell their properties to the U.S. government. This hastened the harvest by whites of the pines and hardwoods of the area's hills and valleys.

Soon the backwoodsmen were displaced by well-to-do planters from Virginia, Georgia, South Carolina, and Alabama. Many of these new Texans, mostly of English descent, had come through French-cultured Louisiana after short sojourns in Acadian country.

If land was cheap, so too was life for the pioneers settling in these forests. Family heads, for instance, who migrated in 1836 and 1837, received 1,280 acres from the government. This liberal land allocation policy enabled subsequent sales at reasonable rates, eventually expediting the development of the region. Many lost their lives in the difficult journey and in the effort to survive the frontier wilderness of these southern woods. Even as I write, one may literally stumble on small carved headstones deep in the forest. On one such marker for a family of three, the dates of death, ranging from 1838 to 1863, are clearly legible. Elsewhere, a spy for the Confederacy was buried in a lone marked grave surrounded by numerous depressions suggesting other burials. Her interment was dated 1895.

About the time of Arkansas exploration, others were crossing the Sabine River at Pendleton Ferry or at Orange. At the more northerly port of entry at Pendleton, just east of today's Milam, the loblolly pine–hardwood forests were first seen by the pioneers. To the south at Orange, they encountered the swamp called Blue Elbow, then a thin zone of longleaf pine flats, and next westward the Big Thicket.

Big Thicket Intruders

That the soujourn into the Big Thicket wilderness was to be permanent and not a fly-by-night passage for most of these Scotch-Irish folk from Alabama and Georgia settlements is attested to by the presence even now of their descendants. Their offspring remain bound to the land. The fight in the 1970s to establish a national preserve in the Thicket often became a feud between these individualists and the agents of the federal government and environmentalist groups. Family lands were not to be readily surrendered.

Once the Big Thicket was breached by pioneering settlers, migration was easy and rapid. By 1880, all of the pine-hardwood forest, the Post Oak Belt, and the Cross Timbers had become the habitat of white, black, and brown men. All but a small group of Indians had moved out of their way.

Westward, precipitation diminishes. Not only are trees smaller, but the greater abundance of bison reported by chroniclers of pioneer days suggests the entrance to the prairie. In stepping into the prairie, one steps from the back door of the southern forest.

Historians Robert Maxwell and Robert Baker remind us of the importance of rivers flowing Gulfward throughout the maritime belt. Foodstuffs, salt, and household goods moved upriver, while cotton, hides, and beef flowed downward for shipment to metropolitan areas in the East. Cooperage staves, shingles, and sawn timbers accompanied the agricultural commodities once the area was settled by migrating whites.[72]

These Gulf-pointing rivers, however, were notoriously unreliable for transportation, much more so than those that flowed from the Appalachian Mountains easterly through the Piedmont, the Fall Line, and the Atlantic Coastal Plain: "In the summer months they became so low that even smaller boats (such as those used by the pioneers) could not navigate them for any considerable distance. In the winter and spring the water level rose suddenly, sometimes overnight, threatening to carry away boats and their cargoes. Sandbars shifted unexpectedly."[73]

Caddo Country

Among these water courses is Caddo Lake, on the Louisiana and Texas boundary. Village names there tell of the attitudes of early settlers in this wild land. Freedom, Equality, and Friendship are examples. So, too, is Uncertain, nestled in a bay of Caddo Lake. Karnack, named for the town on the Nile River of King Tutankhamen fame, suggests the homesteaders' knowledge of the world.

The southern baldcypress–tupelo gum forests that cover Caddo Lake differ from the pine-hardwood mixtures on the drier peripheral lands. Averaging ten feet deep, the lake was early recognized as an important transportation route. In lanes cut through the timber (including one known as Government Ditch), cotton moved from its interior cropland source to the Gulf coast for subsequent shipment to the East or to Europe for manufacturing into cloth.

To further encourage shipping through Caddo Lake, the U.S. government in 1872 cleared the long-accumulated log debris of the lower "raft" that dammed the Red River. By this action, a waterway was created on the Big and Little Cypress rivers to a swamp-side village called Jefferson. So alarmed were people around the lake when the water level was suddenly lowered (by, some said, as much as fifteen feet)[74] by the removal of the barrier that the government shortly thereafter built a quarter-mile dam to maintain a stable pool.

The original dam was a natural obstruction. Timbers lodged with one another as they fell into the river, the result of the caving-in of forested banks on the Red as well as on its tributaries. Sturdy enough for horses to ride across safely, the raft continued to grow. As a result of the greater inundation, in a single year an additional five linear miles of lake shore was added along the rivers' courses, backing up the Red for 160 miles. While the natural dam of organic debris is usually given as the origin of the South's largest natural lake, Indian legend holds that Caddo Lake resulted from an earthquake, notably the tremor of 1811. This late an occurrence as the cause of the damming of the river is unlikely, for the

bottomland hydric vegetation in the region predates that event. Yet germination of the seed from which the present remnant trees originated in
today's lake would have necessitated exposure of the mineral soil, the site
free of flooding, for at least a short time.[75]

Swamp Roads

The lowered water level of Caddo Lake, "logged" in 1873, altered both the economy and cultural attainments of many of the people of
northeastern Texas. Without transportation, commerce was disrupted;
and without transportation, the principal medium for communication in
the swamp country, diffusion of knowledge was hindered. No longer
would steamers and stern-wheelers, fueled by wood and illuminated by
resinous pine knots, ply to Jefferson through cypress trails, like Government Ditch, in Caddo Lake. Sizable boats navigated these waters, giving
it the name Ferry Lake, until the dam's rupture. Black oarsmen, one account notes, pulled, like an ancient galley of slaves, an imitation of a
Roman barque while its owner rode majestically at the prow.

Star Ditch, like Government Ditch, was another route pio-
neers cut through the lake. Beyond Star Ditch, illiterate blacks in the
days of the pioneers unloaded supplies according to playing card symbols
at docks along the way. Marshall, for instance, was the king of diamonds.
Horses and housewares, from as far distant as New Orleans, via the Red
River, would be off-loaded by code cards attached to animals or to goods.
Small craft still ply Star Ditch. Tales have it that a successor to Captain
Shreve in 1873 blew up the remnant raft and Government Dam to assure
that his port in Louisiana would be the terminus on the Red River for
inland shipping.

At first Caddo country, like the bayous of Louisiana, was navigated by white men in pirogues, or dugouts, solid wooden canoes whittled
and burned from southern baldcypress logs by able artisans. These vessels,
skimming the surface of the water, could carry heavy loads through the
shallows where hidden brush and snags would otherwise impede movement. Because of the shallow water and because rowboats were not readily and inexpensively available, pirogues moved people and their goods.

The lake appears peaceful in its baldcypress and water lily se-
renity. For this reason, old-timers remember it as Fairy Lake. In this setting lived the kindly Caddo. These civilized Indians of small stature, resisting encroachment by less-tolerant white and black men, were paid
$80,000 by the U.S. government in the mid-1830s to move out of U.S.
territory. By 1840, the Caddo tribe had dwindled to a few hundred
people, and most of these, having left the banks of the mid–Red River,

settled at first in West Texas. They then wandered to Kansas and Colorado until 1902, when federal allotments were made for each tribal member. This enabled their settling in Oklahoma, where more permanent residence was possible.

A Preacher's Account

A few miles south of Caddo Lake, a man of the cloth, the Rev. Sam McCorkle, chronicled his observations as early as 1849 in the new State of Texas. "I left the Pinery and found myself surrounded with poor blackjack, post oak country," he wrote. And again, "I passed out of the Pinery and got into the high-ridge land, which was of a Spanish brown color and covered with a rich growth, consisting in sumach, sassafrass, mulberry, dogwood, etc. The timber is not quite so good as in the Pinery; it consists in blackjack, black hickory, post oak, etc. The cornstalks in general look large enough for a southern soil. Cotton grows well."[76]

Some commentary on the remarks of the Rev. McCorkle may be helpful. His "Pinery," today called the pineries, comprises the relatively pure stands of loblolly and shortleaf pines on the better upland soils. Rather abruptly in east central Texas's pine-hardwood region, one passes from this tall timber to the ridges, as little as fifty feet above the surrounding forest. The soils, formed from water-lain alluvial sediments, vary in their texture and the depth of each deposit; thus gravel is at the surface on some ridges while on others sand is as coarse as that in a coastal dune. Drought-hardy species like blackjack oak and black hickory, the latter named *Carya texana* by latter-day taxonomists, and the most stunted form of post oak prevail. The branches of older black hickory trees appear to weep as they hang downward: on those xeric sites they have reason to.

The itinerant Rev. McCorkle describes the soil of the ridge as being of a Spanish color, perhaps a reference to the olive-complexioned Spanish ethnics that remain living today in a few communities of pure blood. The "rich growth" in the circuit rider's diary most likely referred to the dense "growth . . . [of] sumach, sassafrass, mulberry." Having listed the understory, which included dogwood, a tree generally given to rigid site requirements of substantial soil fertility and moisture, he lists the scrub species as timber, noting that the site "is not quite so good as in the Pinery."

The comment that corn and cotton grew well on these lands brings into question the reliability of many such candid observations available to historians in the archives of the region. Some were local commercial promotional pieces meant to encourage settling in the region. But, by the twenty-five-bushel-per-acre standard of pioneering times, the preacher's account may have been appropriate.

Throughout the South, the pioneers, in earlier or later times, brought wheat, sugarcane, radishes, figs, citrus fruit, and vines to compete with the trees of the forest. Many vegetative stowaways, including Kentucky bluegrass, daisies, and dandelions, colonized the fields carved out of the woods.[77]

Exploitation Begins

Pioneering Uses of the Forest

The axe in America became the symbol of the free and resourceful spirit of the southern frontier. As time went on, established folks of wealth would use wood, a versatile material, more widely. Better homes displayed it as luxury in handmade furniture and wooden wall paneling. Regional development saw bridge timbers cut from durable hardwoods, like post oak; the iron horse soon rolled on rails of wood covered by a thin iron strap, the rails supported by crossties of wood. Alongside the rails were lines of wooden poles that held the wires over which were telegraphed the dots and dashes of Sam Morse's invention. Little went north, even after cut-out-and-get-out practices had exploited the white pine and beech-birch-maple stands of the Appalachian forests in New England, New York, and Pennsylvania.

As the white pines of the Northeast emblazoned with the upward-pointing broad arrow by Crown foresters (and by Massachusetts authorities after the American Revolution) were cut for transport to British shipyards or girdled before the war by revolutionary vandals, the government looked southward for new sources of pine ship masts, white-cedar decking, and live oak hull pieces and siding. By 1730, the harvests for maritime purposes of these species in North Carolina had become significant.[78]

Before the American Revolution, the British government encouraged sawmilling by granting land to those who would build mills, promising then to buy the lumber produced. These grants were as much as a thousand acres in the coastal pineries of Georgia.[79] Select woods went abroad. Black walnut, hard maple, and wild black cherry probably were among the timbers shipped to Europe to supply the cabinetry needs of a refined people of financial means. Oaks and pines and naval stores were sent to islands of the Caribbean. Small sloops in the American Revolutionary War years carried barrel staves as well as shingles to the West Indies, there to be exchanged for rum, sugar, and badly needed cash.[80] But much wood stayed home.

George Washington's Mount Vernon mansion remains an excellent example of the use and durability of the heartwood of longleaf pine, cut from the forests well to the south of his northern Virginia estate. The exterior planks were beveled and painted with a sand finish to appear as stone. America's equivalent of European nobility used woods of the southern forest to enhance the beauty of their surroundings and to raise the esteem with which they would be held by their neighbors.[81]

Lumber Inspection Begins

Concern for the quality of forest products produced by southerners was early in evidence. In the 1760s, the Georgia Assembly enacted legislation to provide for regulation and inspection of lumber, barrel staves, hogshead staves, and shingles. Requirements included proper dimensions; pieces to be utilized were to be free of sapwood and have squared edges. Inspectors at seaports culled out lumber sawn from loblolly pine, declaring it unmerchantable.[82] Shortleaf and longleaf pines at that time and place were the preferred species.

Specialty uses for southern woods in pioneering times were not uncommon. Rot- and insect-resistant southern baldcypress heartwood was especially in demand. A water main of bored baldcypress logs was installed in New Orleans in 1789. It was used until 1914, and then only a trace of rot showed on the periphery of the logs.[83] So great was the demand that, by the end of the Civil War, the cypress industry was devastated. However, the species' special properties, including its ability to take on a beautiful finish, brought about its rapid rejuvenation in timber commerce.[84]

Curved buttresses of live oak were selected to fit the contours of the vessels that plied the high seas, a technique still employed in building small wooden boats in Greece. Craftsmen carefully selected logs for their crook, and called such pieces "compass timbers." These were sawn for a particular position in the siding of the boat. Bending the wood and straining the superstructure with boards fastened under pressure is largely eliminated.[85]

Shingle weavers got their supplies from the eastern swamps. Because white-cedar in New Jersey was depleted by 1800, further harvests were from the sloughs to the south in the Virginia and North Carolina Dismal Swamp area. Many valuable boles had sunk during logging, but these sinkers were retrieved up through the Civil War years. Such salvage operations were called "mining."

Rails and Rosin

The Virginia rail fence was a prime user of timbers from the virgin forests. No posts to rot, the split rails were laid in zig-zag fashion for stability, only the bottom one in contact with the soil. Or, preferably, the ends of the lowest rail were placed on rocks. To further reduce the necessity for replacement due to decay, fence builders used American chestnut. The remnants of these fences persist to this day. (In the 1950s, I found one in disarray, but not with decay, in the high mountains of North Carolina in a fifty-year-old forest. Perhaps it had marked a farmer's field for sixty years prior to the land's abandonment and the natural reforestation that followed.) But what a cost! A typical fence five feet high requires about seven thousand rails per mile.

Rosin from naval stores production was an ointment, a preservative for ropes, an impregnating gum for roofing paper, an ingredient of ink, and a by-product of turpentine (called "tar" in old manuscripts). Rosin in those days was crudely distilled from the resin in wood and solidified. A cord of "fatwood" heavily impregnated with resin could produce fifty gallons of "tar."

Resin was also an excellent adhesive. One fledgling forester, investigating his first logging chance in a southern pine stand, can attest to this. Backed up to a freshly cut stump by the woods' boss, he was invited to "have a seat" and "talk this matter over." The neophyte accepted the invitation, fell into the trap like a fly on sticky paper, and gave all the flatheads a laugh they enjoyed recalling more than thirty years later. The seat of those britches is probably yet stuck to that stump and well preserved in its resin. Pitch from southern pines also was used for caulking, becoming a commodity for international trade in the age of tall ships. Laps between boards and seams at their unions were sealed with this gum.

By 1849, naval stores were already shipped from the South. Lyell, the British geologist, found on his second visit to the United States "gashes in the bark" from which the resin flowed. In North Carolina, where the resident was soon to be called a Tarheel, a hole in the ground was lined with clay and the resin from the living tree poured into the hole, set ablaze, and allowed to evaporate. When the flame was extinguished, only the heavy dark-colored pitch remained. In the Gulf Coast areas, iron pots replaced the clay-lined hole, and the "tar" was boiled until pitch remained. On the Atlantic coast in those days, most resin was probably collected from loblolly pines; along the Gulf of Mexico, slash and longleaf pines were the principal sources. Often naval stores from Virginia and the Carolinas were first shipped north, then exported to Europe through the ports there.

Camphine was an important commodity for both domestic and export trade. Sometimes it was solely an oil of turpentine and other times a mixture of turpentine and alcohol. Both are lamp fuels equal to sperm whale oil.

Pine Knots and Potash

"Fat pine splinters," another product of the pioneers' forest, were used for torches. The splinter was from the heart, the resin-soaked center of the log or stump of southern pines, and used for kindling wood. Lightwood, another name for the pitch-impregnated heart that ignites readily and burns for a long time, was a necessity for the pioneering homesteader. Indeed, Lyell reports that a "North Carolinian is said to migrate most unwillingly to any new region where this prime luxury of life is wanting." Pine knots, the very dense wood in the zone where a branch extends from the bole of the tree, provided light for nighttime guidance. The "lightered" knots, like the fat pine splinters, burn for hours, emitting black smoke that soon coats a cabin wall with carbon.

Potash was also an early export product of the southern forest. Ashes of sap-filled trees were boiled to a thick brown salt. The saline slurry was then dried and refined to produce pearl ash, an alkali used in the manufacture of soap. Thus was derived the word *potash*, ashes from the pot, now the term for the element potassium in English. (Its symbol, K, is from the German word for the element *kali*.)

An aim of colonial companies was to produce "pot ash" from the virgin forest for the English. The industry never became important, though the chemical derived from the ash of wood was used in tanning leather as well as in making soap. Potential applications for the chemical included the manufacture of flint glass, dyes, saltpeter, bleach, and for printing designs on cloth. The colonists, however, made more money in sawing lumber and splitting staves than in cooking wood.[86]

Furniture and Food

By the mid-nineteenth century, Spanish moss was exported to England for mattress stuffing. Following the example of birds that use only the woody fiber for nests, moss gatherers buried the long strands. After a suitable period in the ground, the exterior coat rotted away, leaving the central thread, the useful part.

Lyell noted how the cabbage palm, its bulging base constricted a foot or so above the ground, grew in cotton fields of the Carolinas. Apparently planted there, the stems he saw were twenty-five to forty feet tall. The cabbage was edible, and the "wood" was employed in boat and shaft construction. The fiber decays slowly and is not attacked by shipworms when fully submerged.

The Florida maple, its range extending far beyond the present boundaries of the state by that name, produced sugar, food, and medicine for the pioneer. Sap was boiled to evaporate the water, leaving a crystalline sweet; seeds were dewinged, boiled in water, and eaten hot; and the dried riven bark was consumed as a pain reliever for ailments of the liver and spleen.

Pioneers crushed the fruit of the farkleberry, or sparkleberry, tree and diluted the pulp with water for a drink. The fruit was also used for cookies. Beechnuts served as a substitute for coffee in the settler's kitchen. Salads and pickled relish were made from the flowers and buds of eastern redbud trees.

Wooden Shoes, Leatherwork, and Treen

Blackgum found its way into the shoe factory. Negro slaves, Porcher wrote, got diseased feet when shod in leather in the hot dusty fields and humid forests. Soles of wood as a substitute seemed to eliminate this malady.

Tannin for the leather industry was obtained principally from white oak, eastern hemlock, and sumac. Other less-desirable species from which tannin could be extracted were utilized locally. In processing, the bark was crushed and soaked, and then the hide absorbed the tannic acid, making the skin impermeable.

Late in the era of the pioneers' forest, use of wood became more sophisticated. As examples, black walnut was bought in Kentucky and Tennessee for Singer sewing machine cabinets; palms in Florida were cut for wharf logs and paper pulp; and dish timbers were taken from maple, black walnut, oak, and white pine trees for woodenware. Woodenware may in some marketplaces still be called "treen," as it was when settlers invaded these southern forests. The word is derived from the Anglo-Saxon *treowen*, meaning made from a tree, *treo*.[87]

Less traditional uses for some woodland plants included dogwood extracts used for disinfecting mangy dogs, a treatment brought from England by settlers. Oil from eastern redcedar scented soap and candles, while wax for these articles came from the southern wax myrtle. Tan-colored sawdust, the product of powder-post beetle activity, was used for baby powder. Yet with all of these uses of products of the southern forest, most wooden furniture, wagons, and tools were imported from the North until well after the Civil War. Indeed, the South's first furniture factory, in North Carolina, was not in operation until 1888.[88]

The Forest as Medicine Chest

An important use of the southern forest was for medicinal concoctions. We have already seen how John Bartram and his son William roamed the woods in search of pharmaceutical plants to send to England and Europe. Although medical botany by the time of the Civil War was considered an advanced art, drug collection remained an important activity in the pioneers' forest. Porcher's *Resources of the Southern Fields and Forests*[89] is largely devoted to this subject. In spite of the title, few words in the book involve use of the forest for lumber or for food. Originally published in 1863 in Charleston for the Confederate militia and its medical attendants, the book considers the forest obviously inexhaustible as a source of drugs for human health.

Poison oak,[90] named then and until recently either *Rhus toxicodendron* or *R. radicans*, was said to be common in pine lands. Possibly no mention was made of its occurrence elsewhere because the forests of the clay bottoms and mesic slopes covered with broad-leaved trees were too dark to sustain its growth. Later, one notes, the noxious climber-shrub-creeper was nearly ubiquitous in the woodlands of the South. Urushiol, the yellowish volatile oil exuded by any bruised, broken, or burned part of the plant except the pollen and surface hairs, is the cause of an "erysipelatous inflammation," according to Porcher, the Confederate medic. How we all would suffer if the toxic agent were present in the pollen we ingest! Severe allergy reactions do occur when heat of a forest fire volatilizes the oil that is then inhaled into the lungs. Porcher noted the use of the plant as a stimulant and narcotic. (Its juice is still used to make indelible ink.)

A kindred plant, smooth sumac, was also a pharmaceutical of that day. The bark was heated in milk and water as a burn treatment that would not leave a scar. Indians mixed the dried leaves with those of tobacco to smoke as a treatment for asthma.

Sweetgum was another multipurpose tree of the southern forest. Its scientific name *Liquidambar styraciflua* literally means liquid styrax. The gummy resin obtained by bruising the bark was considered an antiseptic. Pioneers chewed the gum for its flavor. And magnolia flowers, blossoming at everybody's door, somehow "produced a decided reaction upon the nerves."

Other medicinals from the forest were turpentine, used to treat skin ailments (perhaps it literally burned off the diseased tissue), and the gummy substance derived from the bark of slippery elm, used for treating burns. The elm bark was soaked until the floating mucilage could be skimmed off, leaving the gummy substance. Oil of oleum, a compound in the roots of sassafras, also famous for its tea ingredient, was used for treating constipation. A rumor persisted that drinking the "sovereign remedy" retarded old age. No doubt pioneers were aware of the idea, if not the words, penned in 1586, that it was this tree that produced the "wondrous root which kept the starving alive and in fair goode spirit."

While an extract of witch hazel provided the pioneer relief for bruises and sprains—and still serves that purpose—its consumption was believed to infuse the imbiber with occult powers. Another narcotic was boiled from the green nut shells of hickories. Pioneers, under survival conditions, used crushed husks of hickory nuts to immobilize fish.

Folklore Healing

Folk medicine, or perhaps superstition, encouraged the use of plants of the southern forest. Buckeye seeds were carried in the pocket to prevent rheumatism, and white ash leaves stuffed in one's boots prevented snake bite, a belief arising from the Indians' sacred tradition of the reptile-repelling power of the tree's foliage.

Early visitors to the Appalachians knew the story of ginseng, already made famous by the Chinese as a medicinal agent. Indeed, many physicians of the time considered it a cure-all. Its technical name, from the Greek *panax*, is a literal translation of the phrase *all-healing*. The tonic is derived from its roots.

Charcoal manufacture was called the "blackest job in America." The carbon chips were used for cleaning teeth, thrown into water supplies to remove odors, and taken as a powder for upset stomach. (In addition, much was burned to heat ore in the manufacture of iron.)[91] That so much of the southern pioneers' medicine (and teas and dyes) came from the woodlands caused one historian of the period to remark that "in no other portion of the nation was human life so thoroughly integrated with natural forest resources as in the . . . South."[92]

Lumbering and the Use of Wood

Farming was not always the reason for clearing ground. As the era of the pioneers concluded, lumbering emerged as a social and economic necessity. Timbers were needed for building settlers' cabins and houses in the new towns. Pioneers in the later years dragged logs from the southern forest with timber wheels, high wheels as large as eight feet in diameter, which raised all but one end of the log, or logs, from the ground. Reduced friction enabled the oxen and mules to more easily pull the logs to the landing, or log-collecting point. Four- and eight-wheel wooden wagons aided the effort.

Often the landing was on a high bank of a river. From there the logs were rolled down the bank, tied into rafts in the water, and driven by slaves to mills downstream. Such drives took place on the Savannah River, the logs destined for mills at the coastal city, perhaps fifty river miles below. Similar river rafts were found on lesser streams, like the Sabine River, separating Louisiana and Texas, en route to the Gulf of Mexico. Sometimes flumes of heart pine lumber guided logs to mills at lower elevations. Creeks were dammed at the higher reaches in order to collect a head of water. Opening the dam gate sent a torrent of water to rush the logs to the mill.[93]

To supply settler needs as early as 1608, colonists produced rough-sawn pine boards at Captain John Smith's crude sawmill at Jamestown. A century and a half later, in 1744, a mill was operating in Savannah, and from it, in 1749, wood was shipped to London. Also about that time, masts were being exported to Havana. Pit saws, whip saws, and mechanical mills with gears made of wood and powered by water (the muley saw) evolved. And then came the sash saw, operating with vertical, rather than circular, motion. Although usually powered by water, one built in 1841 in Texas was powered with an engine and a boiler salvaged from a wrecked steamboat.[94] Two or three hands could operate a sash mill. Lumbering was expedited and, with the ability to more cheaply cut logs into boards, timber harvests were encouraged.

All the components of the pioneer house or cabin, from the shingles on the roof to the floor joists, were made of wood. The joists often rested on heart cypress or the naturally resin-soaked heart center of a pine log. Nails were scarce, so carpenters used wooden pegs. These were carved from a species whose wood has an ability to shrink and swell with changes in moisture that differed from the kind of wood selected for the boards or beams to be fastened together. Thus cypress pegs bound pine boards to pine studs. The peg, first dried, then inserted, would take up moisture and, in a swollen state, hold securely the boards or beams through which it was mortised. All tables, chairs, and wardrobes were of wood. Dishes and woodenware, like spoons and oaken buckets, came from the forest. The plow, even its share, was of hard wood; so too were wagons and their wheels and barrels and their hoops. Split rails and round posts were all that was known or available, apart from the dry rock wall, for fencing. Wood was the only source of fuel, except for the occasional tallow in a candle.

As early as 1858 in the Carolinas, plank roads provided all-weather transportation. Short timbers, four inches by four inches by four feet, were laid in trenches dug across the road. Hand-hewn six-inch-by-eight-inch stringers were then set on the planks in the trenches. On these stringers rested eight-inch-wide boards eight feet long. Finally, a blanket of sand covered the wooden roadbed.[95]

It was to gain control of its timber that Spain took an interest in West Florida in 1781. Though wood was used domestically by the settlers, Spain's aim was shipments abroad. There, Spaniards erected a mill, driven by water power probably from the Escambia River.[96]

Some Animal Stories

While the southern fur trade began in Maryland in 1634, subsequently extending southward, pioneers utilized animals of the woods for food and for hides. One man, we are told, killed three hundred deer each year in the Gulf coastal forest. Turkey, too, were abundant, fattening on the acorns of live oak trees. Where oranges were introduced in the 1500s from the Old World into Florida, it soon became apparent that bears considered them tasty. Obtaining them was easier for the bruin, too, than robbing a bee tree and suffering the stings of that theft. Nongame animals, apart from predators (like the lynx) on domestic livestock, seldom were given attention in the early days of settlement.

The confusion over the mammal gopher and the tortoise gopher remained through the times of the pioneers' forest, and indeed does so today. Bartram, the reader may recall, attributed the mounds in the longleaf pine forests to the reptile, whereas it was the rodent that burrowed in its search for starch-rich taproots of the conifer. Bartram, in time, named the gopher turtle *Testudo polyphaemus*, which is now called the great land tortoise.

The diamondback rattler was frequently seen, and always feared, by early settlers; however, it was not technically described and issued a Latin binomial until clearing of the forest was well under way. Hognose snakes, then as now, were confused with venomous vipers, including the pygmy, or ground, rattlesnake and copperhead. Young hognose snakes look like the former, but adults look like the latter. This confusion is due, in part, to the broadening of the hognose's head into a flat, triangular organ when frightened. Coloration for both is copperlike.

One story about the southern toad by Bartram in his travels through the settler regions rates comment because few others, Harper reminds us, have reported his fascinating observation. "When irritated," he wrote, "they swell and raise themselves up on their four legs." That should bluff the intruder![97]

Of Birds and Bees

Wood pelicans, perhaps the wood ibis, decorated the landscape while the noisy Florida barred owl made memorable impressions upon the human residents of these climes. A lone traveler would wish he had stayed amidst his own kind!

The presence or absence of the honeybee in the virgin forests of the South was a matter for notation by early sojourners. Some observers may have mistaken similar social insects for the wax and sugar producers. The honeybee, brought in by European colonists, soon escaped, always seeming to be ten to twenty miles ahead of the western movement of Anglo-Saxons and Spanish settlers. In caves and trees, new hives were formed and these searched out by men. Discoverers of bee trees carved their initials on the bark of the bole, thereby claiming possession until the tree could be felled, the bees smoked out, and honey and wax scooped from the hollow. The Indians, not appreciating this insect introduction into their haunts, felt harassed by the bees. However, to the Caucasian finder of a rich, full hive in the hollow of a large beech tree, it was as though he had stumbled into a camp in Canaan in the days of abundant milk and honey. Today's visitors to the woods of the South yet find special pleasure in robbing bee trees of their honey. A single hive in a beech tree may produce two hundred pounds.

Of Hogs and Frogs

Soon after pioneering settlement, hogs ran wild in the southern woods, consuming acorns and hickory nuts from the river bottoms and the roots of longleaf pine seedlings growing in the sandy hills. Their meanness as the razorback or wild boar and their appetite as the piney woods' rooter became well known. Feral hogs that consumed beechnuts had a special use. With *Fagus* mast as their diet, when slaughtered, the animal's fat would readily boil away. The yield of a quantity of oil was little inferior to olive oil and fit, also, for burning in the pioneers' lamps.

Tales of the pioneers in the Texas Big Thicket, told now by their descendants, may tingle one's spine. Bear were abundant; so too were the red wolf and bobcat. Stubby-tailed cottonmouth moccasins yet abound in the marshy ponds that serve as "frogging grounds." (One will know why the cottonmouth is so named if ever one comes face-to-face with the reptile. The fangs protrude from a mass of white flesh, looking like a boll of freshly picked cotton.) Francis Abernathy says they "lie in the coontail and spatterdock with just their fist-sized heads protruding, the mean eye gazing over the smiling white lip."[98] Reptiles like the canebrake rattler and its dwarf relative, the pygmy rattler, encountered by the pioneer were less abundant than they are today because of the current dearth of predators. The little one is mean, and many a settler's toe or heel were the target of its wrath when dislodged from seclusion underneath a rotting log.

Fire in the Forest

Pioneer settlers, like their Indian predecessors, kindled fires great and small. Like the Indians, they set fires to remove the underbrush, thereby exposing the enemy. This was especially important around the stockades. (These structures were built of wooden palisades or of posts with boards between the posts. Upon the sloping ends of these boards the protectors could rest their long rifles while peering through the woods.) Early migrants into the South also set the woods ablaze to improve the range for cattle and, possibly, for horses. Soon they learned that an acre of land burned within a hundred-acre parcel, six weeks after the fire in the spring of the year would be the pasture for a score of hungry steers. Because the southern forest, especially the pineries, does not lend itself to productive grazing, the slight improvement in fertility by burning the grass or understory was worthwhile. The carrying capacity, though a term not yet coined, would be higher on freshly burned tracts than elsewhere.

Grazing Commons

The southern forest soon became an endless land upon which any and all might pasture. Towns of the Northeast and of Europe had their commons, where the undivided land was available for all to use as pasture for the family milk cow. The South was now one mammoth common. To control the range was beyond reason. And spite fires did occur as disgruntled laborers and feuding factions got away with incendiarism. A crop of trees in a naval stores forest easily became a fire storm of roaring torches.

Economists of the period, and later, seldom dealt, or yet deal, with the cost of natural and "torch-bearer" fires in the South. The burning of Atlanta may have shown on the tally sheets of historians, but seldom have the losses to woods arson been recorded on the accountant's ledger as a cost of the Civil War. Estimated losses of $7 million for torching over five million acres in 1880 alone and an estimated $12 billion for the 150 years of settlement make the work of Sherman's soldiers appear, as one historian noted, "little more destructive than lightning bugs on a pleasant summer evening."[99]

Breaking New Ground Continues

Pioneers set fires to aid in clearing land for agriculture. As the population expanded and people migrated westward, land for food and fiber production became essential. Until the opening years of the twentieth century at the western edge of the Gulf Coastal Plain, the movement was extensive. As I write, more than an occasional tract in the Texas Post Oak Belt or the Cross Timbers to its west is cleared for agricultural pursuits.

Mighty labor went into this extensive conversion from virgin forest to agricultural husbandry. Rice is a tough taskmaster, planters working in knee-deep water under a semitropical sun in swamplands grubbed of timbers and the accompanying reptiles. Efforts to produce tobacco, corn, and cotton on sizable acreages were only slightly less laborious.

By 1880 most of the fertile land of the South and much that was not suitable for cultivation had been cleared. Some was high-graded of its timber and otherwise left intact. Uncut forests, apart from the western edge of the region, were mostly pines of various species on steep mountain slopes and timbers of the frequently flooded swamps and river bottoms.

By the time the pioneers had settled in to stake their claims and to make their homes in the forests of the South or to squat on the ownerships of others, the extraordinarily rich variety and lush growth of flora were recognized. Thus Porcher could write with enthusiam and only a drop of exaggeration: "It is the teeming product of every variety of soil and climate, from Maryland to Florida, from Tennessee to Texas. The Atlantic slopes with their marine growth, the mountain ridges of the interior, the almost infra-tropical productions of South Florida, with the rich alluvia of the river courses—all contribute to swell the lists and produce a wonderful exhuberance of vegetation. These a bounteous Providence has vouchsafed to a Confederacy of States." Prophetically he wrote that what this great wilderness needed was an assist by the "arm of authorities or the energy and enterprise of the private citizens to be made sources of utility, profit, and beauty." [100]

Next we'll see how the migrating lumbermen from the North, the "authorities," and their energy and enterprise did so.

CHAPTER 3

The Lumbermen's Forest

HE WEYERHAEUSER Company went west in 1907 following the cut-out-and-get-out days of logging the Lake States'
forests. Other logging and milling industries and their laborers in the North followed James G. Hill's recently laid
Great Northern rails, some dropping off to begin cutting the virgin forests
in Montana or Idaho along the way. Many came south and scattered
across the region. While the migration began about 1880, cut-out-and-
get-out practices erupted in earnest throughout the South upon the clo-
sure of the Lake States' mills and the burning of millions of acres of its
woodlands in the latter half of the nineteenth century.

Migrating Lumbermen

Even before the great exodus from Minnesota, Wisconsin, and
Michigan, the South's forests had been entered by entrepreneurs from the
North Atlantic states. By 1880, at least five thousand sawmills, mostly
family operations in the Appalachians, were cutting logs in the South.
Yet the South was producing in 1890 less than one-half of the volume
then being harvested in New York, where cut-out-and-get-out was supposedly complete.[1] The mountain harvest, however, had little effect upon
the region compared with the more intense lumbering effort that began
about that time along the Eastern Seaboard, near the shipping ports that
would expedite trade to the metropolises of the Northeast or the timber-
short, high-population centers of Europe. So Tidewater Virginia became
the "cradle of the industry." In time, Paul Camp's harvests there were
significant, cutting 12 million board feet a year.[2]

In addition to the mills built along the Atlantic shore by the major wave of migrating lumbermen, settlers near the Gulf Coast cities erected mills and ports from which they could ship timbers to the North or to nations abroad. Soon loggers exercised their muscles up the rivers that empty at these ports. A little more recently, about 1900, the movement away from the coasts was well under way and, by then too, encroachment was into the last of the South's great virgin forests at the western edge of the southern pine–hardwood region in Texas and at the region's southern extremity in Florida.

Typical of the migrating lumbermen were Hans Dierks, who came from Iowa near the end of the nineteenth century to become Arkansas' largest landowner, and E. S. Crossett who was not far behind in locating in the same state a mill and a city that commemorates his name.[3] Notable exceptions to this chronology occurred, for example, when a sash sawmill, powered by boilers from a wrecked steamboat, began operating in 1841 near Galveston and when the Thompson family mill started to harvest the high-quality timbers in Northeast Texas in 1852.

Exploitation Opportunities

Some two hundred tree species, many with attributes still unknown, evoked the interest of the lumbermen. Clear, straight-grained boards from long-bodied trees came from these forests. Hardwood boles were sawn into lumber that measured two by twenty inches and sixteen feet long, clear of knots and other defects. White oak and yellow-poplar, commonly called "poplar," provided flooring, panelling, moldings, and furniture. "Bay poplar" of the South was likely "tupelo" to the botanist. Pines of all species were sawn into boards without a blemish, one by thirty inches and sixteen feet long. Often the pines, regardless of species, were given local names for the market. Such was "Neches Valley pine," harvested from an extensive tract along a river in East Texas. More widely used names were "Rosemary" and "black pine," probably references to loblolly pine, while "short straw" apparently referred to shortleaf pine.

The demand for the dense wood of the southern yellow pines in the rapidly growing cities of the North and Central States hastened the removal by high-grading—taking the most valuable trees and leaving inferior stems—of the biggest and best of the loblolly and longleaf pines not far inland from the coasts. Next, in time, were harvested the old-growth loblolly and shortleaf pines of the Piedmont Province that had been overlooked by the earlier migrants into the South as they cleared land for farms. The shortleaf pines in this area were among the least desirable because of the high proportion of sapwood to heartwood, unlike virgin stems of other species of southern pines. The zone of sapwood inside the

High-quality loblolly pines—tall, straight, with minimal taper, and few persistent limbs that leave knots in the lumber. These were the kinds of trees that enticed the migrating lumbermen into the region. (Courtesy U.S. Forest Service.)

bark of a tree, in contrast to the interior core of resin-soaked heartwood, exhibits poor resistance to attacks by rot-causing fungi and destructive insects. Sapwood lumber is also more prone to warp. Until the advent of drying kilns, shortleaf pine in North Carolina was used only locally; with kiln drying, millmen marketed the species as "North Carolina pine." We are justly left confused, however, for the earlier indigenous timbermen often referred to loblolly pine with disdain, while speaking highly of shortleaf pine.[4]

Eventually, the loggers moved into the slash pine stands along the lower Atlantic coast and east of the Mississippi River's mouth not far inland from the Gulf of Mexico. The last of the conifers to be cut were the sand pines of Florida; the Virginia pines of the Cumberland Plateau in   X Tennessee; and the pond pines, southern baldcypresses, and the less-accessible Atlantic white-cedars of the coastal swamps. Hardwood harvests for furniture and specialty items occurred simultaneously, both in the uplands of the Southern Appalachian Mountains and Piedmont Province and in the river bottoms of the region. Depending upon markets, many other species were harvested along the way with those listed here.

Specialty Products

The sweet-smelling southern baldcypress and the Atlantic white-cedar trees were used for shakes, shingles, coffins, and other products requiring resistance to rot. These woods were especially important for cisterns and the water towers erected beside the rails for refilling the boilers of steam locomotives. Eastern redcedar trees, occurring in relatively pure stands in the Nashville Basin of Tennessee and in the Cedar Glades of the Ozark Mountains in Arkansas, were important for chests and for closet panelling. Even the soft juniper from the Cedar Keys of Florida was marketed for pencil stock. Fisher Body and Singer Sewing Machine, among others, utilized the various woods from the southern forest for particular purposes. For automobiles, hard pines made good running boards and floorboards, and hickories provided quality wheel spokes. Cabinetmakers used many species for various furniture parts.

By 1920, North Carolina had exhausted much of its furniture-quality woods—various oak species, black walnut, and American chestnut. Some remained to be harvested throughout the 1930s. Most of the American chestnut in the South had not yet been attacked by the blight-causing fungus when the lumbermen entered the southern forests. By the time the harvest was complete, however, living merchantable stems of this species were gone, probably forever.[5]

Products other than timbers from the migrating lumbermen's forest included tannin and Spanish moss. Leather workers required tannin, extracted mostly from American chestnut bark and wood after the eastern hemlock played out in the North. Use of the astringent chemical for tanning skins to make them strong, pliable, and durable peaked early in the 1900s. After that, most of the tannin and tannic acid came from trees in Virginia, western North Carolina, and Tennessee. Spanish moss,

Clear boards from long-bodied, straight-grained timber of the river bottoms of the South that went into flooring, furniture, paneling, and molding (millwork) in the early days of the twentieth century. Sweetgum ("red gum" as labeled here) often was especially valuable for its figure. The board on the right, marked "bay poplar," is probably tupelo gum. The board at far left measured thirty inches wide and fourteen feet long. (Courtesy Southern Pine Lumber Company Collection, Steen Library Archives, Stephen F. Austin State University, Nacogdoches, Tex.)

American chestnut snags in the Blue Ridge Mountains. These trees suggest the importance of the species in the 1930s when the blight killed the larger trees. (Compare with trees in the next three photographs.) Young seedlings, from seeds and from sprout reproduction, often grow to seed-bearing age—a little taller than these living trees—before the blight infects and kills them, too. (Courtesy U.S. Forest Service.)

the *Tillandsia* the explorers also called "old-man's beard," remained an important by-product from these woods through the Great Depression. Families gathered the epiphyte as it grew in winter, selling it for pillow stuffing, for padding saddles and automobile seats, and for packing valuable glassware and china.

Shingle weavers worked the woods throughout the period of the lumbermen. They sought "bull pines," a name given to old growth. They looked for trees with yellowish bark cutting boxes into the boles to see if the grain was tight and without spiral. Those shingle trees would be the genetically "super" trees selected for progeny testing in today's forest.

Preferred Forests

Why did this harvest follow, rather than precede, that of the Lake States? Mosquitoes are worse in the Lake States. Black flies and "no-seeums," minute insects smaller than gnats, are a scourge there. Because the muck swamps and the many small lakes of the northern flats are se-

American chestnut snags. Many species replace the native chestnut stems; the land does not lie bare, as seen in this 1939 photograph. (Courtesy U.S. Forest Service.)

vere obstacles to travel and to timber accessibility, industrialists had to dig extensive canal systems. While the southern woods burned with regularity, fire danger and the prevalence of disastrous holocausts in the North Woods far exceeded those of the South. Soils of the Lake States' forested region are sterile in contrast to the lands of the South. The climate in the North is numbing cold in winter and scorching hot in summer, the growing season short, the logging season short, and the stand rotation age long. The southern yellow pines are heavier, denser, freer of knots, and stronger than the white and red pines of the North. In the Lakes States, aspen, a weed tree (at that time), follows fire and clear-cutting. In the South, another stand of yellow pines comes in after intense fire or clear-cutting of the forest.

Favoring the North were the frozen ground and iced-over rivers that facilitated log skidding and decking in preparation for rafting, during the spring thaws, of the harvested timbers to the mills downstream. The North also was nearer to the markets of the rapidly develop-

American chestnuts. Open-grown, full-crowned, and short-boled trees on ridge tops produced abundant seeds for humans and wildlife. (Courtesy U.S. Forest Service.)

ing industrialized cities of the region. Another advantage for the Lake States was the rail transportation in the North. Many lines in the South defaulted during Reconstruction following the Civil War. And there the tobacco and cotton economy, dependent upon black chattels, remained more important than timber to the region's welfare as long as prices held and soil erosion was not yet serious.

Movement of Men, Mules, and Machinery

The population immigration routes may have been reason enough for the barons of Maine, New York, and Pennsylvania to transport men, mules, and machinery to the sandy flats and mucky swamps of northern Michigan, Wisconsin, and Minnesota. But movement westward instead of south after logging the Lake States could not be attributed to migration. Had Dixie's emerald belt of virgin pine been understood, as in time it would be, money and transport would have been available for de-

American chestnuts. A 1914 photo shows a dense, fairly pure stand of trees with their catkin blooms. (Courtesy U.S. Forest Service.)

veloping the southern industry when the last logs passed from the carriages of the saws of the Northeast forty years before the demise of the industry in the Lake States.

Disease, too, likely hindered movement southward. Filthborne cholera, yellow fever, typhoid fever, typhus, and malaria continued to discourage migration into the region. Some historians also attribute the delay to long-established biases in the North toward southern-grown wood and the adequate, though not abundant, supplies of timber in the North.[6]

We have suggested that the tardy entry into these woods could be attributed to a lack of knowledge of the quality of the forests. On the other hand, long before the period of the migrating lumbermen, the strip of hardwoods and pines in the Piedmont Province, a continuation of the broad-leaved mesic forest of the Northeast that extends into Alabama, had been included in earlier harvests. One might suppose industrialists would have known something of the value of the South's forests from those incursions. In time, as we shall see, men and their families did move from Iowa, Illinois, Indiana, Kansas, New York, and Pennsylvania, as well as from the Lake States, to harvest the trees of "The Great Southland." By then the high resin content of the southern pines, in contrast to white pine, and the easy splitting quality of the hard pines would not be so objectionable.

A Time to Harvest

Two hundred years to cut-out-and-get-out of the Northeast, and forty years to ravage the Lake States. How long, now, to log the South? Little did it seem to matter, for the late nineteenth and early twentieth centuries was a time when care of the resources of this virgin forest, stretching from Virginia to a hundred miles west of the Sabine River into East Texas, was of little concern to citizens of either high or low estate.

The conflagration of Chicago, attributed to the impatience of Mrs. O'Leary's cow, could have created a critical local need for wood. The need, however, would be delayed, for of the Windy City's 121 lumberyards, only thirteen burned in that holocaust of 1871. And lumber stacked in those yards already included some from Louisiana.[7] The great Peshtigo fire in Wisconsin (taking about twelve hundred lives and scorching 1.2 million acres) that burned on the same day as the Chicago fire, along with many other similar pyric catastrophes that consumed the Lake States' forests, hastened the need to import wood. The shortage of trees in the far north that resulted from the extensive burning and the cut-out-and-get-out attitude created economic incentive for developing the forest industry in the South.

Chicago Investors

Products from these forests well before 1880 included poles, pilings, bridge trestle timbers, posts, barrel staves and headings, lath for

The end of a tram spur through a forest of red spruce in the southern mountains of the Appalachian chain. The fifty-year-old stand probably seeded in following fire, for this picture portrays the initial harvest of a virgin woodland. (Courtesy U.S. Forest Service.)

plaster walls, pickets for fencing, shingles and shakes for roofing and siding, and various kinds of naval stores, as well as lumber and tannic acid. Significant volumes of southern baldcypress were shipped to Chicago, probably before southern pine was first introduced into the market there in 1880. About that time, the present giant retailer, Marshall Field's and Company, then a wholesale builder, purchased 2.5 million board feet of yellow pine from southern mills. In 1885 the *New York Tribune* editorialized on the virtues of southern pine for its many uses. Perhaps the story bore a relationship to the fact that the 35,000-ton towers of the Brooklyn Bridge rested—and yet rest—on pilings of southern pine.

By 1888, Chicago investors had purchased, for as little as twenty-five cents an acre, 122,000 acres in Florida. By 1890, the group owned 800,000 acres of timberland in Louisiana, bought for as little as $1.25 per acre. Tracts in Arkansas, Texas, Tennessee, Mississippi, and Florida were transferred for about the same price. Much of these holdings was subsequently sold to Long-Bell, a Missouri corporation, "at a good profit." By 1892, imports into the North of southern pine, called "yellow pine" in the lumber trade, and southern baldcypress approximated a hundred million feet annually.[8]

An Ashe Report on Fire

More important, W. W. Ashe's fire report for North Carolina in 1895 told of the provision of southern lumber for the Lake States as standing timber in the latter region played out. So little was being harvested in the South that Ashe could note that the Tarheel state's total annual production of pine lumber was still less than Michigan's shortage for 1894. "Each year," he wrote, "as the demand for Southern lumber becomes stronger with the increased consumption and the exhaustion of the forests of the Northwest [meaning the Lake States], a larger proportion of our manufactured product will be for shipment."[9] Although the term *sustained yield* was not yet coined, an *American Lumberman* article of the era reported that T. L. L. Temple, copurchaser of seven thousand acres in Texas, was calling for a more profitable method of tree cutting than the "sweep clean" techniques used by most southern yellow pine operators.[10]

Oxen came south along with the Lake States' loggers. About 1904, it is reported, a man journeyed to Moorestown, Michigan, stayed for a week in the hotel there, and bought up every good ox team he could find in the region. These were shipped to Louisiana for logging in the cypress swamps.[11] The first lumber census, in 1869, reported a mill tally for the South of 1.6 billion board feet for the year. It had almost doubled by 1879, amounting to 2.7 billion board feet; and by 1890, the mill scale was 5 billion board feet.

The economic panic of 1907 affected the welfare of the people involved in logging the South. Land and stumpage changed hands, and many a shrewd businessman became a ruler of an estate that equalled in

Oxen teamed to haul logs. Note the red heartrot in the cross sections. The disease destroyed considerable volumes of wood in the virgin forest and subsequent second-growth stands. Its virtual elimination in managed forests has affected the abundance of the endangered red-cockaded woodpecker, which makes its home in infected trees. (Courtesy Southern Pine Lumber Company Collection, Steen Library Archives, Stephen F. Austin State University, Nacogdoches, Tex.)

area that of some nations. The complex economic, cultural, and political problems that they inherited also required the wisdom of the wisest of potentates.

The Lumbering Peak in the South

The year 1909 marks the peak period for the exploitation of the southern forest. More than 16 billion board feet of lumber cleared the South's saws in those twelve months. That amounted to 45 percent of the total U.S. harvest. By 1929, near the end of the period arbitrarily selected for this account as the time for the termination of the lumbermen's forest, the South still produced 42 percent of the nation's lumber. From then on, the harvest diminished each year until, by the mid-1930s, log-

ging the southern woods was essentially complete. When the decline began, over one-fifth of all railroad freight traffic in the South consisted of
forest products. [12]

Major centers of the industry in its heyday were New Orleans,
Mobile, Pensacola, Norfolk, Wilmington, Charleston, and Savannah for
the softwoods. High Point, North Carolina, was the principal marketing
center for upland hardwoods, while Memphis served the interests of the
manufacturers of lumber from bottomland deciduous trees.

So well developed was the industry by 1910 that finished wood
in various forms moved from Gulf Coast ports to Europe. Among these
exports were sixteen-by-twenty-inch timbers eighty feet long. One stick
was so large that it required twelve yoke of oxen and an eight-wheel
wagon to haul it to the port. Extensive deliveries were also made early in
the period to Mexico, the West Indies, and South America. By the second decade of the century, European nations were principal importers.

Even during the period of the migrating lumbermen, turpentine collectors worked the southern forest. Oleoresin went abroad, considerable quantities via the British West Indies. Occasionally disputes
arose over the use of the trees in the forest, for the butt log, the most
valuable in a tree, when chipped for gum naval stores was of little value
for lumber (or so it was thought). Logs with turpentined "faces" retain the
gummy substance that is naturally impregnated throughout the log. Turpentined trees are also fire hazards. To this day, the turpentine industry,
sometimes politicized but producing a product always necessary for the
nation's defense, remains separate from the business enterprises that log
and convert into lumber the southern forest.

Migrating Barons

Today's historians may be too hard on the lumbermen of the
times in calling attention to the abuse of the land by these exploiters who
came from outside of the region to fell and mill the virgin forests. People
in other industries at the time behaved similarly. Cultural historians vary
in their opinions about how much the "carpet baggers of the woods" contributed to society or promoted the general welfare. "Nor did any [indus-
trialist's] concern for the continuity and growth of the ramshacky communities that had, rather incidentally, gathered around their mills and
logging camps and along their jerry-built rail lines trouble an industry
long accustomed to a migratory life." [13] Logger behavior pretty much followed the pattern set in the Northeast and in the Lake States. Few were
the incentives to encourage change. And there was the belief, perhaps a

trust, that the supply of trees was inexhaustible. Cut-out-and-get-out as a policy and philosophy had migrated south with the migrating lumbermen.

Not all lumbermen entering the far-flung empire of the South's "first" forest, as foresters now call the virgin woodlands, should be classed as exploiting barons. Indeed, the philanthropic accounts of some, even before the accumulation of their wealth, could be heard while sitting around a pot-bellied stove in the country stores of the region only a couple of decades past. Many would have joined with Carl Alwin Schenck, the German forester of North Carolina's Biltmore Estate, and exclaim to the heavens, "Excelsior, the higher good," in deciding the future of the lands entrusted to them.[14]

Some early industrial leaders were native sons of the South. Caught between competition with fly-by-night millers and loggers and altruistic motivation, they realized that decisions they made in their day would favorably or adversely affect their offspring. They believed that the economic sins of the fathers, as well as other kinds of misdeeds, "are visited upon the children to the third and fourth generation." These lumbermen highly regarded the Ten Commandments.

The high-grading of the period (taking the trees that would be graded a certain quality and scaled to a preset volume) should not be confused with clear-cutting. The latter is a legitimate regeneration method for shade-intolerant species, such as the southern pines, that require bare mineral soil for seed germination and full sunlight for optimum growth. Had clear-cutting been practiced (which, when properly done, assumes a seed source) and *if* wildfire had been prevented, the South's second forest, offspring of the virgin stands, would have been an economic bonanza within fifty years of the harvest made by the migrating lumbermen.

Not all logging was carried out on company lands. Stumpage, the price of standing trees, at twenty-five to seventy-five cents a thousand board feet was purchased from neighbors. (The 1970s' peak year prices often exceeded $300 per thousand board feet for much smaller, lower-grade trees than those of the original forest.) Courthouse-recorded deeds sometimes camouflaged the real value of the sale with such phrases as "$10 and other goods." To expedite transfer, deeds and bills-of-sale were written on paper sacks and on pieces of one-by-twelve lumber. One story is told of a check written on a piece of wooden plank that a bank considered negotiable. Timber deeds were sometimes necessary for the transfer of stumpage (also the term used for standing trees), for unharvested timber is legally real estate according to the laws of many states. When felled, the trees become personal property and a bill of sale suffices. With deeds, title to lands with ten to twenty thousand board feet per acre changed hands. With bills of sale, negotiations were for stumpage only, often preferred by the lumbermen. Ad valorem taxes would be collected on the former and not on the latter.

The Railroads' Role

Logging with Rails

Many railroads in the region, rebuilt during the Reconstruction period, enabled more efficient delivery of lumber to metropolitan markets. The Chattanooga and St. Louis let all know this, its box cars emblazoned with "The Great Timber Route." Industrialists could now extend those rails into the woods.

In the rush to roll, rails were quickly laid, taking into account the location of raw material as potential freight, accessibility of water for the engine's boilers, wood supplies for its fuel, markets for the distribution of finished lumber, and the possibility of passenger service. Small lines sprang up, often owned or controlled by lumber companies. Their nicknames were frequently better known than the legal titles on bills of lading. The "Wobbly, Bobbly, Turnover, and Stop" referred to the Waco, Beaumont, Trinity, and Sabine line. Although a common carrier, the WBTS served seventeen large sawmills along its fifty-mile run. HE & WT was commonly called "Hell, Either Way Taken"; its timetable called it the Houston, East and West Texas. The T & NO line signified "Time No Object," while one Texas rail with a single Shay locomotive for power was chartered as "The Great Sweetgum Yubadam and Hoo Hoo Route."

The "Grand Dream" seemed often in the mind of the railroad's promoter. HE & WT never got to the dry sands of West Texas; it never got out of a few counties in East Texas. The Moscow, Camden, and San Augustine line never reached San Augustine. Its passenger service, until discontinued in the early 1970s, provided transportation for two or three generations of families over a seven-mile run between a company mill and the line of a larger railroad. Still operating is the Angelina and Neches River Railroad, a wood-using industry-controlled line of a few miles length used solely for moving wood products. Across the South in the days of the migrating lumbermen were hundreds of railroads like these, delivering logs to a mill and carrying planed lumber to the mainline.[15]

Mudlines

Tramroads, called "mudlines," branched from these company railroads. Occasionally a passenger car was attached to a tram locomotive

A Shay locomotive, "The Titan of the Timber" (ca. 1905). An 1882 ten-ton model
pulled forty-five carloads, containing sixty-one thousand board feet in 343 logs.
Workers easily "walked" the geared, wood-burning locomotives back to the rails
after they jumped the track. Eight were in use in Texas in 1883. (Courtesy Forest
History Collection, Steen Library Archives, Stephen F. Austin State University,
Nacogdoches, Tex.)

if the train chanced to pass through a village or come near another line.
Passengers rode in the engine's cab or sat astride the timbers on a log car.
Not infrequently, a short line "with commodious shipping track,"
evolved into a public conveyance, the rights-of-way still serving this
purpose.[16]

    The crude tram rail lines used for moving logs to mills were
laid through rough country for temporary use. Rails were salvaged after
the timber was cut in one area and used elsewhere as new routes for hauling logs were needed. Each day, the steel gang extended the spur, usually
198 feet, into the forest for a new logging "chance." "Six rails up and six
rails down" was the motto of the taskmaster, a "task" defined as the lifting
and laying of sixty rails. A day's task was done for a ten-man crew when

six rails per man were moved. The workers "hit the ground running" as they left the moving train. Lifting and laying was no easy chore, for each rail weighed six hundred pounds while the angle bars at each end were another twelve. Indeed, lifting the heavy iron was a task. Track work went on ten hours a day, six days a week, workers earning $1.35 a day.[17]

Periodically, maybe twice a week, the log loader moved along the temporary tram to a new position near the terminus of the track. Workers used both single- and double-drum cylinders to hoist the heavy timbers onto flat cars. Typically, six men, without regard to race in a time typified by segregated employment, manned the stationary loaders, their booms fixed. Introduction of the swinging boom to more readily lift the logs was an appreciated improvement. An efficient crew and rig loaded as much as a quarter million board feet in a day.

One early engineer told how on Christmas Day, 1910, "cutting was going on way out in the timber and the mules at the logging site needed water and feed." The logging superintendent and the engineer fired up the locomotive and made the run to the corral. They did not get there. A large stump blocked the way, for a rail that had rested on the edge of the stump had settled, exposing the stump between the rails. "Running pretty pert, the engine hit the stump, rocked about, jumped the rails, and headed for the woods. A hundred yards from the rails, still upright, it stopped."[18]

Fueling the Engines, Making Ties and Trestles

Some locomotives were coal-burning where this fuel was available, as in northern Alabama. Elsewhere, lignite fired the boilers in woods' engines for some forested zones. But most fuel was wood. To supply "turnip stacks," Shays, and most other log-hauling rigs, boys were employed to stack piles of resinous "fat pine," the heartwood of trees fallen long ago, at appropriate intervals along the track. ("Turnip stacks" were locomotives with smokestacks shaped like turnips.) The volume of fuel wood consumed could amount to 140 cords per track mile per year.

Cross ties required an abundance of wood. Usually they were hewn from post oak and other hardwood logs or from southern baldcypress timbers that were not good enough for lumber. Because no inexpensive chemical preservative treatment of wooden materials was yet developed, naturally rot-resistant materials were desired. Post oak could be expected to last ten years, other hardwoods for lesser periods, and the heartwood of baldcypress, though a softer, less-dense wood, much longer. Ties were hand-hewn in the woods and stacked along the rail side for either replacement or pick up for later use. For spur lines, only ground and rail faces of the ties were hewn. Bark remained on the sides. At first spaced at three-foot centers, eventually twenty-two ties supported each thirty-three–foot rail. Rails resting on ties of wood often were themselves of wood, capped by thin metal bands. The ties lay on the slightly graded ground, the roadbed usually without ballast.

Trestles also utilized much wood. Company managers preferred trestles to culverts because they were cheaper to build. Fills—requiring vast tonnages of earth—are necessary when culverts are employed. Some dry-land trestles exceeded two thousand feet in length. They were virtually endless in the swamps, utilizing untold volumes of wood of the most rot-resistant species.

Some companies insisted on a continuously regular harvest, necessitating all-weather tram roads. In this event, sand ballast underlaid the six-by-eight-inch by eight-foot cross ties. Here the bed was built up where the rails passed through low swales adjacent to river banks. Steam shovels assisted the laborers in this endeavor.

Trains of the early years rode narrow-gauge rails, some as little as three feet apart; a few were later converted to the four-foot 8 1/2-inch standard-gauge rail to accommodate traffic connecting a main line. Among the locomotives in use was a popular engine called simply "the Shay."

The Shay

Ephraim Shay, a logger in Michigan in the mid-1870s, built in his own shops crude gear-wheel engines for local use. Later, the Lima Machine Company of Lima, Ohio, manufacturers of logging and milling machinery, took over Shay's operation and obtained in 1881 the first patent for the engine. Soon, the Lima Locomotive and Machine Company built and sold throughout the country a geared engine called "The Titan of the Timber." Various models of Ephraim Shay's ingeniousness ranged from 10- to 150-ton capacity and of several track gauges. Grades negotiated by the engine with its full complement of log cars were as great as 7 1/2 percent: more typical, however, were grades of 1 percent.

An 1882 ten-ton model, purchased for $3,000, pulled forty-five carloads of timber at a time. The load of almost four hundred logs totaled over sixty thousand board feet, the volume tally of a clean-swept harvest of about seven acres. Fifteen to twenty cars to a train was more typical, a caboose or "crummy" bringing up the rear for the accomodation of the woods foreman and some loggers. Those who recalled the day of the Shay engine said, "It made ten times as much noise as ordinary locomotives, pulled the load of ten of them, and went one-tenth as fast." A fast log train could take two hours to reach a mill twenty-five miles away.

When Shay engines jumped the track, getting them back on the rails was easy. Poles were placed under the gear treads and the wood-burner fired up, its gears then "walking" the poles back to the rails. Boiler explosions were common, for locomotive (and stationary) boilers had no pressure gauges. Often employees working nearby died in these explosions.

Some of these iron horses were used to build the Panama Canal, completing that task in time to be refurbished for participation in the harvests of the South's virgin forests. They needed to be refurbished, because the cabs and floors of many models were made of hardwood boards from northern species. Service in the tropics of the isthmus led to decay of the wooden parts, necessitating company blacksmiths at the southern mills to replace the cabs with sheet iron. Even then, the floors of the cabs and tenders were usually rebuilt with oak and hickory timbers from the neighborhood.

In addition to the Shay, less-famous geared logging locomotives employed in the region were the Climax and the Heister. These first appeared in 1888 and 1894, respectively. The little Heister was called a "tea kettle."[19]

Oxen, Mules, and Their Drivers

Skidders, the men who drove the mules and oxen, moved out as much as four hundred feet on either side of a tramroad to drag logs to a landing, there to be loaded onto log cars. High-wheel carts, pulled by teams of the beasts, aided the effort. Good slip teams were a mule driver's friend, responding to English terms like *gee* and *haw* for right and left, accommodating the needs of the skinner (as a mule driver was also called) and greatly easing the hardship of his labors. Teams of oxen, requiring less care but being slower moving than mules, were equally obliging to a benevolent ox driver. Yoke-fellows like Rough and Rowdy were famous for their comprehension of the tasks daily before them.

Mules and oxen, each kind responding to its own understanding of human speech, formed uncanny partnerships with mule skinners and bull punchers as they dragged logs to landings. Animals, depending upon their ability to respond to commands, were valued from $5 to $500. Expensive ones were treated with especial respect. Mules like Molly and Dolly even had a lot of affectionate beaux among the human race. Mules were generally purchased in spans, or pairs. As recently as the Great De-

High wheels, sometimes called "big wheels." These were used to haul logs to land-
ings for loading on trains. Skidders usually employed teams of four mules or horses.
(Courtesy Forest History Collection, Steen Library Archives, Stephen F. Austin
State University, Nacogdoches, Tex.)

pression years of the 1930s, a span sold for $200 to $300. One old-timer
recalled how mules were bought and sold at barns, like cars at later-day
used-car lots. Truth in advertising and 50,000-mile warranties had not yet
been legislated. Some mules worked the woods until they were twenty
years old. After oxen were finally discharged from their duties in the
1940s, mules remained the principal source of log-skidding power. (Not
until the 1950s did tractors almost completely take over. Loggers still use
mules, and sometimes horses, for special projects requiring minimal damage to the soil.)

Animals intuitively sensed the operation of the high-wheel
cart, an ingenious device imported from the Lake States for moving logs
to the landing from the site where a tree was felled. As the team moved
forward, the slip tongue of the "cart," as the rig is called in the South, slid
forward, pulling a chain over a drum into a locked position. This raised

the end of the dragged log so it could be skidded over tree stumps, gullies, and other obstacles. High-wheels, with rims as large as eight feet in diameter, lifted logs as large as four feet in diameter. Logs of any length, and as many as four, cradled with chains in the slip tongues, were handily hauled. When high-wheel carts were not available, choker setters fastened tongs, often called "grabs," at the end of a chain to the logs. Animals then pulled these to the landing for loading onto tram cars.

Oxen pulled short logs loaded in wagons to landings from as far away as a half mile from the rails. Teams were likely four yoked pairs, consisting of eight bulls. One yoke was the tongue-steerer, working the wagon tongue. At the felling site, a lead yoke and a swing yoke snaked logs, and another pair of animals loaded the log cart. Skid poles and chains enabled the oxen to cross-haul the logs into place on the wagon.

The resonant, melodious song of the puncher could be heard, along with the crack of his whip, for miles as he alternately cursed and praised his team. The whip, like the song, was never stilled. Yet the thong seldom touched the animal's hide, always an inch or even less away. But if it should meet the hide, the beast was not pained, for the whip was tipped with soft cotton rope. Toward day's end, one heard the song of the bull puncher. The crack of his whip coupled with the groans of his animals as the evening hush fell over the forest gave the air of the fading light an unforgettably eerie sound.

Mules were bred in three sizes and five colors. Small ones could be used around the mill; large beasts, weighing up to twelve hundred pounds, were employed in log hauling. Mules, surer footed than horses, are also more patient, more docile, stronger, and longer lived. The skin of the hybrid is thicker and tougher than that of a horse. Thus, galls from a rubbing harness or trace chains would not form an open sore as they rubbed a mule's hide. That thick skin also may have provided some relief for the beast in the hot and humid days of summer in the southern forest.

Mule skinners claimed their animals were smarter, or perhaps less high-strung, than horses: a mule with a leg caught in barbed wire patiently waits for release while horses thrash around, cutting tendons and arteries, in an effort to get free. On the other hand, a hornet's nest will panic a mule. And if a mule steps in a nest of yellow jackets, the whole team bolts in berserk frenzy. The insects then swarm all over the helpless animals, sometimes literally stinging them to death. Mules are also better at regulating their food intake. Left in a corral over the weekend with a three-day supply of hay and feed, they eat properly, never gorge, and thus are ready for the labor of Monday. Horses in the same corral overeat at first and will not be fit for work two days later.

While some logging by lumbermen of the period was done with teams of four mules, most log wagons had hitches of six. Usually teamsters matched the brutes by color and size. One observer of the scene says "it would have been an unpardonable *faux pas* and a heinous crime to have mixed colors in a hitch." If one died, his mate would be matched by tone and weight. "They worked together in unison like a squad of well-drilled marines. They were pretty, thrilling, and inspiring to watch."[20]

Good mule skinners were almost always blacks. Neither whites nor Latins seemed to get the hang of handling the animals. "Mules and Negroes loved each other, understood each other, and respected each other."[21] The pride of the man was shown in the care of his animals. Gaily colored tassels hung from their bridles, and brightly polished brass ball ornaments decorated the hame tips. A skinner purchased these from meager earnings to make his team the best dressed of all.

Motorized Hauling

A new kind of teamster in time was employed to get logs to the mills. But the introduction of trucks did not foreclose the need for animals in the woods. Skinners used the beasts to cross-haul the logs up and onto truck beds. Not infrequently truck drivers drove their rigs across "raccoon," or "Arkansas," bridges that straddled creeks and gullies between the log landing and the road to the mill. These crude motorways consisted of two logs, hewn flat on the upper side and laid across the ditch. Strategically placed to accommodate the wheels of the truck, the driver cautiously proceeded.

Woods Workers

Flatheads and Other Men

Flatheads felled the trees and bucked them into logs. The title is not a term of derision with respect to a woodsman's cranial features but, rather, is derived from the grub larvae of a wood-borer with that name. The insect girdles the tree as it tunnels through the phloem. The term is applied to pine cutters only, never to the loggers of hardwoods. Flatheads were sawyers only; they were never the mule skinners. On occasion, employers segregated the workers by color and task: the flatheads were black men, the mule skinners white, or the other way around.

Native-born flatheads used double-bit axes, not the single-edge common axe used in the earliest days of logging the New England woods. Flatheads used wedges made of hickory or dogwood, hammered with a sledge into the undercut, to control the direction of fall. They carried a stick eight feet four inches long, with which to measure—with an eight-inch tolerance—a sixteen-foot log, the most commonly bucked length. When working the hard, resinous pines of the Coastal Plain and Piedmont, they carried soda water or whiskey bottles filled with kerosene or turpentine. Pine straw, protruding from the bottle's mouth, served as a brush to spread the solvent in dissolving the pitch that collected on the two-man crosscut saws.

Flatheads used an ax for making the undercut prior to felling trees with the eight-foot saws or occasionally for completely felling trees. Sawyers displayed a high degree of coordination as, in cadence, they pulled the steel blade "with the grace of a ballerina."[22]

The task was dangerous. Bones and backs broke in a moment of carelessness. Pit vipers—copperheads, rattlesnakes, and water (cottonmouth) moccasins—and nerve-poisoning coral snakes snared their share of workers in the woods. Superstition required the burying of a leg bitten by a pit viper, the victim usually dying in that position. And many got blood poisoning through cuts made on bare feet and legs by the rasp-toothed sawpalmetto.

The woods "fo'man," the bull-of-the-woods in other climes, was responsible for his men as well as for supplying the mill with raw material. He stayed with his flatheads and skinners from before dawn until dark. They often drove in the last load to meet a day's quota with the aid of a lantern's light.

But the train boss's hours were even longer. So long was his day that workers prefixed his name with descriptive titles. "Midnight Jake" or "Midnight Sam" began his work sometime between midnight and daylight and ended it between dark and midnight. Workers in the woods worked from "can to can't," from when they could first see the light of day until the last rays were visible in the west.

Paul Bunyan's lumberjacks did not come south with the migration of the lumbermen from the Lake States. Logging in the South, unlike the fictional logging of other climes, was not a romantic job. Flatheads and tie hacks were neither sung about in ballads nor written about in narratives of daring. Tales of tall trees and tough men could have applied, but for some reason these men who lived with their families and rode trams and carts daily to the woods did not encourage the sentiment of songs and myths that won the hearts of many for Paul Bunyan and his lumberjacks of the Lake States, the white water men of the Northeast, the high-climbing topper and spar rigger in the Douglas fir forests of the Pacific Northwest, nor even the cowboy and oil-field worker of the Southwest.

Tie Hackers

Tie hackers, occasionally women, were a migratory lot. Nomads, they roamed from job to job, moving with the tide, yet without obvious reason. Employment for manufacturers of railroad cross ties was advertised widely, leading one to say that "a jug of whiskey and the *St. Louis Globe-Democrat* will break up any tie camp in the world." One old joke still repeated goes like this: "Mama, do tie makers eat hay?" Mama: "Yes, dear, if you sprinkle a little whiskey on it."

In 1881, ties were worth twenty-five cents. In 1886, prices dropped to fifteen cents and twenty cents. The five-year change was brought about by the entry into the labor force of "thumpers," apprentices as young as ten years of age. The two prices offered in 1886 were, respectively, for ties made by thumpers and hewers, the latter being journeymen. It usually took two months to acquire the skill of a hewer.[23]

Prices for hand-hewn ties made some tie hackers well paid. Twenty-five ties in a day, forty for a high roller, enabled a few of these men and women to earn twice the wages of mill-hand sawyers. For some, like J. H. Mitchell in Texas, it was an art like music and painting. While not listed in *The Guiness Book of Records*, Mitchell claimed he made six hundred ties in eleven and a half days with only one cull. As recently as 1950, ties were hewn as they had been when the first rails were laid a century earlier.

Tie hacking frequently was a one-man operation, which the tie inspector could make or break. In order to get a good report from one inspector for the Cotton Belt Railroad, a fellow who knew said, "You had to have a quart of liquor sitting on his table in his hotel room. One time I had a bunch of ties ready for inspection. I hooked up a train and some box cars and took the inspector down the lines and picked up ties. He was culling one maker pretty severely, and the man finally said, 'Mr. G, how many ties have you made in your life?' And Mr. G said, 'I haven't made a damn one, but I've made a hell of a lot of tie-makers.'"[24]

Some animosities arose between tie hackers and loggers and lumbermen. Trouble also occurred between tie cutters and federal foresters. Arguments mostly were over access to timber. As a junior forester for a national forest, I looked into a case of alleged timber theft in a remote compartment of the ranger district. With a forester's hand compass and beginning at one end of the compartment, I crossed the tract, offset ten chains, and returned to the old logging road that marked the boundary of the compartment. I continued to run the line and to offset back and forth until I heard the swish of an ax, its cadence so perfect the axman could have been a drummer in a Glenn Miller band. Abandoning the compass and seeking the sound, I located its source.

Peering through the parted brush, I chanced upon two of the biggest men I had ever seen. Dressed only in their undershorts on that July day, they were hand hewing cross ties from post oak logs (locally called "postes," or "posties," for both the species and its principal product). With rippling muscles in arms the size of twenty-eight inch waists, and with beads of sweat the size of grapes streaming down their shiny black skin, they were hewing a tie with precision. Beginning at opposite ends of the log, they each shaped one side, flipped it ninety degrees, and squared the remaining sides. The ties were carted by horse-drawn wagon about thirty miles to a buyer for a railroad company.

Forest Service officers in those days carried a book of free-use permits intended for local citizens who needed firewood for household cooking and for Monday morning washpots. Those two hackers, whose razor-sharp axes worked the same side of the log their bare legs were on, received a license from this J. F. to cut without cost all of the "postes" they wanted on the 180,000-acre ranger district. No longer could anyone accuse them of timber trespass. (On other compartments, stand-improvement crews were killing the hardwoods in order to release the more valuable pines, but that is another story.)

Mill Operations

The Drone of the Saws

Raising capital for mill expansion and land purchases often required unusual public relations skill and mastery of persuasion. A certain industrial captain of the day, in 1908, prevailed upon the publishers of the *American Lumberman* for publicity assistance. The magazine, one might say, was "commissioned" to provide the story that included ninety-six photographs, maps, and drawings. With that account under his arm, the entrepreneur's presentations to financial czars of the East were convincing. The company made rapid strides beyond that date in its development, the influence of which eventually extended across the South.[25]

The migratory lumbermen's first mills cut perhaps fifty thousand board feet daily. As improvements—like mechanical hogs, band saws, and shotgun feeds—came along, capacity increased to a quarter of a

Young but vigorous longleaf pines with understory brush controlled by frequently occurring fires. These trees provided poles for the rapidly developing power and telephone line requirements of the 1920s and 1930s.

million feet. Power sometimes was generated from bulk wood waste; other times, the mechanical hog, "giving the edgings a closer mastication," enabled more rapid combustion of the trimmings in the burners.

From the earliest days of logging in the South, every pine mill had a pond. When tramroads were laid, trains pulled the logs from the woods to the mill pond. The rail on the pond side of the track was lower. When the retaining stakes were removed from the lower side of the car, the logs rolled into the mill pond. Keeping pine logs wet between felling and milling reduces blue stain fungus infection. The water also washes sand from the bark, hence conserving the teeth on the circular and band saws of the mills. Logs were held in the pond for as little time as possible to avoid water-logging and sinking to the bottom. (In later years, draining mill ponds exposed fortunes in sound, but sunken, virgin timbers.) As laws relating to water rights in some precincts were yet unwritten or ignored, mill men rather arbitrarily formed ponds by damming creeks or created lakes that filled with water piped from a river. Hardwood logs were not put in ponds because the blue-stain fungus does not infect and discolor freshly cut wood of these species.

Planing mills and dry kilns were parts of large operations. "Peckerwood" mills had neither. The rough-sawn lumber of small, and often fly-by-night, operations was air dried and then shipped by rail to mills with planers. Well-equipped planers, even in the migratory lumbermen's mills, included sizers (for standardizing board widths), molders (to make ornamental boards, called "millwork"), edgers (to cut bark from boards), resaws (to cut a board a second time to meet dimension and grade requirements), and lathes (for rounding timbers to pillars and posts).

Saw filers were possibly the highest-paid employees of a mill, earning in the first decade of this century ten dollars a day. This compared with $1.35 to $1.75 as an average wage for mill hands.

One occasionally earned a reward of five dollars for stealing the night watchman's lantern while he dozed and then turning it in at the office the next morning. The Christmas anthem, "Watchmen, tell us of the night / What the scenes of promise are?" took on new meaning. The watchman was reprimanded or fired, and the squealer became the community scoundrel.

Mills shut down when, because of long rainy seasons, an inadequate log supply was delivered to the mill. On the major water courses, where logs were rafted downstream to mills, low water and the resulting logjams also forced some mills to close. These jams were not infrequently a mile long on rivers like the Sabine, on the Louisiana and Texas border, and the Savannah, separating Georgia and South Carolina. To avoid the jams, companies built splash dams to store water for later release. The dam gate was opened when the logs were ready to be rafted to the mill. (River drives did not include hardwood logs, for many species of these porous woods readily become waterlogged and sink.) Mills also temporarily closed for cotton picking, the less-skilled workers badly needed for that brief period of harvesting the fluffy white bolls; cotton was yet king in much of the South.

Scaling logs for accurate volume determination was often a worrisome matter in the South, as elsewhere. Like the popular volume tables devised by a logger-preacher named Scribner in the Northeast, T. F. Herring as early as 1871 developed a scale stick for calculating volumes in the boles of harvested timber in the South. Converted to tabular form, his rule became the official scale for the Kirby Lumber Company in Texas. As Herring's rules did not apply to logs under twelve inches in diameter, Devant tables, derived by another Southerner, were added for accommodating smaller trees. The combination Herring-Devant tables gave volumes similar to the Scribner log rule. Still other company tables were used in the marketplace. Southern mills first adopted in 1883 lumber grading in order to standardize the quality of the boards produced.

How Lumbering People Lived

Camp Towns

Looking back over the trail marked out by the calendar, one focuses upon the people of this time and place. They were hearty and hardy folks. Large numbers of men and a few women made up the woods' labor force, living with their families in company towns or in loggers' camps miles from the mill town. Tramroads often ran through these camp towns.

The camp towns were of three kinds: permanent, portable, and wheel. Permanent camps were of the simplest rusticity, built—in spite of the name—for only a few years' accommodation of the workers and their families. Portable camps were constructed on flat cars for easy removal from place to place. These cabins would, without condescension, be appropriately called shacks. Portable villages also consisted almost solely of tents for the habitation of a company's loggers and their families. One still sees marked on forest maps names like Ragtown, indicating such a town. Names such as Camp Britain, in what is now the Sabine National Forest, also suggest by incorporating the term *camp* the temporary nature of these villages. At Camp Britain, from 1918 to 1933, families gathered in the narrow mud or dusty streets between the lowly homes. Now little survives, apart from the maps, to suggest that any human ever inhabited the area.

Wheel camps were usually crude homes built on the trucks of worn-out railroad cars. One wheel camp listed seventy-five men whose families resided in fifty-four "car houses." The remodeled boxcars were fitted with windows and rented for four dollars a month in the first decade of the twentieth century. Forerunners of the mobile home, they were lifted from the tram tracks and set down a few feet from the right-of-way on either side.[26]

Gentle rises of ground were sought for camp settlements in order to encourage favorable sanitation. Water for camp towns was hauled from rivers or springs. Some camps had wells; others relied on cisterns. Yet the *American Lumberman* could report self-servingly, but

Warped rail along the main street of a logging camp town, fifteen miles from the mill town. Loggers and their families resided in these car houses, an early (before 1910) version of the trailer home. (Courtesy Southern Pine Lumber Company Collection, Steen Library Archives, Stephen F. Austin State University, Nacogdoches, Tex.)

probably accurately, that "sanitation conditions [were] very comfortable and healthy."[27]

Company stores were in the camp towns, too. They likely occupied a portable structure similar to the residences. So did the drugstores with their physician's office. Health care by the itinerant company doctor was provided at a reasonable rate. The fee for membership in one Employee Hospital Association was fifty cents per month for single men and a dollar for families. The more fortunate among the laborers advanced to the company town, where standards of living would be much improved.

Company Towns

The company towns at the mill sites were considerably more comfortable for the residents than were the camps for the loggers. Here might be found tennis courts, baseball diamonds, athletic societies, li-

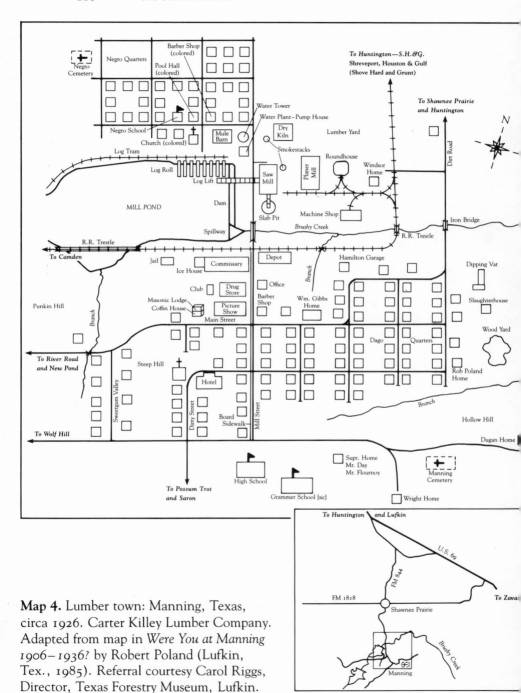

Map 4. Lumber town: Manning, Texas, circa 1926. Carter Killey Lumber Company. Adapted from map in *Were You at Manning 1906–1936?* by Robert Poland (Lufkin, Tex., 1985). Referral courtesy Carol Riggs, Director, Texas Forestry Museum, Lufkin.

braries, fraternal orders, boarding houses, and dormitories for unmarried employees of the company. Most of these facilities were prerequisites for "young men of quality" in a company's employ and not likely to be enjoyed by the mill hands. Hotels did accommodate loggers and other rugged men, providing room and board for sixteen dollars a month in one mill town in 1906.[28]

Home ownership was rare in company towns, but sometimes encouraged. John Henry Kirby, a Texan who became the spokesman for the entire southern lumber industry, was a saint to some Southerners of the period and chief among sinners to others. Thus, his promotion of home ownership by mill workers was significant. In an emotional speech, he called the owning of a home a sign of social progress, the pursuit of happiness declared by the Declaration of Independence to be the privilege of all Americans. The cynic may suggest that Kirby's concern was beyond the boundaries of his many company towns. Home ownership sold a lot of lumber in those days when an American residence throughout most of the land was 90 percent wood. Many companies established fairly modern and permanent communities, perhaps encompassing a square mile or so. Some of these remained company towns through the 1970s, at which time they were sold to the residents. Less well-constructed structures were demolished.

Schools served the pupils in company towns. Because camp towns sometimes were overlooked, across the South into the 1940s were a goodly number of people of both races who, having been reared under these conditions, could neither read nor write. They often had to be taught—into the 1950s—to sign a Forest Service payroll when the national forests hired the one-time children of the camps as laborers. Where rural schools served loggers' families, the buildings were typically one-room. A single teacher held classes for twenty-five or more students of ages six through fourteen, and usually with six grades. Some of those children, now elderly, remember it as a good educational system: six-year-olds learned by overhearing the lessons taught the twelve-year-olds.

Companies located "colored" schools for blacks in the Negro section of the community, often called "the quarter." The teacher there was typically addressed as Professor, a term implying respect where lesser titles like Mister were not condoned by white people. For such schools, even rope was scarce: for one, a crude wood ladder substituted for a rope to reach the bell "tower." The bell was mounted atop a four-by-four-inch post about twenty feet above the ground. A student, appointed to climb the ladder, sent forth the call to study.

Schools for all were expected to run nine months, and teachers were not infrequently paid in part from the company treasury. Some

A school for blacks in an Angelina County company town (ca. 1905). Professor J. W. Hogg provided instruction and, when required, sent a boy up the ladder to ring the bell. Companies often paid part of a teacher's salary. (Courtesy Southern Pine Lumber Company Collection, Steen Library Archives, Stephen F. Austin State University, Nacogdoches, Tex.)

companies, it is reported, supported programs of adult education for employees, perhaps for as many as 20 percent of their people. One who has worked closely with people so educated cannot help but be amazed by the many who have risen to meet the challenges of the technological age, able to stand on an equal footing with colleagues with more, and more formal, education.

House rental in the company town was from six to twelve dollars monthly, wallpaper and electricity included. However, the generator ran intermittently, perhaps from 5:30 A.M. to 10:00 P.M., making unnecessary the use of switches to control at bedtime Mr. Edison's globes. Emergencies and impending births were cause for special illumination: the lights all over town suddenly came on when someone fell ill or the doctor or midwife was called to assist in a delivery. Company towns had telephone service of a sort no later than 1908, when instruments connected the mill office, railroad depot, store, and perhaps the end of a thirty-mile string of wire at a logging camp town or tram camp where a bridge gang was at work.

Water and garbage collection seemed not to be billed extra in these feudal towns. Some homes had wells, and often there was one between each two homes. Many were fitted with outhouses with pit toilets; others had a room with a hinged door in a box below the seat that permitted ready access from the outside of the house for removal of buckets of night soil. This human waste was dumped beyond the limits of the town. The access door had a spring hinge to prevent entry by chickens and pigs that grazed freely in the yards of residences. (The "honey bucket" of homes in towns of the far north, like Nome, Alaska, where permafrost prevents conventional sewage flow in underground pipes, reminds one of the mill town form of sewage disposal.)

Mill town churches, often of several denominations, met at various times in a single structure provided by the company. The log pond served for baptisms. Wood workers' fraternities, like the International Concatenated Order of Hoo Hoo, gathered in an upper room of the church. Public lectures and the "electric theater," sometime later to become the movies, likely shared a community house built by the company. Youth organizations, bands, and book clubs served the people. The Boy Scouts, formed near the turn of the century and later to be considered principally for urban, middle-class lads, was widely dispersed among the rural, backwoods people throughout the South. Companies frequently supported troops. Even before the movement was well established in this country, a British missionary to the Scotch-Irish of the Southern Appalachian Mountains organized troops up and down the coves. Those scout units were modeled after the military style of the movement's English founder, Lord Baden-Powell.

Sawmill companies may have invented daylight savings time. To encourage family gardening, employers rescheduled the mill whistle to blow an hour earlier in the spring so workers could have more daylight during seedtime and harvest. Companies often provided land for tilling. They also may have provided cattle on credit, one head per family, requiring repayment at the rate of a dollar a month. Cottonseed meal, purchased by the company by the carload, was sold to employees at cost, or so it was said.

The mill whistle, sounded by a youthful "whistlepunk," was sundial, alarm clock, and timeclock. It also held families together. Mill wives married for better or for worse *and* for lunch. The "cornbread" whistle blew at 11:15, the cue for women to scurry for the wood stove and have the table spread. A mill hand, mighty hungry at noon, used the whole hour allotted for dinner (still the name for the weekday mid-day meal in the rural South).

Ethnic Communities

To avoid ethnic conflicts, companies segregated people of diverse backgrounds. Though they might work together, their families could not live together. In one Mississippi mill town in 1917, Mexicans, blacks, and whites were segregated. And in that town, the French were required to live apart from other whites.

Some counties in the South contained preemption communities. These sites, often in the remote forest, were special places set aside in the post–Civil War years for exslaves or their descendants. The blacks stayed overnight on the land, hanging a kitchen pan on a tree to bear witness to their ownership and intent. Single men received 80-acre grants; married men, 160 acres.

Company Money

Often the company was the bill collector of employee debts. From a man's wages, a dollar a week would be retained for debt payment, the company charging another 3 percent for its service. Fines too were deducted from wages. In a town of a thousand souls, the company, besides serving as employer, was landlord, banker, barber, benefactor, United Way, policeman, hotel host, doctor, undertaker, educator, city council, utility supplier, family counselor, and storekeeper. Often it was the mint, coining its own scrip to be used in the employer-owned store.

Company "money" consisted of round cardboard or wooden nickels, dimes, and dollars. Metal rarely was used. One side of the "chip" or "punchout" might read "Good for 10 in Merchandise," not indicating the value more specifically. The other side bore the company name, usually its president's signature, and town and state. These coins and similar paper currency (coupons) were used in company stores at full value. But when spent in town and city stores beyond the company's control, they were discounted 10 to 20 percent. City merchants who redeemed the chips at reduced value could only use them in the company store for items they may have neither needed nor wanted.[29]

Some companies used "doolies," thick paper sewn around the edges and dyed various colors. After the value was printed on the doolie and the cashier signed his name, the paper was soaked in varnish. One company paid its workers in cash only twice a year, Christmas and July 4;

Company money, called "merchandise checks," used for paying wages. These could be redeemed for full value at company stores. The federal government eventually outlawed the practice. (Courtesy Forest History Collection, Steen Library Archives, Stephen F. Austin State University, Nacogdoches, Tex.)

another once a month. The choicest employers paid in cash every Saturday night.

Since the company store handled groceries, clothing, hardware, and medicine, there was little need for employees to venture elsewhere for purchases. The discounted value of the tokens assured *that*, for commissary money became known as "robissary" money. In one southern state, in 1937, a law required payment in "good and lawful money of the United States if (the scrip is) presented at a regular payday." That legislation soon eliminated the system there. So, too, did expert counterfeiters. Redeeming from its laborers at fair value a thousand dollars more than it issued on a single payday was enough to convince one company to abandon its use of "funny" money.[30] Subsequent payrolls were met with government minted and engraved cash.

Some companies forbade transferring tokens in order to discourage gambling. Payrolls using company money also impeded the purchase of liquor by laborers, for commissaries stocked only medicinal alcohol. Bootleggers would take some of this "currency," but they had a hard time disposing of it. In some stores, cashiers had the responsibility to approve purchases so that employees would not squander money on "snuff, fancy groceries, candy." Their wages were to be used for buying staple food for their families.[31]

Post-dating paychecks was another scheme used by the migrating lumbermen. They claimed that the practice was necessary because of hard times and customer defaults. The check could be cashed before its date, but at an appreciable discount. For full pay, one might have to hold the paper several weeks. These kinds of activities led to attempts to organize workers, even in the earliest days of southern lumbering.

The company store did have some advantages, even if one owed his soul to it. Mills were often great distances—twenty miles, a day's journey—from a town with a well-supplied "mercantile" establishment. By having company stores, laborers and their families were spared travel time and costs. Poor roads aggravated the situation, and trains did not run to every village. Indeed, some county seats in the forested South still have no intercity public transportation.

Roads of Wood

Wood planks served towns for road surfacing. Usually oak planks, cut at portable mills, were nailed to sleepers, logs laid in the ground or on top of graded soil. These plank roads of two- and three-inch dimensional stock were used extensively for public thoroughfares, especially in Alabama, Mississippi, and Tennessee. No doubt considerable volumes of timber for this purpose moved northward, and so helped to hasten the harvest of the southern forest.

Timbers also provided all-weather roads throughout the region for the loggers. Corduroy roads were common in the woods and camps. With these, the lane is simply "paved" with small logs—three to six inches in diameter—laid snugly on the ground. Eventually, the industry promoted wood blocks for street paving.

Tough Logging Chances

Swamp Logging

Late in the migrating lumbermen's ventures—as recently as the mid-1940s—the interiors of some swamps that dotted the southern forest were first subjected to the logger's ax. Early in the century, harvests with bole-diameter limits had been made along the banks of the rivers that flowed into, through, or out of these swamps. In the 1920s and 1930s, in the interior island hills that rise slightly above the swales, timbermen harvested the pines, the water-loving hardwoods, and southern baldcypresses. Finally, in the least accessible sites, the swamps were dissected with canals dug with barge-mounted draglines that hoisted buckets or pulled pans. Loggers floated or barged out the timber through the canals. Thus, over a wide area the last three thousand board feet or so per acre were removed from land that probably supported six to nine thousand feet upon initial entry at the beginning of the period of the lumbermen. Laborers worked these last harvests two to three decades after the periphery pine cutting on any particular swampy site.

Pull-boats skidded the logs to the canals, resulting in many small ditches emanating like spokes of a wheel from the pull-boat position. The ditches made by the log skidding are narrow and deep. They remain distinguishable today, both on aerial photographs and from small craft. (Though the logs were not skidded in the conventional sense, the term was used for the movement of the logs to a landing for loading onto a conveyance for shipment to a mill.)

Sawyers often girdled the stems a year before harvest. The dead trees, when felled, would float. Some girdled trees, found doty with rot a year after ringing the bark, were still standing forty years later. Tree "fellers" cut the trees that grew in shallow water, working from small boats or from springboards inserted into sawn slots above the buttress at the base of trees. The felled timber was barged or made into rafts for delivery to mills lower on the rivers.

Sometimes a barge was equipped with a steam donkey and winches. From the donkey drum on the pull-boat, a cable line ran to the woods. There the cable was fed through a hole drilled into the end of the log. The timber was then yanked down the pull-boat "road," actually a ditch often more than eight feet deep. Southern baldcypress, the "wood eternal," and veneer-quality tupelo gum thus moved from the swamps.[32]

Legendary Great Swamp Harvest

Such were the techniques employed in the harvest of the Okefenokee Swamp, the gigantic seep that gives rise to the Suwannee River on the Georgia-Florida boundary. Some called the legendary engineering feat "Jackson's Folly," naming the debacle for Captain Jackson, an Atlanta lawyer turned lumbering entrepreneur in the last decade of the nineteenth century. Not until the Civil War veteran drained the waterways in, and out of, the swamp had there been significant success in logging the valuable hardwoods and southern baldcypress that grew in the fibrous organic soils. Jackson intended to reclaim the "land of trembling earth" for agricultural use. That was not to be: heavy timber, miry soil, vermin, reptiles, the low value of lumber, and the lay of the land saw to that.

Jackson's plan to channel water through canals indicated a lack of an understanding of the terrain. The Okefenokee is shaped like a saucer, and a ridge bordering the wetlands in the east forces drainage to the southwest and away from the St. Mary's River, Jackson's intended destination for the excess water. By the time failure occurred, the captain had stockpiled at the mill more than five million board feet of baldcypress. His holdings, amounting to almost 260,000 acres, sold for 68 cents an acre in 1897. (The U.S. government paid $1.50 an acre for the cutover land in 1938. It is now a wildlife refuge.)

Later, between 1910 and 1927, over a billion board feet moved from the Okefenokee by pull-boats and tram tracks. Dummy engines pulled small log trains to the swamp edge, trainmen then switching the log cars to larger locomotives for the thirty-six–mile run to the mill at Hebardville, a town built by a lumbering family especially for this venture.

The fragile soil of muck and peat often failed to support the weight of the trains. Pilings of pine and baldcypress driven twenty feet into the ground sank farther under the heavy loads of logs and engines. Tracks of spur lines sometimes were wholly under water: even so, the trains ran on them.

A Hebard Company chronicler, Robert Izler, tells the story

this way: "A spar tree 60 feet tall was selected near the middle of the set . . . various cables were run from the spar tree to tail trees 1000 feet away. . . . A choker was attached to a trolley that ran on these long cables. The overhead skidder, which was steam operated, provided the power to pick up the logs. The trolley would be swung out to the logs, where the men would set the chokers on the logs. The overhead skidder would then pick up the logs, transport them back to the deck and load them onto flat cars." [33]

River Drives

Though never as dramatic as the springtime river drives down the turbulent rivers of the North, some timbers moved over river routes in the South. Most log runs were on mountain streams, the small mills relocating upstream as the trees downstream were cut. A few river drives took place in the Coastal Plain; for even there the migrating lumbermen, planning to imitate the techniques employed in the North, often measured river depths prior to setting up a mill. Out of 122 Texas mills, for example, only two received logs by water in the years between 1909 and 1915. One of these, at Orange on the Sabine River, was likely typical of the South. Rivermen formed rafts of 1 to 10 million board feet at a point 150 river miles to the north. They then rode the rafts to the mill. Arrival of a raft was reported in the nearest mill town press. Words like "Howard arrived" told the community that the raft and its keeper had reached their destination safely. The saw could continue to spin, and payrolls would be met. And, as for Howard, he and his fellow rivermen hiked back to the camp town from whence they had embarked.

Some enterprising folk went into the salvage business. On that same Sabine River and smaller drainages, salvaged southern bald-cypress sinkers, lost from rafts when waterlogged, later brought a dollar a log at the mills. Salvage of baldcypress took place into the 1940s in Deep East Texas.

Logs of the longleaf pine forests were skidded by animals as much as four miles in the days of the river era to points along the water courses that served as important traffic arteries for moving timber to steam-powered mills. To facilitate the operation, companies dammed creeks. The logs collected in holding ponds, and when water was deep enough for driving the heavy timbers, the dam gate opened. Sometimes ditches, lined with boards to retain their shape and to guide the logs, were placed alongside small and crooked streams. These ditches, similar to the flumes that parallel a river for miles in the western states and are occasionally still in use, sped the logs from woods to mills.

At the end of the ditch, longleaf pine logs were sawn into square "deals" and then floated farther downstream to be gathered into rafts for transport to coastal mills and ports. At the larger streams, logs were floated to the mills below, not unlike procedures employed in the early days of settlement in the Northeast. At the rivers, men chained logs together to make rafts, and a man or two would ride each raft to the mill and then hike back. Sometimes the "pilots" camped on a raft for days. Logjams occurred, though tales of the rugged men who broke them and lived to tell about it seem not to have been passed down to this time.

Freshets to set unbound logs in motion following rains were common, the strong currents carrying the bucked timbers far from the river's edge or far down the river. But the thaw of the terrible winter of 1885 was long to be recalled in the timber industry. The freeze in the central Gulf region blocked the rivers stacked with logs. With the sudden thaw, forty to fifty thousand logs raced to a river's mouth. Even though rivermen stretched booms across the channels, the torrents of water running high out of the river's banks carried great timbers overland into the salt marshes. Many more logs simply by-passed the booms to travel on to the sea. If floods were troublesome, so too were droughts. The mills then ceased running for lack of water to bring logs to the decks.

Harvesting Tall Trees

The Longleaf Pineries

Longleaf pine forests, stretching across the coastal South, have served like a gigantic stage on which has been played the drama of the region's residents. The uniqueness of the species and of its role in the story of the southern forest warrants tribute. Thomas Croker tells this fascinating saga, how the lives of millions have been touched, and how "red, white, and black men have sweated, bled, and died harvesting [its] products."[34] Some folks became millionaires from timbering operations in these woods; others continued in poverty while furnishing lumber for both mansions and squalid shanties.

The original virgin forest probably encompassed sixty million acres, stretching from North Carolina to Texas, interrupted only by the region's water courses. Regenerated longleaf pine acreage in the second-growth forest amounted to about twenty million acres. Perhaps less than ten million acres remain as I write, the balance never having regenerated to longleaf pine following the harvest by the migrating lumbermen. (A 1986 estimate put the acreage at four million.)

Wildfires and feral hogs contributed greatly to the lack of re-production. A razorback, in search of starch, roots as far as thirty feet from a tree trunk and in an hour pulls as many as eighty seedlings from the ground.

Early lumbermen found the forest open and parklike. Let Croker describe it: "Like huge wooden soldiers, lined up in battle forma-tion, the massive trees dotted the rolling coastal plains in a sea of grass. Gentle breezes, laden with a resinous perfume, rippled the long-strawed crowns and generated music both soothing to the ear and slightly mourn-ful. Occasionally the tranquil scene was disturbed by a killer hurricane that crashed ashore from the sea, felling many veteran trees."[35]

Among the timbers harvested were trees for ship masts. These highest-quality stems ranged from twenty-six to thirty-six inches in diam-eter at the large end and between eighteen and twenty-one inches at the small end. The distance between the large and small ends tallied seventy-five to one hundred feet. Even dead and "down" trees were taken, for the heartwood, heavily impregnated with resin, was resistant to rot. These provided timbers for building sills and trestles, as well as for masts. Those timbers still undergird houses and larger structures built during the period.

Many of the logs sawn into deals, today called "cants" (or squared-up timbers), were shipped to European markets. This was an es-pecially important outlet for longleaf pine because of its reputation as probably the strongest of North American woods.

Logging the Longleaf

The era of river logging had relatively little impact upon the longleaf pine forests, for harvests were confined to stream sides. Railroad logging, however, introduced along with the migrating lumbermen, en-couraged rapid exploitation.

From main lines, spurs were laid at quarter-mile intervals, facilitated by township and section surveys in Gulf Coast states (ex-cept Texas) to reach the great blocks of timber in otherwise inaccessible locales. In the first decade of the twentieth century, armies of saw-yers worked long hours to supply the efficient bandmills then replacing many circular saws. By the 1930s, the sixty million acres of longleaf pine forest from the Atlantic coast to East Texas had been clear-cut. Croker estimates that the volume harvested exceeded four hundred billion board feet.

Skidders called the "Clyde" (sometimes pronounced *clive*) or "Lidgerwood" assisted in the rapid demise of the longleaf pine forests. These machines dragged five large logs at once to tram lines, where

Longleaf and slash pines growing on the sterile, droughty soils of the western Florida sandhills. These were among the last of the virgin forests to be entered by the wood merchants. This stand escaped the ax at least through the 1950s. Here a forester takes an increment boring to determine tree age. (Photo by E. Hebb courtesy U.S. Forest Service.)

McGiffert loaders took over. There, mounted on the tracks and straddling a log car, the McGiffert crane lifted the logs from the ground to the rail car beneath it. (The advent of truck hauling in the 1930s and 1940s saw animal loading return as the principal way to hoist logs from "landings" to truck beds.) This was not simply a harvest: Clyde and similar power skidders devastated the land, leaving the forest appearing as though a panzer division had met its enemy there.

Entrepreneurial Decisions

Management Options

Among the early promotional ventures of the Southern Pine Association (SPA) was the use of blocks of heart pine for surfacing streets in the towns of the region. In time, bricks replaced wood. Meanwhile, mill managers organized to protect their many other interests, and that of the entire industry, in trade groups like the SPA. Members were charged five cents for every thousand board feet of lumber produced.

Readers of the records of the times are all too willing to blame the migrating lumbermen for the greed that led to clean sweeping the southern forests. This is an over simplification. At the time, exploitation was practiced because wood was plentiful, the profession of forestry was essentially unknown in the region, and only so much money would be paid for the finished lumber. At this time, too, following the cut-out-and-get-out trends in the Northeast and the Lake States, southern barons could plan to move men, mules, and machinery to the virgin forests of sugar pine and other valuable merchantable species in California. Some did. Cut-over land in the South sold for as little as a dollar or two an acre, and the cash received was often reinvested in West Coast timber.

There were exceptions. The policy of management of the old Southern Pine Lumber Company, for example, was that "this operation asserts that all yellow pine lands are susceptible of a second cutting, with high-class commercial results a possibility, after a lapse of from 12 to 15 years after the first cutting." Fifteen years after the first harvest, "any acre of land cut by this concern . . . will produce 3,000 to 5,000 feet of merchantable" pine timber. "Unripened yet marketable trees" were also to be left for a third cutting.[36]

One may commend or condemn the managers of companies that practiced cut-out-and-get-out. Commend them for their foresight or condemn them for high-grading the woods, for the stems left behind in the first harvests were those not worthy, in the economy of the period, of cutting, bucking, skidding, loading, hauling, and milling. In fifteen years' time, those trees freed from the competition of the earlier overtopping dominant stems often added as much as fifteen inches of diameter increment. These long-boled pines would be worth going to the woods to harvest as the supplies throughout the South rapidly diminished.

One "commercial barony in the vast expanse of the Empire of the Yellow Pine" had some holdings in fee simple (the company owned the land) and others in cutting rights. The Southern Pine Lumber Company, with total land holdings exceeding two hundred thousand acres in 1907, anticipated logging for the next thirty years if the mills ran at capacity twenty-four hours a day every day of the year. (As a postscript to history, the harvest of the company's first forest concluded about on schedule.)

Low Stumps and Labor Concerns

Company policies may have called for low stumps. In spite of such edicts, seldom before 1907 were stumps much less than three feet high. More adamant management brought them down to about two feet after that time. Why so high? The reader who borrows from a museum a cross-cut saw of that day, enlists another person to grasp the handle on the other end, and tries to fell a tree will understand. A man could still stand erect at the end of a ten-hour day if the stumps he left behind were waist high. With shorter stumps, either his work day, his output, or his vigor rapidly declined. Fire and logskidder damage to the butts of trees were other reasons for leaving high stumps: damaged parts of logs were left in the woods.

Among the major problems faced by the lumbermen in the period of their dominance was that of the labor unions. John Henry Kirby, owner of one of the largest lumber companies in the South, opposed unions. Though often considered paternalistic toward his employees, "the Prince of the Pines"—as he was known in legislative halls—remained determined to operate the corporation without interference from labor or government. Other industrialists followed his lead, and a lumber war resulted that lasted three years. Strikes, lockouts, violence, and murder occurred throughout the region between 1899 and 1912.[37]

The bib-overalled workers in the employ of Kirby and his industrial colleagues fared variously. Many a poorly educated laborer rose to the top of the corporate ladder if mechanically inclined and loyal. One company would provide for the widow of a man killed on the job; another would charge the woman for the lumber for the casket. Until such practices were outlawed, many companies required a laborer to sign away his rights to sue in the event of an injury. By signing the waiver, the worker claimed he was able to do the job, that he was experienced and knowledgable of the work. Typical defenses, if a case got to court, were that the worker volunteered for the job, a fellow worker's carelessness contributed to the accident, and the worker himself was careless. Not until the teen years did state industrial accident boards get involved with the wood-using industry, though the U.S. Department of Labor reported that logging and milling accidents were seven times more likely to occur than an accident in all other manufacturing jobs combined and averaged.

National Policies Influencing Forestry

Economic Change

Arrival of the migrating lumbermen in the South did little to relieve the region's deep poverty. Defeat in the Civil War subjected its people to economic distress, many conditions the direct result of federal restrictions on the region's financial well-being. (Freight rate discrimination against manufactured goods moving north was a notable example.) These retaliatory and perhaps vindictive regulations were the opposite of the Marshall Plan, which provided assistance for the defeated enemies of the United States following the Second World War.

The migratory lumbermen, however, introduced a new incentive for people living off the land, bringing to the region a manufacturing industry to use the raw material already in a condition suitable for processing. Of course the textile industry was here, but cotton had to be grown, and most of the freshly picked bales went north or abroad for spinning and further refinement into cloth and clothing. Hence, cotton as a raw material shipped from the South provided remuneration for people beyond the region's bounds. Logs, too heavy for shipment to northern mills, had to be locally manufactured into lumber. Employment opportunities remained close to the source of the raw material.

In contrast to the immediate past, times appeared a little better, though they were still discouraging for many. Field hands found work, but for many the task of felling and bucking, skinning and punching, setting and dogging, and sawing and trimming were skills yet to be learned. Logging and milling are labor-intensive: the estimated cost of labor for lumber processing in 1880 amounted to 35 to 40 percent of the total cost of production. One report pegged it at 60 percent in 1890. Wages were low: workers in the industry were paid only a little more than brick makers, the class of labor listed at the bottom of the pay scale.[38]

The passing of the migratory lumbermen's forest in the 1930s, and with it the smokestack "as sacred as a church steeple," had so drastic an effect on the region that lumber began to be imported from outside of the South. Suddenly sections of the region were no longer self-sufficient in materials for construction of homes and factories, even though logging and lumbering enterprises remained principal sources of employment. There was little else for a laborer to do during the Great Depression.

By 1912, 30 to 35 percent of some once totally forested counties had been cleared of timber, lumber output was decreasing, and the mills then remaining were often supplied with stumpage from adjacent counties. "Stump pastures" appeared, the "mule-tail" residual pines overlooking a wilderness of grass and stumps. ("Mule-tails" were those trees with almost no branches left as worthless by the lumbermen and heard to swish in the wind-swept openings.)

Still Breaking New Ground

As the forests were cleared and the land invaded by both squatters and by legal settlers, farming began. Cleared sites along railroads doubled in value in the first decade of the century, for here access was handy; and from these sites, fruit, cotton, and vegetables could be more readily marketed. Just as the cutting of the forest encouraged the production of cotton on the freshly cleared land, later the decline of the cotton industry ironically ushered in a new southern forestry enterprise, a subject to be considered in subsequent chapters. The irony is that the new industry would produce a fiber competitive with cotton.[39]

Farmland prices ranged from five to twenty-five dollars an acre, perhaps higher than attained in the North because of the mild growing season of eight months' duration and the well-distributed precipitation, averaging forty-seven inches per year. However, the boll weevil was forcing farmers to diversify. Just as the beginning of the lumber industry in the South was first observed along the East Coast, so too would be the passing of this phase of southern forestry. The transition westward into Texas required a generation or so.

Basket manufacturing was singled out in the accounts of the time, indicating perhaps its primary importance as a use of wood in a previously heavily forested area. One record in 1912 said that "very few merchantable trees [are found] in uplands but some of the bottomlands have a valuable growth of hardwoods [species from which baskets are often woven]. Native grasses became abundant where the forests were no longer dense."[40]

While riverboats and barges carrying supplies and cotton plied up the forested rivers far inland until the 1920s, even in the western edge of the region river transportation was eventually abandoned. At least in part this was because of the silting in of the channels which, in turn, was attributed to the cutting of the forests. Slow-running rivers, unable to turn mill wheels, stimulated the conversion of sawmills in the region to steam power. Those sluggish rivers also influenced federal legislation.

The Weeks Act

When intensive harvesting of the virgin forests of the East hastened severe siltation of the country's eastern waterways, John Weeks introduced legislation in the U.S. Congress to remedy the situation. As a representative from Massachusetts, he intended the bill to provide federal funds for purchasing land in New England for national forests. The South, however, benefited promptly and to a much greater degree than did the states of the North, because the government used the authority of the 1911 Weeks Act to purchase cut-over and burned-over lands from industry and individuals to protect streams from further siltation. The first land acquired under the law was in the mountains of North Carolina— the Pisgah and Nantahala national forests. Thus the bill was often referred to as the Appalachian Act. Among other early acquisitions were extensive tracts in northern Georgia and the mountains of Arkansas.

Sediment loads also built up in the waterways as lands were farmed without regard for terracing, contour plowing, and other erosion-control practices. Siltation was so destructive to river traffic throughout the nation that the Weeks Act, the statute designed to protect the "navigability of navigable streams," enabled the U.S. government eventually to purchase more than 11 million acres for inclusion in the thirty national forests in the South. More acquisitions were authorized by the 1924 amendment to the Weeks Act, called the Clarke-McNary Act.

Some question arose about the definition of a navigable stream. Rivers suitable for floating logs to mills were finally ruled navigable. It was appropriate, for streams were still transportation routes for logs. But the rivers were even more important for shipping raw materials and manufactured products for a growing nation. Names of inland towns like Logansport on the Sabine River and Shreveport on the Red River suggest the importance of these watercourses for moving people and goods. Silting in of the rivers upon which the communities depended often played a role in their demise.

The Weeks Act was claimed by some to be unconstitutional; for until its implementation no large tracts of "park" land had been purchased by the federal government from private owners. The acquisition of

Gettysburg Battlefield, the first such purchase, suggested a change in attitude.[41]

Lobbying for the Weeks Act began prior to 1900 with the organization of the Appalachian Mountain Club. When Southerners joined the effort, one disgruntled politician allowed that New England had clasped hands with the South, the latter's sins forgiven and forgotten, and "in the sacred name of conservation, we are witnessing one of the best organized raids on the Federal Treasury in history."[42] Another said of the effort, sponsored by the National Park Association in 1899, that the Blue and the Gray have combined forces in this last phase of the battle.[43]

A National Forest Reservation Commission was appointed to oversee Weeks Act purchases. Not an easy task, for mountain land boundaries described on courthouse documents and blazed on the ground were the work of "half-literate hill country lawyers and county surveyors."[44] Even for literate surveyors, establishing corners and boundaries in rugged terrain using the crude instruments of the day, the job is formidable. Weeks Act purchases in 1912 averaged $5.95 per acre, though prices in that era as low as $2.82 are recorded.[45]

Fire in the Pineries

No great conflagrations seem to have occurred in the southern forests in the decades that closed the last and opened this century. While burning woods as a sport and for economic reasons was now occurring, the lack of long dry spells may have checked any threatening "blow-up" fires. Holocausts, like those frequently occurring in the western United States, are rare in the southern forests.

Fire in the pineries had become a governmental concern by 1894. Early the following year, W. W. Ashe, the ubiquitous forester of the times, wrote a bulletin on the situation in North Carolina. Already, loblolly pine was replacing longleaf pine, he complained, perhaps not realizing the dependence of longleaf pine upon fire at certain stages in its life. (Brownspot needle blight, naturally controlled by fire, was yet unknown.) The species' grass stage, its infrequent seed crops (1845, 1872, 1892), and the consumption by hogs of its deep taproots were known to Ashe.[46] With so many adversarial problems, fire to kill the blight fungus is essential for sustaining the longleaf pine forest.

With the exception of a few observant lumbermen like Henry Hardtner of the Urania Lumber Company in Louisiana, leaders of the industry seemed little concerned about either hogs or cattle in the woods. The presence of the latter encouraged their owners, most of whom were employees of the company, to set the woods ablaze, for burning the litter and dead grass improves nutrition for cattle and allows early spring grazing. Livestock prefer the new herbaceous growth.

The transition from the lumbermen's forest to the forester's forest (discussed in the next chapter) was made possible, in part, by the work of the Dixie Crusaders. Beginning about 1928, men of respect and with educational and promotional ability were hired to roam the rural communities, there to encourage fire prevention and forest conservation practices. While they were state employees, funds for the effort came principally from Weeks Act and Clarke-McNary federal allocations. The Dixie Crusaders, sometimes coached by a professional forester, showed films and gave talks. For some woods dwellers, the movies were their first viewing of a motion picture. One account said, "There ain't been this many people in Junction since the day George Miller got shot."[47]

Two Tales of the Times

Tobacco Road Plantation

Concern for forest conservation had, of course, occurred much earlier, as evidenced in a few isolated quarters. One such effort was on a road actually named Tobacco Road near Augusta, Georgia. There, people planted pines, likely lifted as seedlings from nearby forests. By this old lane—laid out in 1789 for "rolling" hogsheads to warehouses—is a relict stand of loblolly and shortleaf pines. It may be the oldest existing forest plantation on the North American continent, apart from one planted by Russians on an Aleutian isle in Alaska. The Georgia stand was established in 1873 on the Windsor Springs estate of Civil War General W. H. T. Walker. The museum woods in 1948 had a volume of about ten thousand board feet (MBM) per acre. Estimates in 1962 for the five-acre stand that contained about seventy trees per acre, however, were much higher: twenty-one MBM (Scribner scale).[48]

Bear Hunts

While the forests of the region were being exploited for their lumber, naval stores, and other products, they were also important for both local and guide-organized hunting. Clearings and human habitation altered the wildlife of the migrating lumbermen's forest. Game became scarce as cover was removed, yet poachers prospered and hound dogs proliferated to seek out the game that remained.[49]

Loblolly and shortleaf pines. These trees were probably lifted as seedlings from nearby woods and planted on the Fall Line Sandhills near Augusta, Georgia, in 1873. Apart from a remnant stand planted by Russians on an island in the Aleutian chain, this may be the oldest planted forest in the New World. The man standing in this picture taken in the early 1960s indicates the scale for tree height.

Black bear and panther hunting for sport as well as for skins and meat were as important as white-tailed deer pursuits. The bear killed in these woods in the early 1900s typically weighed three hundred pounds, though some would tilt the scale at twice that.

Hunting the bruin in the deep thicket woods of the South was an art and a skill. An account in 1906 told about it. A pack of eight dogs, headed by a monster hound, made the hunt a success or a failure. The lead dog was free to roam; the others were chained together lest they dart off to chase a deer or bobcat. The head of the pack knew the prey and knew that any bear would leave its bed upon picking up the scent of a dog. When the hound approached the bear, its bellow heard afar, the rest of the dogs were unleashed. The chase was on. It may have lasted a half hour or a day. "Standers," hunters on horseback or on foot posted along trails, waited out the pursuit. They remained alert, for a bear can pass within ten feet of a hunter in the brushy undergrowth of the southern forest without being seen. Pursued bear will stop the chase to turn upon the dogs and then run on, perhaps three or four miles, until exhausted. Or the bear may climb a tree to be safe from the dogs. The hunters, if they have heard the baying of the hounds, then drop the bear with a well-placed rifle shot. Wounded animals charge the dogs, sending them sprawling over each other in retreat until the bruin gasps its last breath. Unlike deer, bear remain in thick brush, causing much pain to the dogs. The hounds' skins are cut by the briars and the thorns, and their feet are worn sore.

Every hunter carried a horn, made from a steer's horn, for communication. Scraped thin, and with the narrow end rounded like the mouthpiece of a trumpet, the horn, when blown by a fair bugler, can be heard a mile away. Agreed-upon codes signaled the sportsmen: three blasts to signal come to me, two to answer me, and one to call the dogs.

In 1906, a reporter of such a hunt noted that "the passing of the North American black bear is only a question of a few years. . . . When the forests (of the South) are no more, the doom of the few surviving members of the big game family in the South will have been sounded; and this time is not far away." By that time, one Louisianan had bragged that he had killed 118 bear.[50]

The Period Wanes

Enter the Forester

The account of George Washington Vanderbilt's Biltmore Estate near Asheville, North Carolina, belongs both in this chapter and in the one on the foresters' forest. Vanderbilt, an heir of the Cornelius Vanderbilt dynasty, built his palace, the only such residence in the United States, on a seven thousand–acre tract on the edge of the Southern Appalachian Mountains. At Gifford Pinchot's urging just before the turn of the century, Vanderbilt employed Carl Alwin Schenck, a German forester with a European university doctorate, to manage the lands of the estate. (From 1891 until then, Pinchot, working out of a New York City office, had been Vanderbilt's consulting forester; soon after, Pinchot became the head of the U.S. Department of Agriculture Bureau of Forestry.) About fifty thousand acres of scenic southern hardwood forests purchased by Vanderbilt were added to the forester's responsibilities. Upon the industrialist's death, Mrs. Vanderbilt conveyed the mountain lands to the U.S. government. As a Weeks Act purchase, they make up much of the Pisgah National Forest.[51]

Even before Schenck's arrival, another German-born forester who had attained the rank of chief of the old Bureau of Forestry in the U.S. Department of Agriculture, Bernhard Eduard Fernow, in 1893 said that Biltmore was the only place in the United States where forest management was actually practiced. Largely because of the effort to manage the timberlands of the estate, the State of North Carolina issued three bulletins to encourage other landowners to practice forestry. The circulars concerned economics, destruction of the forest by fire, and volume tables for standing timber. Apart from some reports issued by the Bureau of Forestry in Washington, these may be the earliest publications of a professional nature involving the forests of the South.

Not only was Biltmore the locale of professional forestry practices and of the first professional forester in the South, it was also the site of the nation's first forestry school (opening a month before the program began at New York's Cornell University). Schenck, its director, recruited young men from throughout the nation to enroll in his year-long program. Most already had graduated from a college. Now they would receive diplomas that would make them eligible for a totally new kind of employment in North America. Before the period I dub "the foresters' forest" is over, Schenck's Biltmore Forest School graduates will have left distinguished marks on the forestry enterprise in the United States. They, like Pinchot before them, had learned an important lesson: a wide chasm separates scientific textbook forestry and that which is practically achievable. Managing forests in rugged terrain where roads are few is costly. Equally noteworthy is the lesson each generation of foresters learns about the South: climate, soil, and tree species combine to provide quick recovery of exploited sites and to sustain the production of high-quality timber.

Creation of State Agencies

Even before Fernow, the federal government's forestry bureau head, made his comment about the Biltmore property, he had warned forestry industrialists in the region about the wave of new entrepreneurs planning to migrate southward. They would come to cash in on the green emerald of virgin forest that stretched from the Virginia coast to the edge of the blacklands of Texas. Such prophetic pronouncements encouraged the states of the South to form forestry commissions and services. This was especially necessary in order to have access to federal funds for fire protection, nursery seedling production, and private land management assistance, as authorized under the 1911 Weeks Act. These agencies were essential, too, for locating the purchase-unit boundaries of the newly authorized national forests. While the Weeks Act required the legislatures of the several states to establish the zones in which federal acquisition foresters would be permitted to negotiate with landowners, at least one body of lawmakers—the one in Texas—turned the task over to its state forester.

Unfortunately for the forest resource, these governmental entities were usually created after the peak years of harvest. Louisiana's program, established in 1904, is the notable exception. That state, too, was probably the first to legislate forestry practices: an early law required that two trees must be left on each acre following a harvest. Species and size requirements and whether the residual stems would bear seed neglected to be mentioned in the text of the bill. As far as the law was concerned, leaving two haw trees would suffice. Thus, its main purpose was to alert citizens to the need for conservation practices. The Bayou State also prescribed tree planting for cut-over lands. Many states passed laws dealing with fire, but few such mandates had teeth; and few were the judges and juries that would do anything about arson, euphemistically called "fire trespass." Many state legislators considered state forestry departments a fad of the Progressive Era.

Another and important factor played a role in both the establishment, and the delay in the establishment, of these agencies during the period of extensive harvest. The South's people were philosophically and dogmatically defensive of states' rights. For the federal government to send in assistance was generally not appreciated; for it to purchase land was sometimes an anathema. That attitude was not only toward agents of the national government. Citizens also expressed uneasiness when state employees seemed to exercise authority.

A "Snuffy Smith" cartoon of the period illustrates the point. Aunt Loweezy shouts to Uncle Snuffy that "the revanooers is comin'." Both grab their "shootin' arns." As the intruder comes closer, Aunt Loweezy spots his green ranger uniform with the big badge displaying a tree. She yells, "Don't shoot, Snuffy. He ain't no revanooer. He's a

forestry man." Whereupon, the little mountaineer responds from behind the open window, his rifle at the ready, "Works for the same outfit,
don't he?"[52]

Forward-looking Leadership

At the century's turn, exploitation of the abundant forest resource was under way. However, the price obtained for logs, the distance
they needed to be shipped, and the minimal skill necessary for woods labor foreordained the inability of the forest to continue to bring any sem-
blance of wealth to the region beyond the mid-1930s. With the timber's
passing, so went the mills.

The forests have returned, because of fire protection, some
minimal magagement, and enthusiastic assistance from Providence; but,
for the present, in many sections, mills and their markets are inadequate
to encourage rapid development of intensive silvicultural treatment of
these potentially valuable lands. That such mills will be introduced is a
foregone conclusion.

Leaders of the region's industries sometimes marched to different drummers than did the host of their peers when it came to visualizing
forestry in the coming years. Every state has its Father of Forestry, but for
the whole of the South, the individual usually recognized as its founder
and prophet is Henry Hardtner. While most lumbermen were saying it
would be 150 years before new forests would be ready for cutting, Hardtner predicted sixty years for the maturing of second-growth timber.
Hardtner and a few others, on the advice of Yale Professor H. H. Chapman, talked sustained yield, selective harvesting, and reforestation. On
Hardtner's Urania, Louisiana, lands, laborers planted seedlings dug by
hand from the nearby forests as early as 1920.

Hardtner moved to the area, constructed a mill, created a
town, and gave it a name. As the forests there were to the preacher of the
"new gospel of tree farming" a heavenly haven, he sought the name of a
heavenly body for the title of the town. Urania (from *Uranus* in Greek
and Roman mythology) is the muse of agriculture. (Hardtner probably
had heard of uranium, discovered in 1789, the same year as the planet's
discovery, and first made into metal in 1841.) Theodore Roosevelt called
Hardtner "one of the greatest men the South has ever produced." As a
member of the state legislature in 1910, he encouraged passage of a se-
verence tax on the wood-using industry. Payments to taxing entities
under this system are made only when the timber is harvested, rather
than annually, as with ad valorem taxes.

Well before the final blast of the mill whistle on the harvest

of the migrating lumbermen's forest, the sound of another prophetic
trumpet was heard. Some people responded to the pleadings of Austin
Cary above the drone of the saws. Cary was employed by the U.S. Forest
Service to travel the South, visit with lumbermen, convince them of the
need for reforestation, and to establish demonstration plots to prove that
forestry practices were appropriate. Among those who reacted favorably
was Hardtner, on whose land Yale forestry students spent their summers,
beginning in 1917; T. R. Miller and his partner Ed Downing (both Civil
War soldiers) in South Alabama, on whose lands I began my research career; Gen. Russell Alger from Detroit and his partner M. H. Sullivan in
West Florida, financiers of my early research; Edward Crossett, on whose
Arkansas tracts Yale students also trained; and the Goodyear brothers,
whose Great Southern Lumber Company in lower Louisiana is called the
"granddaddy of them all." These industries gave more than lip service:
the Great Southern Lumber Company seeded longleaf pines and planted
trees on 175,000 acres of its cut-over land as early as 1920. (Alger and
Sullivan named their mill town Century as a reminder of the time of the
beginning of the enterprise when one-half of its output was shipped
abroad, including many ship mast timbers.)

What Now for This Land

Many companies, having practiced cut-out-and-get-out spoil-
ation, were anxious to do something with their land. Many participated
in the 1917 Conference on Cutover Land, held in New Orleans, convinced that these lands would never again grow commercially merchantable trees. Investors from "up East," with a push from the railroads, gave
them assistance for "colonization" of the seemingly useless land. As they
knew well the high cost of pulling stumps prior to tilling for row crop
cultivation, the program encouraged planting Chinese tung trees (introduced in 1905) for the paint market, papershell pecans, and strawberries.
In the mountains, English and Scottish promoters hoped to establish
"idyllic recreational and industrial communities." [53]

One group in Southeast Texas put together about six hundred
thousand acres of cut-over and periodically burned land on which there
was little expectation of ever producing another crop of pine trees. The
idea was to encourage the expanding and overcrowded population elsewhere, both in the North and abroad, to migrate to the "Old Southwest"
to farm and ranch the land. [54] Another group, operating out of Chicago,
chartered trains from St. Louis on which they escorted potential settlers
to visit extensive cut-over tracts that were for sale. Both of these ventures, like many others, failed. In the first case, the tracts became the

Hardwood stand. Many species of hardwoods initiate ecological succession in the southern mountains and its Piedmont foothills. This scene suggests the density of a new forest in the pioneer stage, the stems arising from seeds as well as from the roots and stumps of the trees recently harvested. (Photo by Daniel O. Todd courtesy U.S. Forest Service.)

commercial forest for a large paper mill; in the latter, the land was absorbed into a national forest. Good timber now covers both.

The Forest Service in the U.S. Department of Agriculture by the end of this period in the mid-1930s had purchased eleven million acres, most of it from large industries, for national forests. Previous owners, behind in their taxes, were willing sellers. Whole national forests were purchased for as little as $2.80 an acre. Five to six dollars was not atypical. The federal government did require the payment of all back taxes—sometimes a several-year accumulation—before a deal was finalized. A few tracts still contained virgin forests. These were sold to the government for ten to fifteen dollars an acre. One ninety thousand–acre parcel in Texas that averaged twenty-six thousand board feet per acre went for $12.50 an acre.[55]

In the Great Depression years, the mills that used the timber ran but one day a week. That they ran at all was both a courtesy to faithful laborers and respect for a threat from the bank. For many workers, one day's wages provided enough money for a family's groceries for a week.

The Depression's end and the entry of the forester into the South dramatically altered the situation. The forester introduced forestry, an art based upon sciences, which would now begin to demonstrate how the lands of the region could be perpetually managed for the benefit of people.

CHAPTER 4

The Boat Builders' Forest

HE SOUTHERN forest provided materials for seafaring vessels during periods that overlap the explorers', the pioneers', and the immigrating lumbermen's journeys into these lands of evergreen conifers and deciduous hardwoods. As early as the expeditions of the Spanish explorers, the value of the resinous sap of the southern pines was noted. Caulking for the wooden sides of the tall ships that plied the seven seas could be as precious as the gold carried in the cargo bays. Rosin and resin remain important commodities, though today they are not much used in boat building.

Early explorers found the live oak trees of the Atlantic and Gulf coasts to be valuable ship timbers. These the boat builders used until steel-sided vessels, like the Monitor and Merrimac, replaced those craft whose hulls were covered with shiplap lumber. Live oak provided structural components, decking, topping, and gunwale materials for both the merchant and naval fleets. Tall pine timbers served as masts and the rot-resistant Atlantic white-cedar, baldcypress, and eastern redcedar provided lumber for water barrels and sea chests. Shipwrights used more than a dozen other southern trees for specialty woods.

Half a century after the live oakers pulled out of the southern forest, loggers dragged timber to the wharves, dramatizing the promotional abilities of proponents of using wood for boat construction during the First World War, a time when the nation was unable to provide the necessary steel ships for troop and cargo carriers. Military men along with their armaments and food had to be transported over three thousand miles in submarine-infested Atlantic waters. "Ships, more ships, more ships!" cried the British Prime Minister Lloyd George in 1916 as the United States prepared to join France and England to defeat Kaiser Wilhelm's Germany.[1]

Henry Wadsworth Longfellow's lines from "The Building of the Ship" tell symbolically the variety of woods used in the boat builders' efforts and the variety of sites in the southern forest from which the trees were drawn:

> Timber of chestnut, and elm, and oak,
> And scattered here and there, with these,
> The knarred and crooked cedar knees;
> Brought from regions far away,
> From Pascagoula's sunny bay.

The Turpentiners' Forest

When ships were made of wood, shipwrights used rosin to caulk the boards that formed the decks and sheathed the futtocks, thereby preventing water from leaking into the holds of the vessels. Sails and their cordage were waterproofed with pitch. The hawsers to hold fast the cargo, made from the woven fibers of hemp and other plants, received a coating of tar preservative. And turpentine distilled from the pitch provided a "diffusible stimulant, diuretic, and anthelmintic, in large doses acting as a laxative," as well as lamp oil for those obliged to sail the seas.[2] The gum naval stores industry, operating in the southern forest, provided the rosin, pitch, tar, and turpentine to satisfy these requirements for vessels of commerce and of war.

In colonial America's New England, naval stores extracted from the yellow pines of the South for reexport abroad was big business. Shipments of resin products from Boston and other ports brought significant income to the colonies when sold in Europe. Histories give the date of these first exports as 1608, likely from near Hampton Roads or the Jamestown harbor, the gum at that time extracted from loblolly and longleaf pines in Virginia and North Carolina. Later, pitch pines growing in the northern extremity of the region supplied much of the naval stores foreign market. During the late colonial period, Parliament provided a bounty to encourage export, but only to Great Britain. Prior to establishing the bounty, the Baltic states virtually monopolized supplying the English naval stores requirements.[3]

Regulations governing naval stores in the colonial period dealt with weight and quality of product. For instance, each barrel of pitch had to contain 31.5 gallons, free of trash. The cask in which it was shipped specifically required twelve hoops.[4]

Francois Andre Michaux, the French scientist for whom many trees are named and who named others, noted how tar was made from dead longleaf pines. The trees had to have been "prostrated by time or by fire." Parts of standing trees to be turpentined were first felled for lumber. Pitch was extracted from the tops. Even "the branches of resinous trees consist wholly of wood of which the organization is even more perfect than in the body of the tree." So were described the lightwood or pine knots which were encountered in the southern pineries.[5]

Naval stores refers to the gum and its derivatives collected from living trees. Although the term is still used, little of the oleoresin drained or extracted from southern pines is any longer employed for marine purposes. (*Gum naval stores* are the extractives from living trees. Where dead "prostrated" trees, as in the original pioneer efforts, are subjected to steam distillation to extract these materials, *wood naval stores* result. When paper manufacturers separate the same chemicals as byproducts of pulp and paper production, they are marketed as *sulfate naval stores*.)

The first commercial venture of Europeans as they arrived on the Carolina shores may well have been the production of pitch and tar for treating the wood, the canvas, and the stout ropes of the ships of the seas. They extracted resinous sap from the rot-resistant heartwood of the trees that lay on the ground. As stated above, before the American Revolution, the British, anxious to be independent of European sources of naval stores, stimulated colonial production with attractive bounties. The bounty incentive ceased with freedom obtained for the thirteen former colonies. Then a trade embargo in 1807 and the long Napoleonic wars further reduced the effort to produce naval stores from the accumulation of trees that had collected on the forest floor over hundreds of years. When the British tariff was finally repealed in 1845, farmers quit their land to chip and dip and collect and haul the gum, for by that time gum naval stores had replaced wood naval stores as the resinous materials required by sea-going vessels.

For a while after the War of 1812, most naval stores came from the coastal loblolly pine and longleaf pine forests of North Carolina. By the mid-1800s, however, whale oil for lanterns was becoming scarce. Its scarcity encouraged the development of some forms of resin extracts for illuminating the homes and shops of America while continuing to supply naval needs. About that time, turpentine also went into rubber products and varnishes. In 1880, North Carolinians distilled 6.3 million gallons of turpentine and more than 650,000 barrels of tar.[6] Tripling that figure would be a safe estimate for the entire southern region in that period.

The Method

The first naval stores in the New World were collected in shipping barrels and sent to England for processing. Copper for distillation tubing in the colonies was then scarce, and a greater export market for sealing the sides of ships, for waterproofing sails, and for coating ropes was at the English docks.

At first, when the resinous sap was extracted from the rot-resistant heartwood of the yellow pines that lay on the ground, draft animals pulled the dense, solid interior cores of the fallen trees to a pit for burning. Set afire in the pit, the "logs" slowly simmered over the open flame. The resinous fluid was drained from the fallen boles into wooden barrels countersunk in the ground adjacent to the pit. Tar and oleoresin in the extracted pitch were separated from the burning wood as the heat reached the boiling points for the two distillates. The method, one may suppose, had changed little since Noah was instructed to seal the boards of the ark, as described in the sixth chapter of Genesis.

To make tar, colonists piled the resin-soaked lightwood that remained after the sapwood had rotted away about ten feet high in a circle as much as thirty feet in diameter. Over this was built a crude kiln covering of logs, brush, and earth. The pile set afire, workers then punched air holes into the sides of the kiln to provide entry ways for oxygen for combustion. Heat from the smoldering fire forced the resin through a ditch to a pit outside of the kiln. The procedure took about a week. To obtain pitch, workers concentrated the tar by boiling it in iron kettles.

Distillation required a large—perhaps eight feet in diameter—wooden barrel. From a pipe at its base, workers listened for the progress of the process. They knew the sound of boiling gum. When the gurgling could be heard from the "tailpipes," both water and turpentine were allowed to run from the pipe into another barrel, called the separator. Then, from the overflow pipe in the second barrel, the lighter (both in color and weight) turpentine flowed into a settling bowl. Finally, from this the fluid passed into the bunghole of a white oak barrel for shipment.

Gum Flow from Living Trees

Shortly before the American Revolution, turpentiners developed a technique for obtaining resin from living trees. In those days, prior to the availability of copper for distillation, the stills to which they carried the resin were made of iron. These tubular contraptions, not unlike those used in more recent times by moonshiners in the South's forests, stood by a stream that provided cooling water for condensing the turpentine driven off by the heat beneath the boiler. Tarry rosin remained in the still.

Not until fifty years after the American Revolution did copper become sufficiently available in the United States for its use in stilling apparatus. This enabled development of new markets for the sticky sap of the southern pines. The distillation procedure changed little through the 1930s, with two exceptions. The early-day transport of the barrels on rafts to ports down the region's streams was replaced by ground transportation, and improved stills, made possible by innovative engineering, relegated the more primitive stills of the older times to the scrap heap. Better equipment also encouraged farmers and industrialists to turpentine the southern forest.

Sap collection was facilitated by the discovery that the boles of living trees could be cut with sharp instruments and that the liquid gum would then flow freely from the wound. From this syrupy sap, both turpentine and rosin were readily obtained by fractional distillation.

The first containers for collecting the gum as it flowed from the chipped and debarked areas of the tree trunk were called "boxes." They were made by chopping a deep hole into the base of the tree. (These deep cups, cut with axes, serve to this day as resin collection vessels in primitive societies.) The boxes cut into the tree bases damaged the boles for lumber, and fungi infection and insect entry often occurred at these wounds.

Streaks, similar to V-shaped sergeants' chevrons, were hacked (turpentine farmers use the term *chipped*) with sharp implements into the trees' inner bark and slightly into the wood. Gum flowed from these wounds down to the base of the V and into the basal box. From this cup, laborers periodically scooped out the sticky sap, poured it into wooden barrels, and then transported the barrels to the still for processing.

Chipping stimulates the flow of resin from epithelial ducts two to three inches above the wound. When about two-thirds of the available fluid gum has flowed from the intercellular openings, usually within twenty-four hours of chipping, oxidation and crystallization of the resin begin to clog the ducts. When the gum ceased to flow, perhaps after a week or two, new streaks were made, using a sharp hook-bladed steel tool on the end of a heavy wooden handle. Trees were streaked for three years. By that time they were worked as high as a man could reach. The trunks of the trees in these turpentine "orchards" often became fiery torches when the woods were set ablaze.

Turpentiners used a tool called a hogal or a broad axe to flatten the base of the chipped zone for placement of a crude gutter or apron. The gutter guided the sap into the cup or box.

About 1901, someone reported that French workers, collecting gum from maritime pines, used clay pots, instead of the boxes that Americans carved into the trees at ground line. These ceramic vessels are yet used in Mediterranean countries. Still later, rectangular pans of galvanized steel were designed for the purpose. To reduce the loss of gum with the periodic raising of the chipped hacks, chippers nailed aprons or gutters made of strips of galvanized metal to the base of the fresh hack on the bole of the tree. The apron guided the resin into the pan. Both the aprons and pans were held to the tree with double-headed nails for convenient removal and replacement as the laborers periodically chipped higher up the bole of the tree. These later, more efficient methods were in vogue throughout the region by 1910. They continue with little change until this time.

Unfounded rumors often affected the merchandising of these products of the forest. In the 1800s, it was reported that trees south of North Carolina's Cape Fear River would not "run gum." Growth of the industry in South Carolina and Georgia was therefore compelled to wait until there was assurance that sap in that region indeed would run. So well did it run, in fact, that in time the market was limited to production from longleaf and slash pines in the Gulf coastal zone spanning Georgia to eastern Texas.

The Woods Workers

In 1840, North Carolina produced 95 percent of the country's naval stores; therefore, citizens of that state were called "tarheels," because the dark oxidized gum adhered to the feet of barefoot woods workers. No doubt, development of the industry in the South was encouraged by the plantation slave labor that was conveniently available in states like North Carolina when those workers were not needed to plow, plant, chop, or pick cotton. Following the civil hostilities of the 1860s, the industry, no longer able to work slaves, was obliged for economic reasons to move southward to the Gulf states where virgin stands of longleaf pine, from Florida to Texas, were readily available. Entrepreneurs could afford to streak these untapped woods with wage earners.

When chipping began anew following the Civil War near the port towns of Alabama, Mississippi, and Florida, operators controlled the business through factorage houses. These factors built company towns, similar to those of the lumbermen. Managers then leased to individuals certain tracts to be turpentined and supplied them with the necessary equipment for workers in the woods.[7] The factors contained stills, spirit sheds for storing turpentine, rosin yards, blacksmiths, cooperage sheds for barrel manufacture, wagon sheds, barns, commissaries, and quarters for the laborers.

Turpentine farmers for generations have lived at the locale of the stills, going to the gum naval stores "orchards" by foot, by wagon, or by horseback. Almost always they were strong-backed blacks with a special knack for chipping, for the task was a tough one. Turpentine laborers chipped the trees, collected the messy gum in wooden pails, carried it to wooden barrels strategically placed in the gum naval stores forest, rolled the sealed wooden hogsheads up pole ramps to horse-drawn wagons, and carried out the distillation process. The camps in which they resided with their families had short lives. Typically the accessible orchards were worked out in ten years, the camp towns abandoned, and the turpentiners, like nomads, moved on.

Company owners provided camp houses, along with groceries and work clothes. (With the post–Second World War discovery of acid treatment of the tree wound to stimulate the flow of gum, industry owners were obliged to issue overalls to their workers. Laborers would not work otherwise. The dissolution of one's clothes by the acid, carried in a plastic spray bottle, so scared some workers that they quit their jobs. Some, on the other hand, mistaking the dilute sulphuric acid for the moonshiner's white lightning, were permanently injured by drinking it.)

A caste system evolved at the turpentiners' camps. Chippers, those strongest men who hacked the trees at a rate of a thousand "faces" a week, were the highest on the social ladder. Those lower in the pecking order were dippers and haulers. Women and children not infrequently served as dippers, collecting the gum from the cups or pans and carrying it to the barrels. Woods riders, usually on horseback, served as inspectors and managers of the operation.

Coopers, working near the stills, made barrel staves of several species of white oak. Flexible hoops of split hickory held the staves together. Only species of the white oak group can be used for fluids because the pores in the wood of the subgenus *Leucobalanus* are occluded; the pores are open in members of the red oak subgenus *Erythrobalanus*, thereby permitting liquids to pass through.

Before the advent of sulphuric acid treatment, workers chipped a new streak about every ten days. With the hack they gouged out a zone about 1/2-inch high and 3/4-inch deep on the face of the tree. On one end of the hack's twenty-inch handle was five pounds of iron, a weight that enabled the worker to more forcefully chip the bark with the knife edge at the other end.

Each turpentine laborer was expected to "cultivate a crop" of ten thousand faces during the six months of warmest weather. Turpen-

Slash pine plantation. About one-fourth of the stems in this twenty-three-year-old pole-size pine plantation have been cupped for gum naval stores production. Workers rake the flammable pine straw from around the easily ignited streaked trees before setting the woods ablaze to control the brush in order to facilitate gum collection. (Courtesy Georgia Forestry Commission.)

tiners chipped up the trees' boles about two feet each year. In three or four years, a stand of fifteen to twenty faces per acre was worked out. Large trees accommodated two or three faces.

Aprons and cups were raised every year or two to prevent waste, for the last of the year's gum, hardening on the face below the streaks, did not drain into the cups. Thorough workers, however, scraped this resin, and from it they produced good turpentine and rosin. As much as 25 percent of the season's yield could be obtained this way.

Industrious laborers were often persuaded to switch loyalites and join another operator's work force. Perhaps the wages or living conditions were slightly better or appeared to be. Worker pirating was so serious an endeavor that recruiters were said to have paid with their lives for this practice. This kind of woods work was so rough that turpentine workers were at times recruited from prison chain gangs and convict camps.[8]

Grades of gum have been classified, probably from Revolutionary days, by the color of the skin of indentured blacks. Local operators may have referred to "Betty Jane" or "Uncle Jeff" to designate the quality of either wood or gum naval stores. Eventually colored plates standardized the procedure throughout the region.

Conflict with Lumbermen

For a long time, lumbermen believed that the bleeding of trees for gum production resulted in wood so weakened along the chipped face that it was unworthy of being manufactured into boards. Consequently, much wood was wasted in the turpentined trees left standing in the forest or in the butt logs of harvested trees. Discovery that this was not so is attributed to Bernhard Fernow, the German-born forester who became the third head of the U.S. Department of Agriculture Bureau of Forestry (now the USDA Forest Service) and the founding professor of three North American forestry schools. Fernow at about century's turn publicized this information and, by doing so, encouraged lumbermen and turpentine farmers—as they would in time be called—to chip the trees for a year or two before harvesting them for lumber. Even so, seldom has the part of the log with the chipped face been used for lumber or for pulp. Generally, the resin-soaked remnant remains in the woods unless salvaged for lightwood or pitch wood for urban fireplace kindling.

To facilitate gum collection, turpentiners frequently burned the woods under controlled conditions, as they do today. Brush, vines, briars, and pit vipers were thereby checked. Other times neighbor farmers grazed their scrawny cattle in the open range, burning the forests to improve forage quality, again as they do today. These fires encouraged production of nutritious grass which, in turn, attracted cattle to the open parklike gum naval stores stands. These fires also killed pine seedlings that competed with the range plants sought by the cattle. To accommodate either circumstance, turpentiners raked to the mineral soil a wide circle around each crop tree to clear it of tinderlike pine needles. Otherwise, the "straw" would fuel a minor holocaust, and flames would climb to the crowns of trees with exposed resin-soaked faces, consume the foliage, and kill the trees. Crown fires, high in the trees, race great distances across land.

As noted, many of the old procedures continue to this day. However, present practices encourage the marking of trees for cupping five years before harvest by loggers for lumber. This integrates timber management with oleoresin production. Careful chipping, so that only the bark is wounded, enables the log to be used for both pulpwood and lumber.

Modern Methods

Observers of the naval stores industry had to wait until the 1950s to see much change in the method of gum extraction and collection. Foresters discovered that spraying dilute sulphuric acid on the chipped face stimulates the flow of resin. The sulphuric acid causes disintegration of walls of epithelial cells that surround the cavity-like resin ducts and gum canals in the wood. The ducts contain the oleoresin that, with this treatment, flows for a longer period. Labor costs diminish while gum quantity increases.

Subsequent to the acid treatment innovation and, quite by accident, a forest researcher in Florida found that treating trees with the herbicide paraquat enhances the flow of gum. When the chemical is applied two years before the anticipated harvest of the trees for lumber, freshly cut second-growth stumps yield considerable wood naval stores. Producers of gum from stumps allow them to season for ten years before pulling or blasting them from the ground. The stumps of lightwood are still expected to be useful forty years after the trees have been harvested.

Because of the dramatic reduction in the acreage of longleaf pine in the past hundred years, slash pine is presently the most important species for gum naval stores production. Plantations of this species are now established for this purpose. However, decades after the virgin longleaf pine was cut and into the 1960s, stumps were blasted or bulldozed out of the ground and hauled to destructive distillation plants. There they were shredded to salvage the turpentine retained in the wood.

For commercial measurement, a *unit* equals one fifty-gallon barrel of turpentine plus three and a third five-hundred–pound barrels of rosin. The average crop of ten thousand faces yields about thirty-four units annually.

The Industry's Demise

While continuing to be called naval stores, derivatives of pine resin also serve as industrial solvents and as components in paint thinners, shoe polishes, waxes, inks, insulation materials, pharmaceuticals, and resin. But they no longer are used to the degree they once were. What happened to this industry, once stretching from the Atlantic

Ocean to southeastern Texas and now almost limited to northern Florida and southern Georgia? Production peaked for turpentine in 1900 and for resin in 1908. The decline at first was little noticed: later, the demise was rapid. Florida alone in 1936 boasted thirty-six million faces; in 1958, only four million. So important was the industry politically in 1936 that the U.S. Department of Agriculture provided cost-sharing funds for turpentine farmers. Even with the Naval Stores Conservation Program administered by the U.S. Forest Service, production and prices fluctuated widely. Between 1946 and 1972, one could see in turpentine-farming country a city block area behind a chain-link fence filled with barrels piled two deep of naval stores bought by the government under the Agricultural Marketing Act. When the world price reached the Department's purchase cost, the storage lot was suddenly emptied of its produce. Congressional lobbying by articulate southerners, I believe, effectively sustained the life of the industry. Changing national leadership and, with it, shifting priorities for many segments of American society encouraged its demise.

In a sense, the *gum* naval stores industry self-destructed, for the price controls established by the U.S. Department of Agriculture encouraged the search for substitutes. Chemists sought them in petroleum, in exotic plants (such as the tung tree, introduced from the Orient, its oil added to paint or varnish to accelerate drying), and in *wood* and *sulphate* naval stores. The government, recognizing the end of the industry, liquidated its stocks over a five-year period in the 1970s.

The Live Oakers' Forest

Live "oakers" were workers who earned their living from live oaks. For an account of the live oakers' forest, we return to early colonial times when hundreds of Yankees went south to harvest and hew by hand the durable timbers of *Quercus virginiana* for the boat builders of Boston, Philadelphia, and Maine. Even before John Bartram, the British royal botanist, reported to the king in 1766 that live oak had better grain than English oak for shipbuilding, the industry seems to have been well established for the Atlantic trade. Indeed, only three decades after the settling of South Carolina's coastal village, called Charles Town, live oakers were passing through its port. Their numbers were significant by 1700.[9]

Mules and oxen, later aided by high-wheel slip-tongue carts, dragged the timbers from the southern forests to landings for loading on scows or schooners for the journey to the American North or to Great

A historic forest. Lands and live oak trees set aside by Congress in the early days of
the republic in order to assure timber for shipbuilders are now living museums.
(Photo by P. Freeman Hiem courtesy U.S. Forest Service.)

Britain or France for the building of frigates. Some live oak pieces left
coastal waters after commercial agents dispatched them to the Orient for
the China trade or around Cape Horn for the building of ships for California service. Many timbers went to the ocean's bottom in stormy seas en
route to their intended destination. At the boat yards, laborers buried the
timbers underwater, for total submergence protected the wooden pieces
from aerobic pathogens that attacked the wood and caused it to rot.

The Shape of the Tree

Live oak trees in the boat builders' forest were often six feet in diameter at breast height and with branches extending a hundred feet in diameter from drip line to drip line. As an example of the size of these monarchs, the American Forestry Association's national champion in 1976 tallied thirty-seven feet in circumference, though only fifty-five feet tall. The circle of ground that its crown covered measured 132 feet in diameter.[10]

Seldom found naturally more than twenty miles from salt water, this maritime variety of live oak exhibits an ability to resist foliar damage from salt spray, which is toxic to most trees. It also endures overly ambitious storm tides that cover the soil miles inland with salt water. The tree's leaf waxes protect it from desiccation on droughty sites and, in times of low rainfall, on otherwise mesic soils. Trees of this species also endure sandblasting and sand burial, common phenomena in coastal strands adjacent to estuaries.

Of the dark live oak hammocks, John James Audubon, artist and ornithologist, wrote, "The air feels cooler . . . songs of numerous birds delight . . . flowers become larger and brighter, and a grateful fragrance is diffused." The author gratuitously adds, "But not in the hot, humid and breezeless days of a southern summer."[11]

A natural brace protects live oak trees of the southern lowlands from being toppled by the wind. The brace, layers of dense wood laid down on the leeward, and absent on the windward, sides of the boles brings about the asymmetrical growth that makes the tree valuable for ships' knees. Tree physiologists also attribute this uneven growth to the generous, but erratic, transfer of starch and protein from seed leaves to roots of newly germinated seedlings. The odd shape of the trunk's buttress extends into the roots.

Foresters of the Surveyor General of His Majesty's Wood in North America emblazoned upward-pointing broad arrows on white pines of the New England forests to reserve them for the Royal Navy. So, too, did the Crown express its concern and exercise its rights in the South for the protection of live oak woodlands.[12]

Shipwrights, by order of the Commissioner of Revenues, went to Charleston and Savannah to oversee the selection, harvest, and transport of the pieces that would become knees, keels, and keelsons (structural timbers above the keel) for naval and merchant vessels. Knees in the wooden vessels were typically structural midside supports upon which shipwrights fastened, with wooden pegs, deck beams and shiplap planking.

Naval architects sent with the live oakers going south draw-

A southern live oak woodland containing the kind of trees from which boat builders
hewed knees, keels, and keelsons for the yards of the Northeast in colonial times.
Leaves remain green throughout the year, and the Spanish moss draping its twine-
like cords over tree branches gives the scene an air of eerie beauty.

ings of the boat parts needed at the northern yards. The artisans traipsed
the bottomlands in search of trees with just the right "butt swell" for the
desired component. They usually found the live oaks immediately above
the coastal bottomlands on slightly elevated benches where the trees'
roots are not continuously inundated. Tree cutters also carried the charts
into the swamp borders of sandy, well-drained soil, looking for the
stems whose dimensions and configuration met the specifications on the
drawings. They cut the tree and, on the site, hewed it to a more precise fit
before sending it on its journey to the boat-building communities of distant climes.

 The slope of the trunk and the outward curving form of its
lowest branches as they emerge from the bole of the tree are not the only

characteristics that make this evergreen oak a shipbuilder's delight. The dense, hard, strong, tough wood is perhaps the heaviest of American timbers. It is also among the most durable, decaying extremely slowly. People confined to the holds of the tall ships made from other woods suffered from nausea caused by the odor from structural timbers that had slowly oxidized and rotted from fungi attacks. Sickness occurred much less frequently for those souls confined to the bowels of boats built of live oak.

Treacherous Forests

Northern naval architects in the comforts of their shops and drafting rooms had little understanding of the tasks they assigned the live oakers in the malaria-infested swamps, the water moccasin and alligator habitats of the bottoms, and the alternating high and low waters that flooded the hewers' camps or left them isolated. The writer of one diary notes that he had "feveuorer . . . in all [his] limbs." Virginia Wood, the naval archivist, reports that an expedition "party came upon a hundred alligators congregated in one place, some of them twelve to fourteen feet long. Fortunately all reptiles were in a torpid state, but at night the men were aware of 'panthers' (cougars), wildcats, and raccoons. Fish were plentiful . . . the islands beautiful, a 'constant habitation of the Red Bird and Mocking Bird whose united harmony gives a continual delight to the ear.'" These live oak forests were havens for bald eagles and huge flocks of pelicans and gulls.[13]

Both before and after the American Revolution, the Yankees bargained with slave owners to use for this task their "indentured servants" in the winters, when the tree's sap is down and they were not needed for planting, cultivating, and picking cotton. Cutting the wood in winter prevented "checking"—the splitting of lumber that occurs when freshly cut boards are dried too rapidly. Some artisans seemed to have believed that winter harvests also prevented twisting of the grain. Many were convinced that winter cutting produced harder wood. Disappointments happened: rot or wind-shake sometimes became visible after the trees were opened. Wood was wasted; but worse, the labor of searching for the bole that would fit the architect's specifications and of felling the massive trunk was lost.

Some of the live oakers may have had an assist from the pit saw, that man-killing implement taxing the muscles of two men. One man worked in a hole below the ground and one on a scaffold above as they alternately pulled the saw.[14] In spite of the sawdust the lower sawyer ingested, the sawing may have been less physically taxing than would be the fashioning of the pieces with the heavy broad ax.

Oxen participated in the venture. They came all the way from Maine hobbled in the holds of ships, canvas hammocks cradling their bellies to protect them from falls and injuries while on the rolling craft. The beasts, cleated in order to be able to remain standing on sailing ships, were hoisted and lowered in slings over the vessels' sides.

Not everyone was enthusiastic about using live oak timbers for ship building. North Carolina's surveyor-general in 1709 noted that the shortness of the tree's bole makes it useless for planking. A few trees would "allow a Stock of twelve foot, but the firmness and great weight thereof, frightens out sawyers from the fatigue that attends the cutting of this timber." The government official did acknowledge the species' usefulness for knees and other parts.[15]

Political Importance

Although pharmaceutical botanists planted live oak trees in London's Kew Gardens long before the American Revolution, a century passed before the trees' economic significance was much noted. In 1799, the U.S. Congress, then independent of England's Crown, appropriated money for the purchase of Grover and Blackbeard islands off of Georgia's coast as live oak reserves.[16] As the live oak shortage became more pronounced, President John Q. Adams in 1828 encouraged Congress to set aside lands of the public domain in the Florida territory as a research installation. There the tree's characteristics would be studied.[17] By the time of the Civil War, over a quarter million acres in Florida, Alabama, Mississippi, and Louisiana were set aside to ensure an adequate supply of live oak wood. Federal agents of the times established nurseries to grow live oak seedlings for subsequent planting in depleted forests.

President John Tyler ordered the Federal Bureau of Construction to contract with the live oakers for ribs for ships and straight pieces up to forty feet long for stern posts. These were for U.S. Navy vessels. Meanwhile, thieves robbed both the trees in the forest and the submerged storage bins where components were kept until needed, causing U.S. Navy secretaries to hire agents to watch over the supplies. Navy boats patrolled the coasts for poachers, the cut-and-run gangs who lived in palmetto-camouflaged lean-tos in the forests. By 1820, for example, rustlers had taken the last of the trees of value from Georgia's coastal islands, including those on the reservations.[18] Federal authorities responsible for the nation's welfare worried about the purchase of these wooden pieces by countries potentially adversarial to the United States. Our own shipbuilding wood could be readily used in the construction of frigates of a wartime enemy.

The federal government, in those early days, was so concerned with the theft of the supply of live oak timbers for the construction of foreign fleets that Congress voted in 1817, and again in 1822 and 1831, to fine and imprison the villains who illegally cut trees that had been set aside on lands of the public domain. Yet the thefts continued, the Secretary of Navy's appeals to protect these coastal and island forests notwithstanding.

Until discovery of live oak for boat parts, ships sailing the high seas lasted but a decade or two. The stench in the hold, caused by the decaying wood, became apparent not long after a new vessel left the yards. In contrast, Old Ironsides—the U.S. frigate *Constitution*—would be seaworthy for over a century, so it was said, because of the durable material of which it was constructed. With that promotional publicity, the United States capitalized on the monopolistic edge it held over world markets. (That claim was established by the European overseers of New World colonies as early as the 1600s.) Czar Alexander of Russia was so intrigued by the qualities of live oak that he ordered acorns from America to plant in the Crimea. Western Europeans were especially envious of America's supply of ship wood as their tree inventories dwindled.

The English had not always been envious. For a time, American woods were considered inferior to the British mulberry, live oak, and cedar. Indeed, American-built boats, considered "not substantial or well-built," were not in demand in Europe. Timber for masts and spars for British Navy and merchant ships was not to be found in North America south of 41 degrees latitude, according to a report of the time. For all shipwright purposes, timber in the "southward provinces [was] not of so good a quality" as that of the North, which was, by the mid-1700s, already scarce. The cost, too, of overland shipment of any great distance of high bulk items, like lumber, was prohibitive. Timbers for boat building must be "near water carriage" as well as of high quality. Yet, wood *was* smuggled, usually through the West Indies to Europe. Ships with improper papers (for instance, listing shingles rather than the more valuable lumber found on board) were seized in intercolonial trade, and "chipt" (hewn) timbers found their way to Holland "for a better than ordinary price."[19]

The End of the Oakers

When steel replaced the tough wood covering that gave Old Ironsides her name, those who found, cut, hewed, and hauled live oak timbers passed from the southern forests. Navies all over the world followed the lead of the builders of the Confederate *Merrimac*, turning to vessels with a skin of sheet metal. The General Land Office returned to the public domain the reservations that had been set aside for supplying the tough timbers. Quarter sections of these vast tracts were now opened to settlement: farmers soon grew food or cotton in the rich silty land that lay slightly higher than the adjacent river bottoms. There was no need to fell the trees and drag out the stumps. Newcomers simply girdled the boles and plowed the ground beneath the extensive crowns.

But not forever. In the 1970s, foresters teamed with archaeologists and historians to locate the long-abandoned reserves. Some set-aside sites had returned to forest, the farmer-settlers having given up their crop enterprises. Parks now attest to the earlier presence of live oak reserves in Florida's peninsula and south of Interstate 10 along Louisiana's coast. Louisiana boasts a society to which only live oak trees (not their owners) are entitled to membership. In typical blueblood fashion, restrictions for membership are tight: stems must be at least one hundred years old and seventeen feet in circumference to join the club.

Ghosts of live oakers may yet lurk in the boat yards, for the wooden pieces they hewed might still be buried there. Knees stored in the ooze of the wharves came in handy when Old Ironsides was refitted in recent years for display in Boston Harbor. Divers retrieved seven hundred pieces from the slimy mire of Pensacola's old shipyard. Naval archaeologists in 1945 and 1957 located several hundred more knees and other parts in the Portsmouth harbor. Alas, when exposed to the air, the aged beams split, checked, and cracked. Rotting commenced promptly, giving off a nauseating stench. Case-hardened, from aging in water, the wood components, now as tough as steel, quickly dulled the shipwright's saws.[20]

The Pine Shipwrights' Forest

Midway in the period of the harvest of the vast southern forest by the migrating lumbermen and the Southerners who joined them, a dramatic episode in the life of the nation sped up the cutting of the virgin stands of hard, resin-soaked yellow pines. Kaiser Wilhelm's submarine blockades indirectly and quickly exploited more of this nation's material resources than did the attacks of his troops upon the American soldiers and their allies in the trenches dug into the fields and forests of France. Engaging the enemy in the First World War required "a bridge of ships" from North America to Great Britain and on to the west coast of the European continent. Before the war, hardwood timbers moved from southern ports to German harbors, mostly for military use. Meanwhile, German submarines, blockading the ports of nations friendly to France and England, sunk vessels attempting to run the blockades. Torpedoes from

Well-formed longleaf pine. This was the sort that in the 1940s found its way to European shipyards as mast timber. The flat top indicates maturity. (Courtesy U.S. Forest Service.)

those vessels devastated both commercial and military fleets of the Kaiser's adversaries. Something had to be done, and the effort included a dramatic attempt to build a floating trestle of ships from the New World to the Old. The United States agreed to perform the improbable feat.

Southern lumbermen quickly exhibited enthusiasm for the project, partly for patriotic reasons and partly because the products of their export markets lay at the bottom of the sea with the vessels in which their timbers were to have moved to European markets. An intercepted note from a German emissary to Mexico heightened interest. The note—sent three months before the United States' entry into the fray—implied that sinking of merchant ships sailing in the Gulf of Mexico would soon commence.[21] Wood exports from southern states, especially those along the Gulf shore, would be further reduced. Economic vigor of the mills of the South had depended upon those exports to the U.S. Northeast as well as to ports abroad.

Congressional action established the Emergency Fleet Corporation, providing the agency with $50 million with which to purchase light cargo ships of the 3,000-ton class. Eventually, between 475 and 750 million board feet of the finest quality yellow pines were harvested for this purpose.[22] Much planking went into docks and housing at the shipyards while whole trees became pilings for the wharves. Shipwrights fashioned finished dense pine lumber into the decks, sides, and superstructures of the ships.

A Blustering Wind

At first, the southern leadership expressed optimism. Louisiana's Great Southern Lumber Company's superintendent claimed he had six hundred thousand acres to dedicate to the task. Others said twenty-five to fifty ships could be launched every day in the South. Within six months, six billion board feet were available in the woods of the region. Boasters claimed that seasoning of the yellow pine was not needed: the heavy heart would cure in the thirty-six days between the harvest of the trees and their arrival at the wharves. Salesmen's puffing was not forbidden. To encourage the capture of a contract, one entrepreneur boldly stated that longleaf pine is the only southern pine that gets tighter when in water. Yet patriotic posters seemed necessary to encourage diligence in the task. One such sign told the reader that "the government must have wooden ships . . . without timbers, ships cannot be built."[23]

Problems occurred at every proverbial swing of the ax or whirl of the saw. Southern lumbermen knew little of shipbuilding. Few ocean-going boats had been made of wood since the days of the live oakers, and those ships of antiquity were assembled in the North or in naval yards abroad. Most southern labor was unskilled as artisan craftsmen and the ones who were, by 1917, had been drafted into the military or urged to employ their abilities more profitably elsewhere. No southern shipwrights and few journeymen carpenters were available for the shipbuilding tasks now at hand. Building boats of wood, or of any material, was not just a problem for the South. The nation had made few vessels of commerce, even of steel, in recent years. The country had abdicated those opportunities and responsibilities to the British. Nor were many ships of war built in any yard carrying the flag of the United States. Boat building was almost a lost art on the American continent.

Squabbles slowed the effort to build ocean-going vessels of southern yellow pine. Problems were especially acute between the lumber industrialists and the government overseers of the project. Leader of the overseers was George Washington Goethals, an Army general who had gained fame for his leadership in completing the Panama Canal a few years earlier. He offended the lumbermen by complaining that they were working too slowly. "Birds are still nesting in the trees which must go into the lumber out of which to build ships," he said. Responding to the criticism, the lumbermen suggested that the general was not really interested in wooden boats. This was likely so, for he reasoned that an extraordinarily long time, running into months, would be required for seasoning the timbers. Apparently he had not been informed that the resin-soaked heartwood of longleaf pine requires little seasoning. Even trees chipped for turpentining could be promptly made into ship timbers.[24]

Millers, a bit optimistic, claimed that in seventy-two hours they could shoo the birds, cut the trees, mill the lumber, and have it at dockside if the government would cease changing the architectural plans while the ships were under construction. The lumbermen implied, too, that Goethals, because of his success at the Isthmus, was controlled by the steel shipbuilders.[25]

Sufficient numbers of railway flatcars were not available to haul the timbers. Perhaps the federally authorized freight regulations, operating discriminately against the South as they had from the time of the Civil War, played a role. And farm and backwoods women, the only labor available and unaccustomed to this kind of work, operated the sawmills with great difficulty. The industrialists felt that Gen. Goethals was slack in using his office to facilitate the building of the bridge of ships sought by Britain's Prime Minister Lloyd George.

To add to the difficulties, southern mills had already contracted with the Department of War and the Navy to supply seventeen thousand carloads of lumber for barracks in the United States and in

France. Almost eighty million board feet went to Fort Riley, in Kansas, alone. Between four hundred million and one billion board feet were to go for cantonment construction, at six hundred board feet per soldier, from the southern woods. "Two weeks from coastal breezes to the siding of a barracks in Kentucky" was how one merchandizer put it.[26]

This harvest of virgin timber in the days of the First World War was almost totally heartwood, sawn from trees grown for perhaps two hundred years with twenty or so annual rings per inch of radius. Cut into boards, resin-soaked heartwood warps or twists little. It resists fungus and insect attacks. (In contrast, the lumber used for the barracks of the Second World War, unseasoned for lack of time, was almost wholly sapwood and from relatively young trees in the second-growth southern forest. These stems, at the time of the 1940s' urgent harvest, grew six or so rings per inch. The rapid decay, warp, and twist of this lumber gave the southern pine industry a reputation that it still has not overcome.)

Mill managers and government agents argued over the price of wood, the former insisting that thirty-five dollars per thousand board feet was inadequate for the rare marine-grade timbers. The new eight-hour federally mandated work day, businessmen complained, inordinately cost mills that, until then, had been operating on ten-hour schedules. Their former salesmen's puffing aside, they now admitted that no single mill could supply all the parts for a ship.

The federal authorities listened attentively, allowed 10 percent profit over costs, and warned mill owners and managers that they could commandeer the saws and planers. Navy procurement officials then ordered the mills to allocate to the Emergency Fleet Corporation all timbers twelve-by-twelve inches by twenty-four feet or larger and any cants (squared timbers) longer than thirty feet. The bureaucrats seem not to have realized that some of the cants sawn at the mills were too long for railways to handle. To find these timbers, and some fourteen-by-fourteen-inch sixty-foot beams that were required components for a ship model called the *Ferris*, woodsmen traversed the forests. Essentially every slough and hillock was searched. They also looked west.[27]

Competition and Optimism

The Southern Pine Association (SPA) endeavored to coordinate the war effort, seeing that battleship decks got the required southern pine, that lumber was available for barracks, that timbers were earmarked for shoring trenches in France, and that wood could be had for small boats as well as for the arks of war.[28] The association's Southern Pine Emergency Bureau helped maintain order between Goethals's office and the mills, a necessary task inasmuch as the best timber was preempted for the war effort.

Western lumbermen competed for the opportunity to build the "jitney ships" for the war effort, even for the far-distant Atlantic trade. The still new Panama Canal encouraged this venture for those whose yards were on the Pacific coast. Southern millmen also needed timbers that only western trees could provide, dimensional stock of a size rarely available in the southern pineries. Timber contracts were signed between the Southerners and the owners of mills in Washington and Oregon. In time, railroad flatcars delivered fifty million board feet of Douglas-fir from the Pacific Northwest for inclusion in Gulf-built boats.

The Sinking of the New Industry

Two of the South's migrating lumbermen, Henry Lutcher and Bedell Moore, effectively induced the boat builders to proceed at full speed. With holdings on both sides of the Sabine River, near Orange, Texas, the Lutcher and Moore Company had readily available the necessary timbers of high quality. Inasmuch as boats had been built on the launching ways near the company mills since the Civil War, craftsmen understood the task. So it was that in early 1918, the 5,000-ton *War Mystery*, built for the British Cunard Line by the Daugherty Company, was launched at Orange. Said to be "the largest wooden ship that ever took water," she was 330 feet long, displayed a forty-eight–foot beam, and was underlain by a fifteen–by–fifteen–by–thirty-eight–inch keel at a depth of twenty-seven feet. Construction required but seven months.[29]

Another transport launched there was the *City of Orange*. She was 250 feet long, forty-three feet wide, and displayed a hold twenty-three feet deep. Construction required one million board feet of longleaf pine. The five-masted schooner was equipped with two auxiliary 100-horsepower diesel engines. Douglas-fir trees from the Pacific Northwest provided the spars; components for the bow and stern came from Lutcher and Moore's nearby lowland live oak forests.[30]

Shortly thereafter, at the Houston yards, the *Nacogdoches*, named for the oldest town in Texas and christened by President Woodrow Wilson's wife, slid into the ship channel.[31] Shipwrights built the *Nacogdoches*, a 280-foot vessel with a forty-six–foot beam, in seven months using 1.5 million board feet of select yellow pine from the yet-virgin stands nearby. Upon the launching of a sister ship a month later and amid much publicity, one lumberman boasted, "Eight months ago the buzzards and wild turkeys were roosting in the pines from which this good ship

Bonham was built, they being the only birds in this neck of the woods that roost in tall timbers."[32]

By mid-1918, many boat-building projects were well under way, creating a new industry in the western Gulf coastal states of Mississippi, Louisiana, and Texas. But many of the ships contracted for at the fifty-two yards in the South, from Hampton Roads to Aransas Pass, sailed nowhere. Only eighty-four vessels, including those assigned the western yards, were delivered to the government by Armistice Day. With war's end in November 1918, the frantic need for ocean transportation had passed. While some lumber industrialists pushed for peacetime use of the vessels, thus requiring completion of those on the docks, their lobbying had little effect. Steel could do a better job. Bankruptcies followed as thirty thousand workers sought employment elsewhere and mill managers calculated the return on their investments at less than 4 percent. Salvage firms removed the machinery from the ships, towed the vessels to sea, and burned their hulls to the waterline. The unused lumber inventories, now much lower in value, found use in school construction and other civilian pursuits as the nation returned to normalcy.[33] Little is recorded about the seaworthiness of these ships. One account told of leaking hulls, blamed on the gaps between the green timbers that covered the sides and decks.

The End of the Boat Builders' Forest

Many species other than the resin-producing and lumber-producing southern pines and live oaks contributed to the building of ships to serve the naval and merchant mariners. Eastern redcedar, southern baldcypress, and Atlantic white-cedar, all coniferous species with durable and relatively soft wood, provided for specialty uses like cabinets or water containers. Black locust trees, with extremely hard wood and heartwood unaffected by fungi and insects, contributed to the shipwright's store of essential materials. Perhaps another dozen species growing in the southern forest added to the naval architect's inventory. Among them were ship masts cut from tall, straight, longleaf pine timbers. They were marketed abroad for this purpose even into the 1950s. When navies and fleets of commerce all over the world replaced shiplap lumber with steel covering; when screw propellers, powered by petroleum-fueled boilers, replaced the sails for the tall ships and the masts and yards upon which to hoist the sails; and when war no longer claimed lumber for cargo and troop ships, the boat builders' forest faded into history.

Entrepreneurs now looked elsewhere for uses for wood from the southern forests.

CHAPTER 5

The Foresters' Forest

ALT WHITMAN'S telling lines intended for those who encroached upon the virgin forests of the Northeast described as well the South at the conclusion of the migrating lumbermen's harvest there:

> We primeval forests felling, . . .
> We the surface broad surveying,
>   We the virgin soil upheaving,
> Pioneers! O Pioneers.

Poets were not alone in describing the changes wrought upon the land by the cutting of the trees holding the soil in place. In 1917 a publication of the Geological Survey of Georgia acquainted its readers with the destructiveness of the loggers' practices.[1]

The bulletin noted that in the Piedmont Province, especially, filling of stream channels by erosion from slopes cultivated following the timber harvests was so severe that adjoining rich bottomlands were rendered "wholly uncultivatable." With total or partial clearing of watersheds and subsequent tilling of hillsides, drainage channels were dramatically altered, expediting the movement of silt to the rivers that cut through the Coastal Plains adjacent to both the Atlantic Ocean and the Gulf of Mexico. Not only did the removal of the forest expose the soil to the impact of rain and rapid runoff, it aggravated flood conditions by increasing the amount of water in the ground, some of which would have transpired to the atmosphere from tree foliage had the trees remained standing in the woods. Frost heaving of the unprotected soil also encouraged its movement into streams and consequent siltation. Tenant farming, so common in the region of the cut-over lands, added to the problem, for those who do not own the land are not likely to husband it.

Perhaps Patrick Henry's comment had been forgotten: "He is the greatest patriot who stops the most gullies." Fellow heirs of the Virginia patriot a century later received the rewards for the shifting agriculture practiced so long in the South, for a "westering man didn't think he was much of a farmer unless he had exhausted two or three farms in a wandering lifetime . . . the swollen, dirty rivers testify into either sea." [2] Timber cutting always preceded cultivation as farmers broke new ground.

Soil erosion was not the only serious problem for the professional foresters now entering the southern forest. Fires that had been set both accidentally and intentionally for a variety of reasons, the absence of seed trees and seedling stock with which to begin regeneration of a new forest, and a dramatic lack of understanding by some of the lumbering entrepreneurs about how trees grow suggest the urgency of the times for the arrival on the scene of someone educated in a college forestry school. A society suffering from economic depression emphasized that urgency. This chapter endeavors to tell what was done to solve these pressing problems.

Unlike foresters of the Rocky Mountains, the southern forester was not to be solely the caretaker of the public estate. And unlike those professionals of the Pacific Northwest, the forester was not to be the logging engineer. The tasks were to manage the lands, whether public or private, for goods and services, but principally for the former. The goods would be wood for lumber, posts, poles, piling, plywood, and paper. In the words written several decades earlier by Agriculture Secretary James Wilson in his instructions to Chief Forester Pinchot, the foresters' task would be to look after the forests "for the greatest good of the greatest number in the long run." Both government and industry foresters saw the job that way.

The task of beginning to rebuild the southern forests coincided with the occurrence of the Great Depression. Together, the catastrophic condition of the once-great forest and the national economy had a devastating effect upon the South. Without money, fire control, and knowledge of silviculture, there seemed no way that the lands now bare, appearing like the treeless western plains, could be regenerated to commercial forests to provide fiber for future generations. As we have noted, some owners of large cut-over areas promoted the idea that these cleared lands were now suitable for agricultural crops, for here growing seasons were long and winters mild.

The lands would be reclaimed to forests. Foresters were lead-

A vast cut-over tract. Many of these tracts, without a source of seeds for a future
forest, were left by the lumbermen for foresters to regenerate to merchantable trees.
They planted seeds as well as seedlings. This was not clear-cutting, a legitimate
silvicultural practice that depends for regeneration upon seeds blown in by the wind
or carried in by wildlife from the walls of timber at the sides of the openings. (Courtesy Forest History Collection, Steen Library Archives, Stephen F. Austin State
University, Nacogdoches, Tex.)

ing participants in the effort, their activities principally commencing with
the termination of the lumbermen's enterprises. They led the way until
the 1970s, when changing cultural and political attitudes dictated the
end of that leadership role. From then to the present, others have told
foresters how to manage and utilize the South's forest.

Forests and Waters

Watershed Protection

To do something about the destroyed watersheds that led to
the silting in of river courses, statesmen introduced various legislation.
Congressman John Weeks's bill, when passed into law in 1911, enabled

Weir boxes mounted in Ozark mountain streams. These measure water flow during and following rains. Foresters also use weirs to compare water flow associated with silvicultural procedures. (Photo by Bluford Muir courtesy U.S. Forest Service.)

the federal government to buy private lands to grow trees for the protection of navigable streams. The first tract purchased was an 18,500-acre parcel in the Applachian Mountains of North Carolina. The act also provided money to the states for fire prevention and suppression to protect the headwaters of those streams.[3] And every state participated with its

Coshocton wheels. Sediment and water runoff are measured by these instruments following silvicultural treatments. This sampling device measured soil and water movement before and after prescribed burning in the Piedmont Province. The rate of the flow of water and sediment regulates the speed of the wheel's rotation. Mounted on precision bearings, 0.01 of a sample passes through the slot (*at the pencil point*) as the wheel spins, and is collected below in a container within the wooden box.

own matching funds in the fire program made possible by the act. Federal and state governments hired foresters to administer it. Eventually, over ten million acres in a dozen southern states were added to the national forest system through the Weeks law appropriations.

Long before Congressman Weeks (who later was elected to the U.S. Senate) called the nation's attention to the need for watershed protection, the changing water flow brought about by forest removal was reported (in 1849) by the U.S. Patent Office which, at that time, carried on the government's agricultural services. The seminal study by Ambassador George Perkins Marsh, entitled *Man and Nature*, first published in 1864 and reprinted in 1874 as *The Earth as Modified by Human Action*, still served foresters as a managerial bible seventy years after its appearance in print. The ambassador's writing, based upon his observations while serving in capitals of Mediterranean countries, stressed "the connection between forests and climate." So too did a report by the Bureau of Forestry head, Franklin B. Hough, issued after Congress allocated two thousand dollars to study the forestry situation. Cutting over forest lands, the book and the report claimed, altered climate.[4]

Other federal agencies promptly opposed the Bureau's, and later the Forest Service's, allegations that cutting trees diminished rainfall. The U.S. Geological Survey, the U.S. Weather Bureau, and the U.S. Army Corps of Engineers had as much difficulty showing the foresters to be in error as the foresters had in proving their point; however, the injurious effect of timber cutting upon soil water and upon soil and water separately could be readily shown. Since that time, forest influences as an academic subject have been mostly concerned with hydrology rather than climate. Foresters would now be expected to manage lands with an understanding of the effect of their procedures upon the waters of the region. Nowhere was this more important than in the Southern Appalachian Mountains, the Piedmont Province, and the Mississippi River watershed. In these places, inappropriate land use led to disastrous soil erosion and stream siltation.

Forest Influences

The Forest Management Act of June 4, 1897, gave the securing of "favorable conditions of water flows" as a reason for lands of the public domain to be withdrawn from entry by homesteaders, miners, and lumbermen. Withdrawn from entry, the lands could now be included in the national forest reserves. The General Land Office, at that time the agency overseeing the reserves, outlined in its *Forest Reserve Manual* how forests regulate the flow of water. Vigorous stands of young trees, the document suggested, were most advantageous. The evidence remained scanty. Seedlings planted in Louisiana on homesteaded tracts under the Timber Culture Act of 1873 (which gave to settlers a quarter section— 160 acres—of land of the public domain, provided that forty acres would be planted with trees) did not survive to provide the proof. Rice and sugar growers probably little intended for the seedlings transplanted from nearby woods to survive. Their obligation to the General Land Office satisfied, the land now could be legally plowed and planted with income-producing food crops.

While the argument continued among government agents and agencies over the relationship between forests and stream flow, land degradation in the region attributed to overcutting worsened. Formal research was not necessary to show that river siltation was clogging shipping channels, resulting in port closings, and that local economies were suffering. Rails replaced rivers, once the most important and least costly roads of commerce, partly because of siltation that followed timber harvests and cultivation of cut-over land.

To find answers to the question of land use and water relationships for the South, the U.S. Forest Service established the Coweeta Hydrologic Laboratory in the Nantahala National Forest in the southern North Carolina sector of the Appalachian chain. Agency scientists selected the site principally because it received the greatest amount of precipitation of any area in the continent east of the Pacific Northwest's Olympic Peninsula. Some 120 inches (almost three times the average for the South) fall as rain and snow on the upper reaches of the range.

Taking leaves from the books of experimental results in the Wagon Wheel Gap studies in Colorado, dating to 1910, and more recent studies in the San Gabriel Mountains in California, researchers began in 1934 at Coweeta to study the effect of various land-use practices upon water runoff and soil erosion. The effort eventually aimed to show how manipulating vegetation could optimize production of water that is clear and clean for human consumption and industrial use. Clear water, free of sediment, was sorely needed for textile manufacturing in the communities below the Appalachian Mountains' rim, and clean water, free of harmful microbes, was essential for the people living in those communities.

Most notable among the many experiments conducted at Coweeta was the establishment of a precipitation equivalent transpired by the foliage of deciduous trees of the zone. Research foresters learned that if all trees were cut and left to lie so that the soil was not disturbed, the flow of water through the weir in the concrete dam at the bottom of the watershed increased the equivalent of seventeen inches of precipitation per year. Stream flow continued at the higher level if each year's sprout growth was cut back. But, when trees were permitted to resprout and grow, the original, much reduced, stream flow was again reached in seventeen years.

From these data, foresters developed silvicultural recommendations for integrating timber and water management. An optimal quantity of each is then attainable with minimal damage to the forest or to the watershed. Thus, on high, cold ridges where soil is deep (not always the case at the summits), low-grade pines, like table-mountain and pitch, join post oak and other scrub trees. To optimize water production, foresters harvest these stems. Water flows then increase. In time, these low-value species will be replaced by trees of higher value; though, when that occurs, production of clear, clean water diminishes. While this relationship prevails for the mature oak and hickory forest in the Southern Appalachian highlands, it should be considered a proportional—not an absolute—amount of evapotranspiration for the forests of the southern region.

Long before multiple use was a congressionally established principle, foresters in the South wrestled with how best to utilize the land for timber and at the same time encourage percolation of precipitation into underground aquifers from which communities at lower elevations withdraw water. Care of the woody vegetation takes on special significance where aquifers outcrop on arable land.

For example, sandy soil grows excellent watermelons, though its highest and best use may be for receiving water for subsequent percolation to a subterranean reservoir. Cover on the land enhances infiltration significantly. Rules of thumb suggest that a liter of water infiltrates into the floor of a hardwood forest in about thirty seconds, into the needle litter of a pine stand in three minutes, into a grassy field in thirty minutes, into a freshly cultivated field in three hours, and into the compacted soil of a footpath in thirty hours. Hence, watershed managers may recommend maintaining broad-leaved species, even if composed of weed trees, on the land to protect water supplies. Where water does not infiltrate, it runs off the land, taking valuable topsoil with it. Watermelons or higher-value crops protect the watershed only when the foliage covers the land.

The foresters' concern for water increased as the period progressed. The Federal Water Pollution Control Act, passed in 1956, encouraged cooperation by the states to prevent and control water pollution. Subsequent legislation in 1972 contained in section 208 a call for a plan to "identify, if appropriate . . . silviculturally related non-point sources of pollution." To satisfy the law's intent, foresters established *best management practices*, procedures useful on both government and privately owned lands. Such recommended practices included establishing water bars on logging roads to direct water flow, prompt regeneration of harvested lands to provide protective cover on soil, harvesting on the contours of the land, skidding upgrade, and specifying minimal distances from streams for harvesting trees and skidding logs. Erosion and sedimentation remain primary nonpoint source pollutants for the region's streams.

Litigation ensued when the U.S. Army Corps of Engineers, responsible for all of the waters of the country, failed to enforce the Clean Water Act. The Corps is now jointly authorized with the Environmental Protection Agency to enforce implementation of the law.

Burning the Woods

Fire: Friend or Foe?

Intentionally set fires burned regularly when foresters arrived on the southern scene. Many men came to the region upon graduation from the schools of the North. They came from the North because few colleges in the South provided a forestry education, and in the South the Yankee-trained young men could find employment. But their academic background provided little understanding of the South's culture or silviculture where woods burning is concerned.[5]

As soon as sufficient fuel built up to support a woods fire, someone ignited the litter. Typically, this occurred at three-year intervals, some 5 percent of the forested area burning each year.[6] Accidental fires were innocently set by farmers burning stubble from their fields, by women washing clothes in pots over open fires in their yards, and by loggers and hunters warming themselves on cold and wet days. Sparks from logging equipment set a few. So, too, did the sun, solar rays magnifying as they struck the curved glass of a bottle dropped along the way. Tinder-dry leaves and grass readily blazed from the radiation. While lightning-set fires are rare in the region, they usually occur in the Southern Appalachian Mountains. Ordinarily rainwater quickly douses the flame that races down the bole of a tall pine and jumps to the ground as a tree violently explodes when struck by the electrical discharge.

Fires intentionally set by others in the early days of the foresters' entry into the South had detrimental economic significance, but few were the judges and sheriff's officers who thought so. The powers-that-be simply considered woods arson a prank, justifiable revenge, accident, or appropriate procedure. Owners and tenants of small farms burned the residue from the previous year's crop before planting the spring garden. Others burned to control the cotton-destroying Mexican boll weevils and to kill ticks, red bugs (the obnoxious chigger), and snakes. These fires often escaped to the forest. Cattlemen burned to get early spring grass, both in pastures and in the woods, where beef cattle roamed freely or at minimal cost to the owner of the animal.

Cattlemen also set "self-defense" fires. During the fire season in the spring, some stockmen on the open range started fires so that cattle running loose with their new calves would come to the fresh grass that came up soon after the older herbaceous material was burned. The cattlemen could then easily round up their stock for branding. But another man's animals might migrate to the fresh grass and, in so doing, receive an incorrect brand. To avoid losing the wandering cattle, almost every stockman set the woods in which he ranged his cattle ablaze in self-defense. Not until state legislatures across the region passed fencing laws to protect highway travelers was defense burning of the South's rangelands unnecessary.[7]

Cattlemen lost their animals in sandy longleaf pine lands that had been subjected to fire to improve the grass. Before the new grass and forbs thickened, heavy rains splashed sand particles from the soil onto the sparse herbaceous ground cover. Animals feeding upon the succulent new growth consumed the sand. Cattle autopsies on the range showed that sand particles stuck to the blades of grass consumed by the livestock prevented digestion of the grass. The cattle died.

Burning the woods by schoolboys, drunks, and nesters may have been a prank, but burning the woods to get back at the sawmill boss, the neighbor, or the revenuers and foresters was arson. Incendiarists enjoyed setting fires on either side of railroad tracks for thirty miles or more. National Guardsmen sometimes assisted in suppression, and after the Second World War, they occasionally employed war-surplus C-47 airplanes (admittedly a bit awkward) for fire detection. So concerned was the U.S. Forest Service about the reckless abandon in which the woods were set ablaze that in 1920 it transferred from California a district ranger to turn things around. H. N. Wheeler was able to evoke strong emotions against woods burning. He preached Billy Sunday–style for fire prevention.[8]

Although industry and government agency personnel aggressively endeavored to prevent fires, results were slow in showing. Sometimes the effort backfired. Champion Paper and Fibre Company had an enamelled sign posted along roads that read, "Fire the worst enemy of the forest—Champion Paper Co." Unfortunately, the word *fire*, in red paint, faded, leaving passersby to understand that the community's principal employer was the forest's principal enemy.

Nesters who lived in the woods and ran livestock there were too tough for the sheriff. "To make bad men good," Paul Hursey, an early industrial forester said, "you'd pay him $10 a month for looking after your acreage." One national forest ranger recorded twenty to twenty-five fires a month on a 180,000-acre district in the three autumn months of 1942. In the war years, the ranger and "a dozen local old men" were all who were available to fight fire. "We put out 290 forest fires that year," he reported.[9] Mills, too, periodically self-destructed—by careless or intentioned fire.[10]

Judges and the public may have believed that burning the woods was appropriate for the reasons noted earlier. Opening the understory so that game animals could be seen was another reason considered justifiable by the bench. One sure way to get off on an arson charge almost anywhere in the South was to insist on a jury trial. Most of the jurors selected likely would have participated in woods burning or would have associated with someone who had.

White people learned woods burning from the Indians who had been pyromaniacs in the South, burning the woods to expose or rout the enemy or to enhance opportunities for a successful hunt by removal of the understory brush and trees. Closely related to these reasons for burning the woods was enemy arson during the Second World War. Nazi agents set fires in the forests of the Atlantic Coast so that Axis U-boats could see their targets when they surfaced in the night.

One law that did make a difference in fire occurrence was the requirement that spark arresters be placed on all locomotives, both commercial coal-burners and loggers' wood-burners. Conviction of companies under this legislation helped reduce the number of fires attributed to the railroads.

Fighting Fires

Early forest fire statistics may be unreliable because the limited number of fire crews fought only small fires. They let the large ones, those that burned simultaneously with the small fires, burn themselves out. However, in the winter of 1954–55, nearly five hundred thousand acres burned in and around the Okefenokee Swamp in Georgia. Later in 1955, about six hundred thousand acres blazed within a ten-day period.[11] Fire fighters were often stymied in their efforts to locate and get to fires. One might search for hours in dense smoke before locating a fire burning low to the ground.

Hundreds of rivers in the region were crossed by ferries. Where neither bridge nor ferry existed, state forestry agencies strung cable lines so that fire fighters could cross. These over-river carriers also helped the general public get from one place to another. One simply pulled oneself across by a wire attached to a line above the cable.

Spiked trees served as fire lookout posts until the Civilian Conservation Corps (CCC) enrollees erected towers. The tallest trees at strategic places—like the highest point on a ridge—were selected, spikes for climbing hammered into the bole, and a seat nailed on a limb near the top. Some of these lookouts were struck by lightning. A forester of the times commented dutifully, "Of course, during lightning storms, one did not spend much time up in a spike tree." [12]

Foresters took advantage of the respect Southerners had for the Holy Scripture in encouraging fire prevention and other conservation practices. The federal Forest Service published a popular bulletin that cited the Bible's admonitions about stewardship of the land, a circular re-printed and freely distributed many times over. Reducing woods burning was its principal objective. The *Southern Lumberman* [13] summed up the theme in an article by a regional public relations forester employed by the U.S. Forest Service. He noted the passages from Genesis, Ezekiel, Levi-ticus, Isaiah, and the Revelation that speak of the cedars of Lebanon, groves of trees in Beersheba, and the inadvisable use of trees in war. The conclusion of St. John's Isle of Patmos vision in the last book of Christian Holy Writ was an appropriate epitaph for citizens of the Bible Belt: "In the midst of the street of it, and on either side of the river, *was there* the tree of life, which bare twelve *manner of* fruits, *and* yielded her fruit every month: and the leaves of the tree *were* for the healing of the nations." [14] As foresters made the rounds of rural schools to talk about fire prevention and to hand out this kind of literature, they felt rewarded. The leaflets, car-ried by the children to homes that had little else to read, seemed to have an effect in reducing the number of wildfires that devastated the forests.

To protect lands from fire, companies banded together and as-sessed themselves a fee for fire suppression. Two cents an acre a year in the 1930s was typical. The companies did not pay on their bottomland acreages, because the moist-site land was not likely to burn. The com-panies that paid were provided priority suppression services, causing prob-lems where lands of an assessed company were intermingled with tracts of those resisting payment of the fee. The fund was usually collected by the state forestry agency which, in turn, gave priority to the fires on land on which the "tax" was paid.

Foresters throughout the South in 1939 were envious of the Maryland State Forest Service which, at that time, had radio communi-cations. No agencies farther south had wireless service until the State of Texas bought two RCA transceivers, black boxes with antennas. Its Forest

Service then initiated two-way communications, signalling between recently erected CCC lookout towers. The Federal Communications Commission required operators of the shortwave sets to have first-class licenses, a requirement that discouraged development of radio communications.[15]

Men fought fires with hand tools—flaps made of discarded mill belting, potato hooks, toothed rakes made of mower blades, and backpack water cans. The fire fighters typically dropped back to natural barriers, like roads, creeks, or fields; raked a line; and set a backfire. Cleared lines, dug through the litter to the soil, circled the fire so that it would be pushed into a road or stream bottom and burn itself out. By the late 1940s, jeeps with a fire plow mounted on the rear and farm tractors were used to plow lines from which to set backfires, but these vehicles were useless in rough terrain, wet ground, or heavy brush. Sometimes the foresters persuaded farmers to hook their mules to spring-toothed harrows to plow a fire line.

Local labor was often enlisted to fight fires. State governments paid some workers for the effort. Regretfully, that payment encouraged the practice of setting the woods on fire for the employment that was then made possible. One sly national forest district ranger suspected that his own laborers—timber markers, weed-tree girdlers, and trail maintenance men—were participating in this practice. Their wages, ordinarily forty cents per hour, declined to thirty-five cents while fighting fire, a much more exhausting task than the others. The ranger called all of his crews together, announced that when anyone had worked forty hours, his "week" was over. Sunday and Monday night spent fighting fire at thirty-five cents an hour was not nearly so enticing if the balance of the week could not be worked at forty cents. The wildfires suddenly ceased to burn.

Eventually throughout the South fire trespass (the euphemism for arson) was effectively checked. The Cooperative Forest Fire Prevention Program with an assist from congressionally mandated Clarke-McNary funds aided the effort.

Prescribed Burning

Before the arrival of foresters, few were the people who recognized that proper burning of the forest resulted in better seed catches, more rapid growth of seedlings that seeded-in following the fire, and release of valuable trees from competing vegetation. Under the guidance of foresters, prescriptions for fires were written, whereby the purpose of a fire was established and its design spelled out. So, for example, it became common for a fire intended to prepare a seedbed to receive longleaf pine seeds in the lower Coastal Plain to be set between nine and eleven on a winter morning when the temperature was between 25°F and 50°F, the relative humidity above 50 percent, the fuel moisture 7 percent, and the wind steady and out of the north at eight to twelve miles per hour. Such a cool fire, running with the wind along the ground, burns only the ground cover and is not hot enough to injure seed trees. Austin Cary, the U.S. Forest Service's traveling "evangelist" for managing the woodlands recommended such site preparation in 1920.[16]

Even with firm prescriptions (not to be confused with controlled burning, where only standby suppression crews distinguish the set fire from a wildfire), many foresters objected to the use of fire for any reason. A state forester, V. H. Sonderegger of Louisiana, heatedly fought with Professor H. H. Chapman of the Yale Forestry School about such fires in the forest. Sonderegger had been diligently endeavoring to prevent and suppress wildfires throughout his state. Meanwhile, Chapman was demonstrating the need for fire to prepare seedbeds for the regeneration of southern pines, to reduce the brush in the understory of these forests, and to control the spread of brownspot needle blight on longleaf pine seedlings. The arrival of the professor with his students from the North at Yale's Urania, Louisiana, camp each summer called for more patience than Sonderegger could muster. The two argued publicly in the local press and in the *Journal of Forestry*. In the end, Chapman won. Foresters in Louisiana soon were using prescribed fire to improve game habitat, to reduce the risk of wildfire, and to release valuable trees from plants competing for soil moisture, light, and nutrients, as well as for the purposes noted above.[17]

Smokey Bear, the bruin saved from the blazing New Mexico woods to be enthroned in the National Zoological Park in Washington, D.C., picked up where Sonderegger left off. To this day, many laymen and a few foresters object to the use of prescribed fire. They believe that prevention, presuppression (preparedness for fighting fire), and suppression of all fires are essential. Others see that, even in mildly burning wildfires, good may come. Indeed, many of the forests professionals began to manage in the 1930s existed only because of the relatively cool wildfires that had, here and there through the years, burned over the land. By those fires, the soil was scarified to receive the seed for germination; seed-bearing trees were released from vegetative competition for soil moisture, nutrients, and light; and the forthcoming seedlings were freed from overtopping vegetation, able to grow straight and fast.

So the biggest hindrance to the establishment of some southern pine reproduction was said to be "not wildfire," but "no fire." Or fire at the wrong time. In those days "Red" Jared, a district ranger on a southern national forest, requested permission to "prescribe" burn a stand of longleaf pine in which seedlings lingered in the grass stage because of brownspot needle blight, a fungus infection. It took two years for the regional forester's office in Atlanta to reluctantly approve Jared's request for a twenty-acre trial. When two hundred acres "accidentally" burned, because of high and drying winds, Jared said, "It just got away." The beautiful stand that promptly emerged from the grass by the control of the seedling-stunting brownspot needle-blight fungus was a memorial to "Ranger Red" decades later.[18] The U.S. Forest Service also objected to the use of fire for enhancing habitat for bobwhite quail, as Herbert Stoddard discovered when he sent for review the manuscript for his still-definitive work on this game bird.[19]

Professional Foresters: Their Education and Work

Industrial Foresters Join the Ranks

While many second-growth forests throughout the South had been regenerated because of the occurrence of wildfires, millions of acres also lay in ravaged waste as the result of incendiarism. Fire often killed trees left from previous harvests that could have provided seed for a new stand. Fires killed seedlings before they could grow sufficiently tall for their terminal buds to escape the lethal heat. Fires killed seedlings and saplings before the bark was thick enough to provide insulation from the heat, and fires consumed the seeds that had dropped to the ground before the seeds could germinate. In some areas of the Coastal Plain, one could see treeless land stretching for miles. Unto this good land came the foresters.

Among the first professional foresters employed by industry in the South was a University of Michigan graduate named Paul Hursey. His story is not unlike that which could be told in every state by early-day foresters who saw in the South an opportunity to practice the profession for which they trained. Hursey left a forestry-related mapping job that paid $200 a month to go to work for a Texas industry at $125. He recalled, "I went down there [to Texas] and met Mr. [Ernest] Kurth, and spent two or three days looking over the timberlands. I told him at that time that I thought he did not have enough land and timber to go on sustained yield. And he said, 'If you don't think I have, take a six-month leave and spend the time down here to determine it thoroughly.'" Hursey's work, upon entry on the job in 1937, "comprised mostly of looking after trespass (timber stealing), fighting fires, marking timber (for cutting), making management plans, and laying out railroad trams." In that year, only four other industrial foresters were employed in the South.[20]

Those few industrial foresters carried on much like their employers, the migrating lumbermen. Hursey logged from railroad camps, using Clyde four-line rehaul skidders that "left nothing on the ground whatever." Mules and trucks hauled logs to the rails where they were lifted by rapid loaders or McGifford loaders onto flat cars pulled by oil-burning main line locomotives. The Clyde had four lines, or cables, going out from it, each manned by a horse that pulled the line as much as a quarter of a mile from the track. Mule skinners carried the lines out and set the tongs. Cable drums, around which the lines wound, were steam driven and usually fueled with wood.

Skidders of the early period of the foresters' tenure also included donkey engines on a flat railroad car on which was mounted a windlass with a steel cable as long as eight hundred feet. At its end were tongs. The tongs, often called "chokers," were carried out to each log by a boy, affectionately known as the "whistlepunk," riding a horse or mule. The lad gave the tongs to the man in the woods and, as the older person attached the tongs to the log to be dragged in, the whistlepunk loudly signaled the windlass operator to start pulling in the logs, dragging, jerking, and hurtling them to trackside. Many times the boys would get tangled up with the cable; some were injured seriously. This method of logging tore down all the young timber, leaving the land looking like a battlefield.[21]

But Hursey saw the transition from oxen and mules and Clydes to caterpillar tractors to bring out the logs. The first tractor arrived in 1940. "The logging superintendent . . . was so delighted with it that he threatened to shut down the team haul and run all of the mules out of the lot. The teamsters came to me about it, and I put on a study. . . . It wound up that the logs could be hauled for a mile from the track more economically by mule than by tractor."[22]

When the first foresters arrived, some virgin timber had not yet been cut. Within these forests were trees over forty inches in diameter earmarked for special projects, such as "walking beams"—the part of the oil-field rig that tilts up and down and throws the "sucker rod" up. Companies got a fancy price for them. Some longleaf pine tracts ran to forty thousand board feet per acre; loblolly and shortleaf pines exceeded fifteen thousand board feet, with more than a thousand feet in many of the trees.

Early foresters in the region tried to tell industrial landowners that it would be to their benefit to practice forestry. Foresters in state agencies conducted tours and put on demonstrations solely for the industrial leaders, showing them how to harvest stands of pines and hardwoods in order to have the most lucrative income in the long run. The professionals also set up exhibits on much-traveled roads to show that forestry could be a paying proposition. Plots of various species, planted side-by-side, with appropriate signboards told the story. In spite of these efforts, loggers continued to cut timber according to a diameter limit. Diameter-limit cutting (i.e., harvesting all trees above a certain girth) took the genetically superior trees and left the inferior ones to supply seed for the next crop. One of the newly recruited Yankee foresters recounted how a company would sell a tract this way, and if it did not cut out the estimated volume, the buyer simply went to another tract and there made up the difference.[23]

These "show-me" projects were in time successful. Indeed, the purchases of southern lands and mills by national and international corporations can in part be attributed to these tours conducted by foresters for landowners, financiers, politicians, and the press. So enthused were the new corporate owners of these lands that they hired foresters and trained them in public relations to tell the story that growing trees does pay. With interest rates at 4 percent and less and a potential shortage of wood for the growing population, it could be shown to be so.[24]

A great boost for forestry in the South was the organization of soil conservation districts in the 1940s. District programs publicized forestry practices, emphasized planting trees on abandoned agricultural croplands, and even paid for the trees for farmers to plant. State foresters and foresters in the Soil Conservation Service assisted the districts in carrying out their mandate. So, too, Agricultural Extension Service (later the Cooperative Extension Service) foresters, employees of the land-grant colleges in every state, allocated time to any landowners who sought expert advice on the management of their woodlands. These specialists also set up demonstrations and meetings throughout the region to educate the public. Their publications reached a wide audience among landowners.

As the big mills of the migrating lumbermen faded into history in the late 1930s, foresters witnessed the return of the small portable sawmill with horse or mule logging. The "peckerwood" mills both received their logs and dispatched their lumber in trucks. Buyers purchased timber to ten-inch stump diameters or "all merchantable trees" for these mills. Landowners were willing to sell by such rules. And foresters were challenged to turn this around. They have been only partially successful. Too few landowners heard the Florida state forester's couplet, "As grows the pine tree tall and straight / So shapes the future of our state."[25]

Educating the Foresters

Before any rigidly professional forestry schools had opened in the South, Carl Schenck's Biltmore Forest School on the Vanderbilt estate in North Carolina was turning out men whose training was largely practical. The school operated from 1898 to 1913. Though most enrollees were graduates of other colleges, they also received baccalaureate diplomas from Biltmore. The educational program was based on German master schools in which a forestmaster took his young men with him on his daily rounds, the apprentices riding at his heels, watching him, and hearing him lecture.[26] About 350 youths passed through the Biltmore program, many providing senior leadership for the profession by the time the foresters' forest emerged in the South.[27]

At the beginning of the more-or-less intensive management of the South's forests, two undergraduate schools and one graduate professional educational program in the region were turning out graduates for assignments with government and industry. The University of Georgia program was established in 1906 by a gift from financier George Foster Peabody, a philanthropist who endowed a fund specifically to improve education among rural southerners. Later, in 1925, Louisiana State University enrolled students for a forestry curriculum. Duke University's School of Forestry for a long time was the principal producer in the South of foresters with graduate degrees. By the end of the growth period of the foresters' forest in the 1960s, every state in the region had at least one professional forestry school, and almost every institution awarded advanced degrees.

McIntire-Stennis legislation, named for a congressman from Vermont and a senator from Mississippi, provided funds, beginning in 1963, for many southern schools to engage in research. Prior to that time, most experimental work at academic institutions was financed with agricultural college appropriations at land-grant universities.

Yale University's School of Forestry students, from the earliest days of its charter, traveled to the South for practical studies in the woods. In 1909, they worked on the lands and in the mills of East Texas. So significant was this event that Gifford Pinchot, the nation's chief forester, visited the students' summer field camp to observe the practical exercises. In later years, students carried out field studies on the lands of Henry Hardtner near Urania, Louisiana, and still later they studied timber management on the lands and lumbering in the mills of the Crossett Company in south-central Arkansas.[28]

The GI Bill, enabling veterans of the Second World War to

attend college at minimal personal monetary sacrifice, encouraged many young men (me among them) to enroll in forestry schools. These schools bloomed across the South, as they had elsewhere in the nation, providing industry and government at all levels with new professional personnel employable for about the same salaries they would pay subprofessional technicians. Most foresters trained in the South remained there, while many from the large graduating classes of the old, established schools of the Northeast and the Lake States delighted in the opportunities to practice the profession where trees grow faster than anywhere else in the nation.

Toward the closing of the period designated here as the time of the foresters' forest, the professional field was overcrowded, causing new graduates to seek employment in about twenty-five occupations for which their education adequately provided the background.[29] Many elected to accept subprofessional employment upon receiving forestry degrees, anticipating later promotion from technician to technological ranks.

Whether professionally educated people should accept technician tasks for a livelihood has long been debated, and those who do have been considered déclassé. Professionals, as technologists, deal with the *how* of assignments, based upon their knowledge of the *why*. A technician's work involves only the *how*. Foresters give directions on *how* because they know *why*. Technicians follow directions without necessarily understanding *why*. But both were and continue to be essential to forest management.

Forestry faculties argued over the distinction, some defending the need for new graduates to first have field experience, while others pointed to the upward mobility of foresters into managerial positions for which their education counted little. Some professionals of the period chose to reject promotions in order to work in the woods, the reason for which they entered the profession. One conclusion to the debate, that continues yet, went like this: "Professional forestry work becomes subprofessional only when it is repetitious beyond the point of providing any new wisdom or insight into nature and people. The true professional uses his experience, whatever its character, to add to the breadth and depth and effectiveness of his professional abilities."[30]

Professional foresters are what they do. A week in the life of one of them in this period was as fascinatingly varied as counseling a lumberman in his office or a logger at a stump in the woods, speaking to a Lions' Club on "Timber Feast or Famine," chasing smoke before directing crews into the forest to fight a fire, fighting the fire, investigating the cause of fire, surveying a boundary or drawing a map, talking to schoolchildren about fire or teaching field hands to sign the payroll, searching out timber thieves and insect infestation, checking out a timber-marking crew or serving as its foreman, cruising a compartment or checking aerial photographs for "ground truth" (verifying by ground inspection the accuracy of information gleaned from aerial photographs), handling correspondence, or counseling Boy Scouts on a merit badge. Foresters supervised road, bridge, and trail crews and instructed stand-improvement laborers. National forest officers issued free-use permits to farmers who had squatted on the land, gave standing timber to communities for school and church construction, and issued leases to land on which schools and churches would be built. Above all, the forester in the period that this chapter describes was expected to be a community leader.

Nursery Establishment

One of the earliest tasks of the foresters was to select lands for nurseries, to collect seeds, and to grow trees for planting. In the late 1930s, federal funds provided by the Clarke-McNary Act of 1924 enabled state and federal officials to search for land suitable for seedling production. Nurseries require minimal slope, the finest loamy soil with good internal drainage, and a location not too far south (where seedlings will not harden off, or become dormant, before lifting) and not too far north (where ice storms and short growing seasons impede production). Local funding added to a government's allocation sometimes encouraged the selection of a site (for a nursery would bring employment to communities suffering economic depression).

To scrounge and make do was common in the operation of a nursery. The need for a motorized grading table required one nursery-managing forester to salvage a worn out fabric belt from a sawmill and an old motor from a school shop.[31] Dire circumstances encouraged innovation in order to get a job done.

When a young forester in the employ of an owner of a vast acreage of industrial cut-over land laid out plans for a company tree nursery, the executive was aghast at what he considered would be the labor requirement. Finally, after much discussion, the forester understood the dilemma: the lumberman thought that a whole pine cone had to be planted to produce each seedling. To collect and then bury in a nursery over a million cones on each acre of nursery bed indeed would be cost-prohibitive.[32] The industrialist told this story years later, unembarrassed that earlier he had not realized that a single cone may contain hundreds of winged seeds. This lack of knowledge demonstrated by some industrial leaders of the time was a characteristic that haunted them for decades, even as they finally realized the value of the second-growth forest emerg-

Slash pines planted west of the species' natural range into Texas. These trees grew well until annonus root rot, caused by a fungus of the genus *Fomes,* began to devastate the stands. Damage is minimal until a woodland is thinned. (Photo by John Frazier courtesy University Information Office, Stephen F. Austin State University, Nacogdoches, Tex.)

ing from the soil. Much of that forest they sold following the cut-out-and-get-out harvest for as little as two dollars an acre.

Problems for the Foresters

Dealing with Lawbreakers

Among the many duties of foresters was searching the woods for evidence of timber stealing and other violations of law. One of the most trying tasks involved adverse possession. A resident sometimes insisted his house, often a shanty, was on his own land, that the house did not stand on land belonging to an industry from which the government or another company had bought the land in recent years. Threats and guns disturbed the calm. Sometimes, if the new national forests were involved, only the federal courts could decide ownership. In one case, federal marshals were sent by a judge to protect a forester while he again ran a line to check the bearing, distance, and location of the witness trees that designated the metes and bounds of the disputed tract. The forester already had been chased by the rifle-toting, land-claiming squatter, whose wife, also armed, participated in the threat.

The federal government lost so much tax money to moonshine operations that the Secretary of Agriculture in the late 1940s issued an order that was passed down from the Forest Service chief to the least of his agency's people. All stills on national forest land were to be reported. To have complied with the directive would have negated two decades of effort by southern foresters to be friends of the people whom they came— many from out of the region—to help. To have been a squealer could have cost one's life. It certainly would encourage spiteful incendiarism, for moonshiners effectively prevented fires near their copper vats, lest a wildfire attract fire fighters. Foresters, considering themselves land managers, not lawmen, usually bypassed the creek cove and traversed the ridge if a trickle of smoke appeared as they cruised timber, surveyed boundaries, or marked trees for sale. The smoke from the white-lightning maker's cooking, on the other hand, did attract the attention of revenuers.

To avoid suddenly coming up on a still and spooking the operator, foresters circulated among country stores a few days before beginning a task in a management compartment of a forest. Talking loudly enough to be heard by the customers of a mercantile establishment as they sipped soft drinks, the foresters made sure the community's citizens soon would know where and when work would begin in a section of the woods. The message was understood. Foresters stumbled onto a few active stills but encountered many more sites where only recently coils and kettle had been removed.

Insect Epidemics

Early-day foresters faced the southern pine beetle. One of the earliest recorded attacks occurred in Texas in 1939. It was in a remnant virgin stand of timber, with eighty trees to the acre that averaged twenty-six inches in diameter and six merchantable sixteen-foot logs. The beetles ruined several hundred acres. A forest entomologist, dispatched from the Southern Forest Experiment Station headquarters in New Orleans, recommended cutting a swath one-half mile wide in front of the direction of

From the Mark and Brand Records in the South's county courthouses. Drawings and descriptions such as this mark on a pig's ear were common. The description in beautiful 1907 penmanship reads, "Mark of Bill Courtney a resident citizen of Nacogdoches County residing at Lingo [which cannot now be located] about 11 miles S.E. from the town of Nacogdoches: Mark: Two swallowtails in right [ear], and swallowfork and underbit in left [ear]." Bill Courtney then signed the book with "his X," his "mark" there noted by the county clerk.

attack. Every pine tree on the north side for 180 degrees around was felled. That stopped the attack.[33] Except for the size of the swath, the method remains the most effective known, in spite of the millions of dollars spent since 1960 on research on the beetle's control.

Occasional loblolly pine sawfly attacks occurred. One, involving between seventeen and nineteen thousand acres in the early 1950s, was quickly controlled with crop duster aircraft that sprayed dichloro-diphenyl-trichloro-ethane, or DDT. The planes refueled and reloaded at a railroad siding and on a highway.[34] Though effective, the nonbiodegradable insecticide will not likely ever be employed for this purpose again. Congressional action precludes its further use in the United States.

Piney Woods Rooters

Foresters ran up against piney woods rooters that had been turned loose by a mossbacked farmer who had taken an old sow and put her on company or government land. Shortly she would be ready to drop her pigs. The farmers would go out and hunt them in the fall and keep them reproducing perpetually. All that was needed was one sow to get started with an identification mark like a swallowtail or a fork in an ear. The "brands" were cut in with shears when the sows, with their pigs, were rounded up each year. Fights occurred over animal ownership, though weapons seemed to be limited to fists.

The piney woods rooter, the notorious razorback hog, especially appreciates the roots of longleaf pine seedlings. They have more nutritional value than corn. One big boar, observed ten hours in a single day, pulled eight hundred seedlings from the ground. The high starch content in the root is to the hog what a carrot is to a rabbit. The wild pigs also consume acorns and hickory nuts, the mast of the river bottoms. Near such sites they would chase deer from the place. They would also

Hog-proof fence. Controlling wild hogs will continue to be a problem for foresters, especially in longleaf pine country. The mean razorback boars may consume as many as eighty seedling roots in an hour, feasting upon the starch-laden "carrot." The hog-proof fence provides the evidence: feral animals roamed and rooted freely along the public road. (Courtesy U.S. Forest Service.)

tree foresters. Workers in the woods have been gored by the tusked feral boars roaming freely in the southern forests.

A story, perhaps apocryphal, tells of a South Alabama hog roundup by early-day foresters on a company experimental tract. The acreage required fencing with net wire to protect grass-stage longleaf pines. The foresters trapped the pigs in vain. Identified by the ear nicks, the trapped animals were taken to their owners, only to be soon found again on the range. Not until a sheriff was enlisted, though reluctantly, to deputize the county's best-known hog thief to gather in the hogs were the foresters able to continue their research. The well-known thieving scoundrel got few piney woods rooters, thanks to a willing, though again reluctant, editor who headlined with "second-coming" type (the compositor's name for the large bold headline type reserved for the return of Christ) in the county weekly the appointment of the sheriff's deputy. The story revealed to the local farmers the nature of the new lawman's responsibilities. The "deputy," I suppose, got few; the farmers claimed their feral stock; and the silviculturists returned to their experiments.

Mid-Period Developments

National Forest Purchases

Industrial owners, in spite of the optimism of foresters convinced that their lands could grow merchantable trees again, were anxious to sell cut-over lands to the federal government for inclusion in new national forests. Occasionally virgin timberlands were available for purchase under the Clarke-McNary Law of 1924, an amendment to the Weeks Law of 1911. Purchase-unit boundaries were drawn with the lumbermen's intent in mind, acquisition supervisors negotiating with landowners over price.[35]

Owners sold to the federal government in the Great Depression years for various reasons. Some needed money to pay debts, including taxes and wages long overdue. They could not and did not want to pay taxes on cut-over land. Sellers also wanted money with which to begin anew in northern California. And, surprising as it may appear today, many were convinced that these devastated lands would never again grow merchantable trees in commercial forests. County governments were glad the lands were purchased by the federal government because the Forest Service required payment of back taxes before accepting the deed for the land. Bankers stood by to receive their share of the sale, often earning interest from a loan for the tax settlement, when the deal was closed.

As noted above, the lumbermen later regretted selling their lands to the federal government for national forests, but at the time they were unwilling to trust those who told them how well trees grew in the South. This regret was indicated by lobbying in the 1950s by at least one regional chamber of commerce. The organization, after persuasion by its wood industry membership, endeavored to encourage Congress to require the Forest Service to return these lands to their earlier owners. The legislation might have succeeded if the former proprietors had not insisted that the rejuvenated forests be returned for the same per-acre price the denuded lands had brought in the 1930s' transactions.

Enter the Papermakers

Many new pulp and paper mills sprang up at about the time of the entry of foresters into the region. Satisfactory fire control, better protection from timber thieves, pine plantation establishment, cheap labor, a rapidly increasing raw material supply, and some understanding of forestry practices encouraged industrial leaders to look southward. A second forest in the South, established without much of an assist from humans, appeared. An expanded industry would be needed to consume the new wood. While earlier mills in the region had made paper from hardwood trees, now the sulphate process could produce kraft paper for boxes and bags and bleached kraft for newsprint. These mills could effectively utilize the extensive second-growth pine forest emerging from the ground.

The industry credits Dr. Charles Herty, a paper chemist from Savannah, Georgia, with formulating a manufacturing process that extracted resin from the pulp. With it the shiny blobs one still occasionally sees on grocery sacks and newspaper sheets were largely eliminated. When the first southern pine mill utilizing Herty's process was built in Texas in 1939, orders to procurement foresters stated that "no wood could come into the mill that had five percent heart content."[36] Heartwood, the interior dead wood of the core of a tree, is resin soaked. Because the oleoresin in it gums up the vats, only small, round wood bolts—logs under twelve inches in diameter and thus relatively free of heartwood—were utilized. At first, even resinous heart knots were chopped with axes by hand out of pulpwood sticks because the paper makers could not disburse the resin in the knots before the milky mix spread out on the Henry and Sealy Fourdrinier brothers' paper-making machines.[37]

Herty, a southern native, was also an erstwhile publicist. Recognizing that two-thirds of the newsprint utilized in the United States came from Canada, he sought, by speech and print, to capture these markets for the South. Southern bleached kraft, made by the sulphate process from hard yellow pines, could be produced for one-third the cost of northern newsprint. Although northern U.S. and Canadian paper men resented his effort, many eventually participated financially in the venture. Risk-taking entrepreneurs, "soon to be bankrupt fools," became multimillionaires. But Herty didn't live to see the first of these mills roll out its first sheet.

Civilian Conservation Corps

Men of the Civilian Conservation Corps (CCC), dubbed "Roosevelt's Tree Army," in the Great Depression years between 1934 and 1942 planted thousands of barren acres across the South.[38] Foresters led the crews of enrollees—men eighteen to twenty-five years old—as they dibbled (planted) the bare-rooted stock. Each man carried his own trees, made the slit in the soil with a steel tool, closed the planting hole, and moved forward another six feet. Like a long line of infantrymen stalking an enemy, twenty-member crews and four leaders stretched across the open fields, each person planting eight hundred trees a day at six-by-eight-foot spacing. Years later, one could occasionally understand how the demanding quota was met: a dozen pine trees might emerge from a single stump hole. The dibble, the tool that expedited planting, had been designed by Red Bateman, forester for Louisiana's Great Southern Lumber Company.[39]

CCC enrollees, working from racially segregated camps, also installed telephone lines for both the national forests and state agencies. State agency wires usually ran along public roads, providing communications for fire suppression long before the federal government set up the rural phone system similar to the Rural Electrification Administration cooperatives. CCC men set up the fire towers, some rising 125 feet, erector-set style. They fought fires and deadened broad-leaved weed trees by girdling them with axes. The men, often called "boys," built foot trails and converted logging tram roads to truck roads. Such roads are readily discerned today: railroad spikes, commonly found following road grading, still puncture log truck tires. CCC enrollees laid in the wing ditches along the roads, using pans pulled by mules. They labored by contract on private industrial land as well as in the forests and parks of all levels of government—city, county, state, and federal.

Perhaps the most lasting witnesses to their efforts are the recreational areas in which they built picnic tables, bath houses, pavilions, and piers at old sawmill log ponds. Even where former owners had blasted log pond dams when milling operations ceased so that destructive downstream floods could not later occur from ruptured dikes, the CCC rebuilt the dams if the area was to become a recreational site. Again they used mules and pans to ease the back-breaking manual task.

The attack on Pearl Harbor brought an end to this organization, considered by many to have carried out the greatest conservation effort ever attempted. As of the day that "shall live in infamy," enrollees no longer worried about jobs. Many men of Roosevelt's Tree Army went directly into the armed forces as they left the camps following the declaration of war. The CCC regimentation experience would serve them well. Others hastened to jobs supporting the war effort. With the beginning of war and the end of the Great Depression, the nation's war effort superseded the Corps as an employer.

The Second World War Years

TEE-*pee*-WEE-*pee*, the pronunciation of the acronym for the Timber Production War Program, utilized foresters during the hostilities of the 1940s. As the mills seemed unable to obtain enough trees to operate full blast, the foresters' job was to persuade small landowners who held considerable volumes of timber to release their stumpage for the war effort. The War and Navy departments required vast volumes for barracks at home and abroad and for containers in which to ship military armaments. Ninety percent of the lumber and paper production of some mills went to the military during the Second World War years.

Wildfire, including sabotage incendiarism, was worrisome. Without the CCC to fight fire, volunteer forest fire fighters services were organized. Along the Atlantic coast, alert to fires believed to be set by Axis mariners, the War Forest Fire Cooperation Program took responsibility.

Foresters not in the armed services, usually those deferred by draft boards because they had children, kept the mills running to provide wood and paper for the government. Southern foresters were dispatched to West Texas's Pecos region, traversing the area by donkey and car to collect guayule seeds for secret rubber plant research in California. When rope hemp imports for the Navy were cut off, at least one forester was employed to determine how much hawser could be made from West Texas's abundant supply of yucca. "The most trying job was to make estimates of the fiber in the leaf and [to figure out] how to convert it to a usable unit." To encourage cork production for the war effort, the government distributed *gratis* throughout Texas cork oak acorns from Spain and California in ice cream cartons to anyone who would plant them. Many of the trees derived from these seeds are today probably called live oak.[40] Varieties of *Quercus virginiana* growing on an assortment of sites complicate identification.

Other foresters likely played a role in assisting farmers to gather bois d'arc wood. In 1942, U.S. Army clothing manufacturers ran low on olive drab dye, badly needed for uniforms. Texas's Red River County farmers were pressed into service to provide the wood (known to many as Osage-orange), while also adding to their income in that economically depressed place and time.[41]

While the battles were raging abroad, the U.S. military fenced in prisoners of war at scores of logging camps and recently abandoned CCC camps across the South. The POWs came in handy. One example may suffice. An ice storm in December 1943, followed by many days of rain and another more severe freeze in early February 1944 in East

Texas laid fifty million board feet and thirty-five thousand cords of pulpwood on the ground.[42] The ice storms that glazed over the thousands of
acres of pines and hardwoods broke out the tops of the trees. The weight
of the ice uprooted millions of others.

Because industry was short on labor, its leaders persuaded the
government to send in POWs to salvage the trees for pulpwood. Otherwise, they warned, the dead trees would be a serious fire hazard in the
spring transition period—after the ground dried but before foliage
emerged and the grass turned green. Five hundred POWs from Hitler's
Afrika Korps were assigned the salvage job. They did their tasks like
trained woodsmen, though they were from all walks of life. Without a
Doyle log scale to aid them in determining how many board feet were in
trees of a certain size, the German soldiers figured out for themselves the
expectation of the daily quota of logs to be salvaged. When each man had
cut five thousand board feet, they quit for the day. (Perhaps the Geneva
Convention failed to consider power saws when establishing maximum
logging quotas for captured troops.)

Government guards watched the wood cutters from the panzer
division while the wood-using industry provided transportation and super-
vision. When two-man power saws weighing a hundred pounds were introduced, the POWs taught their company-employed foremen how to use
the equipment, for the POWs were already familiar with the chain saw,
a German invention. The Texas Timber Salvage Program lasted about
eight months, wood deterioration making the downed timber unmerchantable after that time. One can still see, as I write, the deformed tops
of many trees in the area, monuments to this natural disaster.

Lumbermen had other troubles during the war. Black laborers
protested working conditions, making it impossible for the mills to meet
the War Department's demand for lumber. To overcome the situation,
the Army assigned wounded black soldiers, home from the Africa or
South Pacific campaigns, to communities in the Southeast. Their task
was to encourage loggers to work more industriously. The Army allotted
food for the southern families—often those of black preachers—that
would provide housing accommodations for the black soldiers. The urging
of the disabled soldiers dramatically improved the labor situation.

Government versus Industry

Ideological Inroads

The years of developing forestry professionalism in the South
witnessed struggles between the economic and political ideologies of

laissez-faire free enterprise and socialism. Young foresters were not keenly aware of the political antagonisms encountered by their elders over the government's proposals to regulate silvicultural practices on private forest lands. Foresters, regardless of political persuasion, took jobs where jobs were available, wherever trees grew, in order to grow trees for future generations of Americans.

So strong were the feelings, however, that one of the few forestry schools in the region adamantly discouraged its graduates from entering federal service. The agency of Pinchot was too socialistic for its alumni, as evidenced in the 1940s by U. S. Forest Service Chief Lyle Watts's advocating federal regulation of the harvests on private timberlands. When, in 1949, all junior foresters were called to the Atlanta office of the regional forester for orientation, some called it "indoctrination." At that time, one of the newcomers to the service inquired about whether all personnel were expected to promote federal regulation of private lands. A staff person responded in a kindly manner, "Yes, otherwise one would do well to find employment elsewhere." The push for regulation died with the appointment of the next chief, Richard McArdle, during the Eisenhower years.

When the Supreme Court of Maine considered state regulation constitutionally permissible, Austin Cary, the itinerant forester, said that it "might be thoroughly good law, but that it would not necessarily guarantee good forestry or promote increased wood production." Yale Professor H. H. Chapman added that regulation by a state or the federal government would work only if forestry became financially profitable. "The main trouble," he said, "with efforts to force owners to practice forestry against their will is that the public is in reality attempting to get something for nothing." He believed the government wanted cheap houses and paper at the expense of forest landowners.[43]

Even before the Second World War, industry endeavored to convince foresters of the alleged socialism of the Forest Service. An executive of the Southern Pine Association in 1941 admonished the forestry students at Duke University, all of whom were in graduate study, that "the forestry schools of the country are engaged in preparing young men for government jobs and socialistic objectives rather than in training them for the work and unlimited individualistic opportunities attainable in private forestry fields." He was correct in his reference to government jobs, but, I believe, grossly in error about socialistic objectives. Schools trained students for jobs, and essentially all professional forestry positions were in government.

In concluding his speech, the industrialist spoke of green gold in the South: "Although some zealots would attempt overnight to change our concepts of property and individual rights, the [wood-using] industry confesses to conservatism. We must see virtue in the profit motive as a potent means of promoting the public weal. To the extent that forestry graduates find profit in the pursuit of their profession, they can in proportion contribute to the profit of other citizens." For those with the "stamina and sturdy individualism of our forefathers," green gold awaited them in the southern forest. Whether in government or industry, the South was no place for a socialist to practice forestry in the mid- and latter-years of the time of the foresters' forest.[44]

Industry Organizing

The wood-using industry during this period believed it suffered its share of persistent annoyance from the government. To bring about peace, the pulp and paper industry created the American Pulpwood Association (APA) in the Great Depression years. One of the new organization's early efforts was to negotiate minimum wages for pulpwood producers. In the South, twenty cents was agreed upon, in contrast to twenty-five cents in the North and thirty-five cents on the West Coast. When an Alabama lumberman was sued by the National Industrial Recovery Administration (NIRA) over the wage and hour agreement, the district court's dismissal of the case played a role in the U.S. Supreme Court's judgment that the law that established NIRA was unconstitutional.

Pulpwood producers also got in trouble with the Internal Revenue Service when the companies they supplied were sued in a class action for collusion, a blow that hurt contractors—pulpwood cutters and those for whom they worked. APA came to the aid of its members, as it also did over troubles with labor unions.

The APA strived diligently in education, providing safety and volume-scaling training for woods workers and high school children likely to become pulpwood cutters. One instructor, the day before a scaling demonstration, prepared a one-cord pile to show how clever woodsmen could cheat an unwary contractor. When the students gathered, the instructor kicked a key bolt in the stack of wood, the whole pile then shaking and collapsing and losing a foot in height.

The industry group, pointing out that twenty-four thousand pulpwood trucks and eleven thousand wheel saws were working in the southern forest, tried to get major equipment manufacturers to accommodate their needs. Interest was scant. "Vac Sink" research, designed to separate bark from wood chips, and efforts in the South to chemically debark pulpwood sticks failed. APA was successful, however, in encouraging Congress to speed up the ten-year cycle survey of timber availability in the South, an effort for which the U.S. Forest Service received a $2.5 million appropriation.

Company funds enabled the prestigious Battelle Memorial Institute to investigate causes of pulpwood shortages in 1955 and 1959. Battelle said that men who work harder produce more; the sophisticated researchers called it "crew aggressiveness."[45]

While APA worked with the industrialist side of pulpwood production, the Southern Pulpwood Conservation Association (SPCA), organized in 1939, labored diligently to educate landowners about growing trees for the industry's use. The SPCA went out of business when it became obvious to company leaders that industry's pulpwood requirements were being met.

Labor and industrial leaders disagreed on regulations relating to work. Congress sided with the workers, reducing the number of employees a company could have without the necessity of complying with federal laws. Safety, taxes, and bookkeeping were involved. Industry responded by contracting much of its woods work, loaning laborers money with which to purchase trucks, chain saws, and other necessary equipment.

The Forest Farmers Association, organized in 1941 with responsibilities similar to those of SPCA, continues as a strong motivating force in the South. It serves as lobbyist for the small landowner, promoter of forest research, and as educator of the public.

Social and Cultural Changes

Enter Women

Not until the early 1970s did females enroll in the South's forestry schools and subsequently enter the professional ranks.[46] It remains unclear whether the transition related to federal legislation and court orders forbidding discrimination in employment, to the blooming conservation movement, or to the changing times regarding sex roles. Many believe that the young women matriculating in the schools were doing what their mothers would have done, had the times permitted when their parents went to college. In such a view, neither feminism nor governmental decrees, apart from how the changing times influenced them, had significance. The young women, like most foresters since Pinchot's era, entered this field of study for altruistic reasons: they were concerned about the care of renewable natural resources entrusted to the nation's citizens.

At least one school's faculty opposed their entry, insisting that administrators find ways to exclude them. Lectures would need to be re-cast, field trips would require accommodations for women, and summer camps—forestry courses in remote facilities—would have to be restruc-tured. Current students, always concerned about employment opportuni-ties, envisioned increasing competition for jobs, especially with affir-mative action that necessitated minority quotas in placement. And some did not appreciate women in their formerly all-male clubs.

Administrators had other concerns beyond redesigning camp facilities, for this was a time when plaintiffs threatened or filed discrimi-nation lawsuits with seemingly little provocation. School deans also wor-ried over the inevitable when boy meets girl, hoping married faculty would not become involved in illicit activities.

A three-week regional silviculture field trip I taught at the time suggests the problem administrators faced. One coed registered for the course, every night of which would be spent on the ground during a 3,000-mile sojourn in a thirty-passenger school bus. She was told that an-other female—her sister, friend, even her mother—would be required to go along, though not required to enroll in the course. Unable to locate another female willing to go, she sent her mother to plead with me, the dean of the forestry school. "Tell me," the mother asked, "Why must there be two girls?" "To protect the professor," was the reply. "Who is this professor you cannot trust?" she asked. "It is I," I said.

On the job, too, early women graduates faced unusual prob-lems. One Jane Doe, assigned to a very remote U.S. Forest Service com-pound where she lived in a small trailer house, knew all of the families of the men with whom she worked, and they knew her. The conviviality was such that she made the rounds of the other foresters' homes for eve-ning meals. Alas, the personnel officer in the regional forester's office thought this assignment unfair to a single young lady. In his "wisdom," she was moved to another district where foresters lived throughout the town in which the ranger station was located. Wives did not know Jane, unspoken animosities developed, and she resigned discouraged. In an-other case, a woman was transferred because a forester's wife objected to her husband working with the woman forester in the woods. The female forester's new assignment: visiting information specialist in a recreation area. She was angry. She went to forestry school, she said, in order to work in the woods.

While some women worked in the woods, employers often se-lected tasks for them for which management believed the women espe-cially well suited. Many operated the computers, "crunched numbers," worked on management plans, and carried out public relations tasks. State agencies often assigned women to urban forestry jobs.

Environmentalism

Late in the period, from the mid- to late 1970s, rather arbitrarily here designated as that of the forester, environmentalism moved to the fore. The reincarnated Thoreau, no longer confined to Walden Pond, became the movement's high priest. Rediscovered were the words of his fellow transcendentalist, Emerson, in lines from "Waldeinsamkeit":

> I do not count the hours I spend
>   In wandering by the sea;
> The forest is my loyal friend,
>   Like God, it useth me.
>
> . . . .
>
> Aloft in secret veins of air,
>   Blows the sweet breath of song,
> O, few to scale those uplands dare,
>   Though they to all belong![47]

Transcendentalism and pantheism returned with the environmentalists. The woods were to be again romanticized as Americans worshiped God in nature, or simply worshiped nature. The movement was strong in the South, though not among native southerners born before the Baby Boom generation. Well-educated sojourners from the North and West encouraged its development in the region.

Foresters got caught in the dichotomy of altruistic motivation that would both assure wood for homes and paper into the unmeasurable future and at the same time provide for wilderness preservation. Until now, foresters had been the "good guys" protecting the environment. Now, rather suddenly, they became cast as villainous utilitarians—whether in the employ of industry or government—interested only in getting all the wood possible from the land at the least cost. They were now the "timber beasts," concerned solely with board feet. Foresters in turn, from Pinchot's day, have accused their adversaries of espousing sentimental nonsense.

Wilderness enthusiasts saw in the last two lines of Emerson quoted above a dogma in an unwritten code of environmental ethics. The lands purchased by others and on which others pay taxes are for all to enjoy. The more radical among them lay down in front of herbicide-dispersing tankers, walked through a hunter's deer lease at dawn during deer season beating on cans, and sued the federal government to prevent the buyers of timber growing on national forest lands from harvesting their purchases.

They filed lawsuits in courts across the South to force the Forest Service to abandon clear-cutting practices, modeling their arguments after the successful (for them) suits in the West Virginia federal and appellate courts over clear-cutting on the Monongahela National Forest. One federal judge in the region ruled adamantly on the plaintiff's side, enjoining the Forest Service from allowing a harvest to continue even after Congress had passed legislation specifically permitting the practice. In this case the appellate court, sitting in New Orleans, reversed the decision.

The dichotomy of a forester's attitude toward nature—a thing of beauty and yet sought for its utility—continues. C. S. Lewis, the Cambridge don, phrased it as though he were a forester of the time when he wrote, "We do not look at trees as Dryads or as beautiful objects while we cut them into beams. The first man who did so may have felt the price keenly, and the bleeding trees . . . may be far off echoes of that primal sense of impiety."[48]

That "primal sense of impiety" for the destruction of the forest, even if utilized by people, is what René DuBose saw as the reason "for the emergence of a grass-roots movement . . . that will give form and strength to the latent public concern with environmental quality." The movement in the South would be powered by romantic emotion as much as by factual knowledge.[49]

That romantic emotion encouraged the U.S. Forest Service's study of potential wilderness areas on national forest lands. As almost all such woodlands in the South had been purchased in the 1930s as cut-over, burned-over, or plowed lands, the probability of any of these holdings being virgin, and therefore worthy of wilderness designation, was nil. Congress, to satisfy the demands of a vocal, but small, public required a second study of the federal lands to determine which tracts were roadless and in a nearly unimproved and unimpaired condition. The new Roadless Area Review and Evaluation (RARE II) resulted in significant acreage being recommended to Congress by the Administration for permanent set aside as units of the National Wilderness System. Many of these parcels were in southern national forests. Wilderness under the new legislation no longer need be those traditionally envisioned pristine landscapes. Cut-out-and-get-out tracts reforested with seedlings but five decades past suffice. Even as I write, environmentalist groups challenge the Forest Service in courts and in Congress to include additional tracts in the system. In 1990, wilderness in the southern national forests amounted to 747,500 acres, or 5.5 percent of the total ownership. Considerable additional wilderness is in the Department of the Interior's national parks and wildlife refuges.

Recreational Concern

For foresters, the problem of recreational set asides—parks, wildernesses, preserves—relates to the diminishing per capita land base for producing commercial timbers. As population doubles in half the time of the previous doubling, both for the United States and for the world, a greater number of people *want* more land reserved. But they will *need* more lumber, plywood, and paper. Whether such reservations are luxuries, foresters and other environmentalists may find debatable; but no one argues about whether wood for homes and paper for communication are necessities. The wants and the needs are for the same people. It is not a case of preservationists *versus* forest-product manufacturers: the preservationist wants a panelled den and the wood-using industrialist likes to visit tall timber for pleasure and inspiration. Rather, it is a case of only so much land for both business and pleasure for the same person.

The National Park Service was established in 1916 both to provide "public pleasuring grounds" and to preserve unimpaired areas of natural and significant uniqueness judged from a geological, biological, archaeological, or historical viewpoint. The intended meaning of a "public pleasuring ground" (the wording of the bill to establish Yellowstone, the first national park) remains ambiguous; but Yellowstone, Grand Canyon, Crater Lake, Mt. Rainier, and Sequoia national parks provide some idea of the desirability to preserve such unique natural phenomena by this classification within the Department of the Interior. However, scenery, no matter how spectacular, may not be "unique," if unique means "one of a kind"; nonetheless, it may be deemed worthy of being set aside. One example to illustrate the varying viewpoint, the South's Big Thicket, may suffice.

The Big Thicket

The Big Thicket was a choice piece of real estate to a number of lumber and pulp and paper companies in Texas. It is not easily pinpointed on a map. Some early settlers called everything for a hundred miles west of the Sabine River that was not in open parklike longleaf pine the Big Thicket.

Early settlers found pure pine stands where Indian and natural fires excluded hardwoods. They also found pine and hardwood stands where fire had once cleared the land to expose mineral soil for pine seed germination, but where, after the pines were established, fires did not burn and the shade-tolerant broad-leaved trees invaded. A third principal

Loblolly and shortleaf pines. This woodland suggests the species may grow well in two- or even many-aged stands. But unless they are released from the shade of the overtopping canopy, most of these three-year-old seedlings will die in another year or two.

kind of forest was composed of hardwood climax cover types—oaks and hickories or beech-birch-maple. The climax cover types would be the kinds of forests that would occur thoughout most of the South if people and fire were kept out of the woods. But the forests making up the Big Thicket were subsequently cut, the pine and pine-hardwood types for lumber and the pure hardwoods for lumber and garden spots. Under the deciduous trees, settlers found mellow soil rich in organic matter and with crumblike particles especially desirable for holding water and nutrients. These crumbs, perhaps the size of garden peas, were glued together by the fecal casts of earthworms.

All of these forests—except those along streams—began as

pine stands, were subsequently infiltrated with hardwoods, and in time, with humanity and fire excluded, became mixed-hardwood types. Most of the area had been harvested at least twice by the time of the concern for the set aside. Trees forty years old were frequently twenty-five inches in diameter. It is said that rattlesnakes grow so old in the Big Thicket that they grow whiskers.

Here were the pros and cons expressed by environmentalists, foresters, and wood-using industrialists for converting Big Thicket private lands to a preserve:

PROS	CONS
Near population center (Houston) to serve as a "public pleasuring ground"	Land needed for commercial wood-using industries
New tourist industry with resultant economic incentive	Necessary to displace many residents
Desirable to preserve Big Thicket vegetation and animal life	Samples of typical Big Thicket vegetation not likely to be entirely liquidated
Unique natural phenomenon (subjective opinion)	Not a unique natural phenomenon (subjective opinion)
Parts of Shenandoah, Great Smoky Mountain, Grand Teton, and Big Bend national parks are not in natural unimpaired condition.	Not in natural unimpaired condition
	Recreational use would require eliminating dense understory by bulldozers, fire, etc.

The alternative considered by Congress was the "string of pearls" concept, whereby several small units would be established in which the natural vegetation would be unimpaired. Further, the State Forest Service, an agency independent of both the State Parks and Wildlife Department and the industrial holders of timber rights would manage the land. Holders of timber rights (not unlike holders of mineral rights), would have first option on harvested materials.[50] Finally, Congress set aside ten units, many joined by streams, as the Big Thicket National Preserve, the first such unit under the jurisdiction of the National Park Service to be so designated. The preserve's promoters call it "a string of emeralds."

Multiple Uses

The Multiple Use Act of 1960 required the U.S. Forest Service to give equal attention to water, range, wildlife, recreation, and wood. While the act was intended to be the rule for all national forests, southern units continued to emphasize the production of wood. Foresters in the mountains of the Southern Appalachians, the Ozarks, and the Ouachitas exercised some concern for water in silvicultural operations applied there, but grass and forbs for livestock and playgrounds for people did not evoke much enthusiasm among the federal foresters in the region.

Foresters who had migrated to the South or had participated in much outdoor recreation in the North and West had difficulty understanding why anyone would want to fight the red bugs, ticks, briars, and snakes in these forests unless they got paid for it. To them, hiking and camping in the Coastal Plain and Piedmont would not be a fun vacation. That attitude prevailed until construction of the dams for the many lakes provided water recreation which, in turn, created lakeside recreation areas.

This chapter opened with a discussion of the integration of watershed and timber management, two of the five legislated uses for national forests. Some forestlands are leased to municipalities for water storage. On national forests and private lands, ranchers lease tracts on which to graze cattle, fencing the allocated parcels. Income from the federal Land and Water Conservation Trust Fund, created in 1964, is spent improving campgrounds built by the CCC and developing new ones, but wildlife habitat improvement is, next to timber, the most remarkable change for the period. While the federal Multiple Use Act is applicable to national forest lands, many industrial managers in the South adopted the multiple-use theme for the care of the several resources for which they were accountable.

Concern for Wildlife

Improving Wildlife Resources

Forests are prime habitat for many kinds of game animals and songbirds. Encouraging population increases for many species became a proper and profitable intention for the land manager. The pine and hardwood forests of the South were made into good breeding and feeding grounds for a variety of wildlife, bringing pleasure to sport hunter and bird-watcher alike. Of primary interest for the hunter were white-tailed deer, bobwhite quail, gray squirrels, and American woodcocks.

Fox hunting, always a popular sport in the South, required new techniques as the numbers of the cunning little carnivores diminished. Now fox hunters, mounted upon galloping horses, pursued hounds that followed a scented trail. Early in the period, in the 1930s, a Negro lad, mounted on a mule, dragged a fox pelt through the woods. The hunt was successful if the skin was faithfully followed to its destination.

White-tailed Deer

Midway through the foresters' tenure, say the late 1940s, foresters could work daily in the woods for a couple of years without seeing deer tracks or any sign of the game animal. It is different now.

As deer returned to the pine-hardwood forests of the South because of better law enforcement and diminished numbers of predators, the percentage of big game animals with trophy racks appeared to decrease at a frightening rate. Genetics and lack of adequate protein in the diet were responsible. To counteract the nutritional deficiency, foresters put protein in strategically located feeders. Trophy bucks would come to the feeders, seeking out high-protein supplemental feed. Hunters prize bucks with many-forked antlers arranged symmetrically. Because the tendency for spiking is inherited, small animals with these prongs are often culled from the herd. Removing them enhances the proportion of older deer with forked antlers for potential harvest in another year. Currently, most industry land and much land held by small private owners in the South are leased for hunting rights.

Bobwhite Quail

Earlier times saw the cutting of forests for agricultural pursuits as well as for lumber. The openings made by cropping and "high-grading" harvests, when loggers did not think about future stands of timber, resulted in a patchwork quilt of logged sites, burned areas, grazed lands, and plowed fields. This variety of cover made possible an abundance of upland game animals, among them the bobwhite quail.

In the 1930s a team of forest game managers in the Southeast began recommending fire for improving the habitat for, and therefore the numbers of, bobwhite quail in the pineries of the Coastal Plain. While their early work showed the need for prescribed burning in the longleaf pine forests, later studies subsequently alerted managers to the usefulness of this forestry tool in other timber types. Fire is a lot cheaper than plowing the soil for game-food plots, planting cereal grains and woody cover in these openings in the woods, and then fertilizing the cultivated cover crop. Game-food plantings, however, often supplement the diet made available by appropriate burning.

Foresters also came in conflict with Audubon clubs over the use of insecticides to control the notorious imported fire ant. Especially destructive is the ant upon bobwhite quail, infesting the nests at hatching time. Even so, the use of chemicals for the insect's control meets with opposition. Equally serious is the killing of bobwhite quail by Cooper's and sharp-shinned hawks durng the predators' northward migrations in the spring. Ironically, the necessary woods burning exposes the game birds to the hawks.[51]

American Woodcock

A bird not often sought by hunters in these parts is the American woodcock. As its habits become better known, one anticipates greater use of the southern forests for the excitement of the hunt for this elusive quarry. Woodcocks winter in dense brush cover, called a "picket fence" by those whose trousers are shredded in the attempt to locate this favorite of the sportsman's dinner table. But under the brush must be an opening for a foot or so above the soil. The brush obscures the woodcock from overhead predators while the cleared ground enables its escape from surface enemies.

Forest game managers are able to create favorable habitat for this bird with carefully prescribed fire and by coupling controlled grazing of cattle with fire. To retain the flocks in pine plantations after crowns close, they periodically thin the stands of trees. The hardwood sprouts that arise after thinning compete with the conifers for soil moisture and nutrients, but these broad-leaved trees become the picket fence, the vertical vegetation, so important for habitat for the bird.

Red-cockaded Woodpecker, An Endangered Bird

The red-cockaded woodpecker began to be missed in the southern pineries as fire prevention encouraged dense growth of understory brush and vines. Its appearance on the U.S. Fish and Wildlife Service's endangered species list eventually was also attributed to the silvicultural practices of foresters. In thinning stands to enhance the vigor of residual trees, the forester's priority was to remove trees with disease. Thus, stems with red heartrot, caused by the fungus *Fomes pini*, were sent

Red-cockaded woodpecker at its nest-site tree. Birds may work for more than four years to excavate a cavity, usually in a tree infected with the fungus causing red heartrot. The cavity will be used by subsequent generations until wind topples the tree. Storms often break the trees where they are weakened at nest height. (Courtesy Dr. Richard Conner, U.S. Forest Service.)

to the mills. So thorough was the sanitation harvest that, by the 1970s, the shelf conks of the fungus and the ellipsoid scars on the boles of the trees were gone from the woods. So too were the woodpeckers. Few foresters knew that the birds, nesting in colonies, make their houses in hollowed-out boles of living pines. Red heartrot creates the soft tissue so readily carved away for the nest. This is the only woodpecker in North America to make its nest in a living tree, though some closely related flickers may do so.

In this case, good forestry adversely affected wildlife management. Once the problem was discovered, foresters began to retain diseased trees for nests, even though their retention would result in losses of valuable wood.

To accommodate the bird, foresters also prescribe fires in order to reduce the density of the woody vegetation hugging the ground, thereby improving colony sites. Resinous sap from the wounds created by the bird, however, coats the bark of nest trees. If the sap is ignited by a forest fire, flames climb the tree, burn its crown, and destroy the nest.

Potential activity sites can easily be destroyed. Consequently burning must be carefully prescribed and loose pine straw and dead leaves raked from around the bases of nest trees with visible resin flow for a distance of about ten feet. For colony sites—where several pairs of the little woodpeckers may be found—foresters safeguard the trees by plowing a fire lane around the area. Glistening, whitish patches twenty to sixty feet above the ground and clearly visible two hundred yards away indicate the nesting holes.

Ivory-billed Woodpecker

In the 1960s, foresters began to emphatically recognize their responsibility for the care of rare and endangered species. Sometimes now the type of forest harvest is determined by the present threat to animals and plants. However, no silvicultural procedure would have saved the ivory-billed woodpecker, for its habitat, some believe, required for each family at least five hundred acres of undisturbed virgin forest of mixed southern pine, baldcypress, and hardwood trees. The almost total harvest of the southern forest eliminated the bird's habitat. Ornithologists consider its present range limited to the high mountains of Cuba.[52]

Appearing like the ivory-bill is the pileated woodpecker, a smaller edition of the ivory-bill and sometimes mistaken for it. The pileated (pronounced *PIE-lee-ATE-ed*) is a regular inhabitant of the forests of the southern Coastal Plain. Unlike the pileated, ivory-bills working on pine trees would be readily identifiable because they strip the bark in their search for adult beetles and insect larvae.⁵³ The eighteen-inch bird with the crested pileus is neither endangered nor threatened.

Bee Trees

In these forests, folks have long sought bee trees for free and tasty honey. An early-day industrial forester tells about running a compass line in a river bottom, hearing a crosscut saw on company land, and discovering an old man and a boy cutting down a tree. It was a family affair, for the mother of the boy and other kin watched nearby: "Finally the old man saw me. He stood there. I came up and passed the time of day with him, introduced myself. I didn't say anything about cutting the tree. It was an old stupid [crooked] post oak. Finally the old man stood as much as he could take and he said, 'What are you going to do about it? It ain't hit the ground yet.' I told him to go ahead and cut the tree."⁵⁴ The bee tree robber knew his local law: in those parts, trees were not considered stolen until they were severed from the stump.

Bee seekers "course" the bees to locate their hives. They then mark the trees, returning at night to cut them and to smoke the bees out to get at the honey. No better woodsman is there than the fellow who can return to his personal mark a mile or more from a trail with only the aid of a torch. Occasional wildfires have been attributed to the endeavor; so too some bad stings.

Timber Scarcity and Timber Abundance

Incentives to Practice Forestry

Motivating owners of small forest tracts has been a concern to American foresters and the wood-using industry since the beginning of the conservation movement. In the South, as in other tree-growing regions, nonindustrial timberland owners have rarely invested in forest conservation measures. As a result, their woodlands grow only half as much volume per acre as industrial forests. Since farmers and other nonindustry owners control over half the nation's woodland, production on these lands must increase if the nation is to meet anticipated timber needs a generation hence.

Timber famine has been a scare cry for a century. As recounted above, in 1873 Congress would grant 160 acres of public domain, provided the recipient of the farmland grant would plant forty acres with trees. Though unsuccessful because much of the land was not originally forested, the species of trees were not specified, and nurseries to produce seedlings were lacking, Americans were alerted. They began to grasp conservation, as defined by leaders of the day, as "the wise use of resources."

As the nation grew, so did the consumption of wood products. Again, in the 1930s, when a Senate report documented serious timber shortages, greater efforts to manage our forests followed. Some money was earmarked to encourage forestry on private lands.

In both periods, the idea of stimulating farmers to grow trees was apparent. Beginning in the 1930s, too, the Forest Service, the Soil Conservation Service, and the Agricultural Extension Service established demonstration farm forests to show owners of small tracts that forests could be profitable. At that time, few landowners considered the economic benefits attractive, nor are they likely to today without financial incentives.

Organizational lobbying took over in the 1940s to endeavor to do what laissez-faire economics seemed unable to do. Incentives to manage the South's forests have always involved industrial sponsorship. The thrust principally involves capital gains taxation. Industrialists lobbied for such tax breaks to encourage small, private landowners to grow trees that the industries, in time, would buy and utilize. So industries, not the landowners of small acreages, provided the financial support for the many groups that educated the members of Congress, the press, the taxpayers, and the small landowners. The lobbying paid off in congressional allocations for certain silvicultural practices on the parcels held by nonindustrial landowners.

To qualify for federal assistance, owners had to own fewer than five hundred acres of forest. But too few applied for the funds available. Congress subsequently redefined *small* as fewer than one thousand acres. Parcels as small as an acre were eligible for government aid. Typical allocations, handled jointly by state forestry agencies and the Agricultural Conservation and Stabilization Service provided up to $2,500 to a single owner. This was a reimbursement for 75 percent of the costs of several silvicultural practices. Federal allocations of the Forestry Incentives Program (FIP) were sometimes supplemented by state appropriations or by the wood-using corporations. Money available, depending on practices and management prescriptions, ranged from $20 to $130 per acre.

FIP practices included site preparation prior to planting, tree planting, and conversion of forests of low-grade weed species (such as scrub oaks) to high-quality stands (such as the southern pines). Direct seeding on clear-cut or burned-over land and the use of chemical injectors to reduce the number of undesirable stems in mixed conifer-hardwood forests were other appropriate practices. Prescribed burning for certain purposes was also authorized.

Even with the many incentives for the nonindustrial private forest landowners to manage their woodlands, success has always seemed beyond reach. By the end of the period here referred to as the foresters' forest, the 41 percent of the South's 188 million acres of timberland owned by nonindustrialists and nonfarmers and the 30 percent owned by farmers remained poorly managed. National forests, making up 6 percent, and other public ownership's 4 percent remained behind industry's 19 percent in a sustained effort to produce fiber from these lands.

Growth Divided by Drain

Foresters had a lot of help in the heyday of their efforts to *grow* trees, not just to *protect* them. *Life* magazine[55] in the late 1940s devoted a full-page editorial to "the vanishing forest," regretting the passing of Eden. While calling for more landowner education, expansion of the national forests, and better "custodial care," the magazine also informed its readers about the growth : drain ratio (G/D), how much wood is grown in contrast to how much is harvested and lost to fire, insects, disease, and allocated to purposes other than fiber production.

G/D remained constant through the times of the explorers and the pioneers. At the time the migrating lumberman moved southward, G/D for the region hovered around one. Fire, insects, and disease removed about as much wood each year from the virgin forest as was added to the trees by incremental growth. Growth rings still visible in the remnant stumps typically show fifty or more rings to the inch of radius, suggesting that growing stock was annually adding wood at about one-half percent simple interest.

Arrival of the industrialists changed that: the ratio probably dropped to 1/100 or less as loggers felled the large, old trees and skinners and tram engineers moved them to the mills. For every board foot of increment, one hundred board feet were sawn into lumber or pulped into paper. By the mid-1930s, when the industrialists, about on their predicted schedule, concluded the cut-out-and-get-out task, G/D was again close to 1: but this time the ratio occurred because there was neither growth nor harvest. Fires prevented establishment of new seedlings, and few trees remained from the virgin stands on which to add girth and height. Again, G/D began to change, this time with the arrival of the foresters. Congress gave them a boost.

Clarke-McNary Act funds, enabled by the 1924 legislation

but infrequently provided by Congress to control fire and to assist land owners, were now released. These funds enhanced the opportunities for trees to grow and thereby improved the G/D ratio. Increased budgets for silvicultural practices and fire control on the national forests that had been established in every state of the region also encouraged the employment of foresters to manage the timberlands.

Operators of paper mills, for a century and a half located mostly in the Northeast, and plywood manufacturing plants, located in the Northwest, finally discovered the South. These owners bought up cut-over and burned-over lands from the migrating lumbermen and their heirs and hired foresters to protect corporate interests. That, too, improved the G/D ratio.

President Eisenhower's Soil Bank Program, funded by the government, provided an incentive. Farmers could now be paid ten dollars an acre to plant trees on land not needed for crop production. The federal treasury then allotted eight dollars an acre per year for ten years if the farmers retained the trees on the land. Pine plantations sprang up across the South. Many worried that, when the ten-year obligation was over, the trees would be cut and the land returned to food and other fiber crops. Few such acres reverted. Later, when soybean prices soared, landowners did cut the pines to grow the valuable legume.

So effective were these and other collective interests that by the mid-1950s, G/D for the region exceeded 2; in some zones, where mills no longer existed to efficiently utilize the new stands of second-growth timber, G/D exceeded 3. By the late 1970s, new and large paper and plywood mills so stimulated harvests that G/D dropped again to about 1.

A ratio of 1 when forests are intensively managed provides for a sustained yield of wood. The figure alone can be misleading, for the same ratio prevails where there is no growth and no harvest, the case for both a virgin forest and a wholly devastated woodland.

New Developments

Advances in Mensuration

Foresters early recognized the need for mensurational techniques by which they could ascertain the quality of a site for growing trees. Curves by which field workers could determine site index (SI), the average height of the dominant and codominant trees in a stand at fifty years of age, were devised for many commercial species. While not included as part of the definition, SI curves, in their derivation, were assumed to be for even-aged natural stands, pure stands of a single species, and unmanaged stands. Introduction of plantations required new curves, usually based upon the total height of *all* the trees in a plantation at twenty or twenty-five years of age. *Site quality* is the term this most often defines. Southern tree plantations are typically of one age, of a single species, and managed.

Basal area, the cross-section in square feet at breast height (4.5 feet above the ground) of all of the trees on an acre, became the measure of stand density. Much more useful than the number of trees or the volume in board feet or cubic feet per acre, basal area per acre provided the forester with a guide for thinning stands of trees. Foresters would then repeatedly allow a stand to grow, say, to 120 square feet per acre and then thin it back to 80.

Tree measurement scales for standing trees were adopted from log scales, like those called Scribner and Doyle. Mensurationists tabulated the tree scales according to *form class* (FC), a term relating to taper. A tree with a diameter at breast height of fourteen inches and an inside bark diameter at seventeen feet (the top of the first log) of eleven inches has a ratio of 11/14, which equals 0.79, or FC 79. Trees with little taper have FCs in the mid-80s; those with much taper are in the 60s. The volume of wood in a tree, the value of its stumpage, and the quality of a tree depend upon this statistic.

Foresters in time learned to determine these kinds of data from low-level aerial photographs. Subsequently, much such information could be gleaned from high-altitude or Landsat pictures obtained from the National Aeronautics and Space Administration. Infrared photographs became especially useful, temperature differences between living, sickly, and dead trees showing on the film. Appropriate salvage or silvicultural procedures could then be determined.

Advances in Silviculture

Developments in silviculture during the heyday years of the forester in the South included seedling production improvement, tree quality enhancement, and advances—and necessary retreats—in chemical pest control. Fertilization, regeneration, and tree growth stimulation were major objectives.

Seedling production in nurseries had to be improved for the foresters to carry out the mandate to replenish the land with trees. Among the problems to be solved was getting seeds to germinate after they were released from their cones or fruit in drying sheds. Birds provided a clue. Beneath fences and utility lines, redcedar trees, for example, erupt from the soil in neatly arranged lines soon after jays and other seed eaters consume and drop the seeds. The bird's craw scratches the seed coats as the berrylike cones are ingested, and stomach acids soften the hard outer layer so that, upon passing to the soil, the seeds readily germinate. Small concrete mixers, the interiors lined with sand paper, served like a craw as the seeds were tumbled within them; and brief immersion in dilute hydrochloric acid imitated the low pH juices of a bird's stomach. Seeds of some species, observers noted, had to overwinter in soil before they could germinate. To simulate germination at the nursery, seeds were stored in refrigerated sheds for long periods between layers of sphagnum moss or sand. The "stratification" effectively substituted for nature's technique. Now, nurserymen refer to any seed treatment as stratification.

To enhance the growth of trees, southern foresters developed fertilizer regimens, finding that certain sites responded favorably to nitrogen and phosphorus amendments. Remedies for insect infestation and disease infection had to be accomplished, both in the forest and at the nursery. In the nurseries, nematocides controlled the noxious nematode when nursery beds covered with sheets of plastic were chemically fumigated.

Of major importance for the period was tree improvement, the utilization of relatively crude techniques for enhancing the genetic characteristics of seedlings coming from the nurseries. Tree improvement reversed the effect of earlier high-grading of the woods, when the biggest and best of the trees were harvested, leaving the inferior to perpetuate the forest. After loggers made several such excursions into the woods, only inferior trees remained to produce seed for the future forest.

Now, foresters sought the biggest and best trees, those with good form, rapid growth, small branches (which produce small knots), horizontal branches (ones at acute angles produce larger knots), nonpersistent branches, and drought hardiness. They also sought trees that evidenced frequent and abundant seed production (cones on the ground under a tree hint at this) and those that showed evidence of being relatively resistant to insect and disease damage. Foresters also looked for stems with superior wood quality, those trees with minimal juvenile wood (produced when trees are young), greater strength, and superior gum production for naval stores. Paper makers wanted trees with optimal fibril angles, the degree of which relates to the quality of pulp for paper, for these traits, too, pass from one generation to another by inheritance. (*Fibrils* are the microscopic material making up cell walls.) Seeds from these superior trees were collected and the progeny arising from them measured for such characteristics. Foresters then set aside the best stands of trees as seed-production areas and established seed orchards of hybridized and control-pollinated stock: pollen from the strobili (flower) of one high-quality tree was injected with a syringe into a plastic bag covering the female strobili of another especially desirable tree. Nurseries across the South in time produced seedlings from the seeds arising from these crosses and labelled them as superior.

Reforestation techniques went from hand planting in cut-over areas to tractor-drawn machines on land that had first been cleared of its brush and windrowed with bulldozers and other heavy equipment. Often the planting sites are burned before the planter's rider drops the seedlings into slits in the soil made by the machine. Wheels attached to the rear of the planter pack the soil around the little trees.

During this period, foresters introduced chemicals to control weed trees that sap the soil of its water and nutrients and which, over-topping smaller, more valuable trees, exclude light. Ammate, the trade name for ammonium sulfamate, was perhaps the first employed. The yellowish salt was simply placed in "cups" cut with axes into the bases of undesirable deciduous trees. Moisture in the atmosphere dissolved the saline material. Some people expressed concern about wildlife consuming the salt, but in the days of its introduction, there was little concern for wildlife. Few deer were in the woods, and no evidence of toxicity to animals had been presented. By the late 1940s, 2,4 dichlorophenoxyacetic acid (2,4-D), a compound synthesized by industrial chemists working with Army Chemical Warfare scientists during the Second World War, was readily and inexpensively available. The synthetic hormone, modelled after the natural plant-producing auxins that had been discovered in the 1930s, effectively killed many species of brush without injuring grasses and conifers. By causing cells to expand rapidly and burst, the herbicide literally caused the tree to grow itself to death. (Ironically, the Army's interest in the wartime research was for a chemical that could be sprayed on rice paddies in Japan to starve the Nipponese into surrender, not as a weed killer. But rice is a grass; 2,4-D killed the broad-leaved weeds in the fields without injuring the grain. Only for later military expeditions did it occur to the Army to use herbicides as defoliators of clumps of trees where snipers might otherwise escape the surveillance of aerial observers.)

Next came an improvement over 2,4-D. The herbicide 2,4,5-trichlorophenoxyacetic acid (2,4,5-T) was more effective on more species. This is the chemical, code-named Agent Orange during the Vietnam conflict, which, because of the allegations concerning its toxicity, was withdrawn from the market.[56] Numerous other herbicides (early called "silvicides" and "dendrocides" by foresters) have taken its place.

With regret, foresters recognize that their zeal to release the pines in order to enhance production of wood for construction and paper

Pond pine, a serotinous tree, in a pocosin—a swamp-on-a-hill—in the Carolina coastal area. The focal tree is of unusually good form for this species. Compare with trees in the next two photographs. (Courtesy of U.S. Forest Service.)

Typical pond pine in dry land. (Courtesy North Carolina Forest Service.)

may not have been the wisest practice. The deadened trees later would have been useful for railroad cross ties and pallet lumber. Their fruit would have also fed some wildlife.

During the period of the foresters' forest, foresters sometimes drained wetlands. Usually this draining preceded converting land from bearing low-value species to bearing those of higher use. The pocosins—swamps-on-a-hill—in the Carolina coastal area lent themselves to this

Pond pine site logged, burned, drained, and planted to slash pine (*left side of road*) and loblolly pine (*right side*). Foresters now must deal with the loss of wetlands by such conversion intended to enhance wood production. (Courtesy North Carolina Forest Service.)

conversion. Scrubby, short-boled pond pine, if the water tables were lowered, could be replaced by loblolly pine. At the other extreme, some diking was done, mainly in experimental trials, to encourage tree growth on dry sites and to preserve wetlands.

As the period closed, integrated pest management attracted attention. With so much of the poorly managed southern pine forest being devastated by the southern pine beetle and the more effective insecticides (like DDT) no longer available for insect control, foresters began to depend upon combinations of methods for reducing populations of such destructive nuisances. Other predator insects and microbes, along with woodpeckers, take their toll on various detrimental insects.

Proper silvicultural procedures, especially those involving thinning of timber, were known to be ecologically effective for reducing insect infestations but were economically inappropriate. Thinning enhances the vigor of the residual stems, thereby curtailing food for beetles that attack physiologically weakened trees. While thinning may have been the best remedy for costly predicaments involving several tree-killing insects, leadership seemed unwilling to promote the procedure over a single end-of-the-rotation harvest. Periodically returning to the same tract with laborers and machinery raises the cost of the harvest. That, in turn, reduces the value of the landowner's stumpage.

The next generation's forest, the subject for the following chapter, will hint at ozone and acid-rain problems in the southern forest. We know only that we have a potentially serious phenomenon with which to contend.

The advances noted above are but a few developed during this period of exploitation and amelioration of the forests of the South. The two U.S. Department of Agriculture Forest Service experiment stations in the region expanded their interests. Branch offices and experimental forests were established, led by station directors and their staffs at Asheville, North Carolina, and New Orleans, Louisiana. In addition to studies already noted in these pages, scientists engaged in research involving wood physics, wood chemistry, tree diseases, wood-destroying fungi and insects, timber-production economics, managerial techniques, tree physiology, hydrology, and soils. Station scientists often teamed with academicians, corporation researchers, and private institutes to solve problems encountered in the region.

Energy Forests

A few foresters in 1973 saw the "energy crunch," brought about by the oil embargo of the Organization of Petroleum Exporting

Countries, as an opportunity to use the vast land resource of the South for growing energy forests. These stands of timber were to be primarily managed for the production of fuel wood. Foresters recalled that wood was the principal source of energy fuel in the United States until 1875, when coal took the lead. Wood remained more important than hydropower until 1945. Energy specialists, too, in their quest for "new" sources of fuel to convert to readily transmissible electrical energy considered the forest. The forest as a living solar receptor is abundantly able to take the sun's rays—the only source of all of earth's energy—and, through the photosynthetic process, produce wood.

Just as the development of petroleum, lignite, coal, and peat depended on photosynthesis, with the green chlorophyll of living plants acting as the chemical catalyst, so does the development of trees today. During the carboniferous era, dead and decaying plant life was suddenly buried, excluding the oxygen of the atmosphere. Decomposition of the vegetable matter, requiring oxygen, did not occur. Instead of oxidation and the returning of the organic matter to the atmosphere as carbon, oxygen, and hydrogen elements, chemical reduction took place. In the reduced state, the organic matter's three organic elements that make up carbohydrate were bound together and locked up in the molecule. The miner and the well-driller now extract this as coal, oil, and gas from deep within the earth.

Unlike nonrenewable fossil fuels, energy forests are renewable. Carefully managed, an acre in the South may produce as much potential energy each year as three tons of lignite. Chemists can convert wood by hydrogenation into methanol, an alcohol, or into methane gas. Both of these destructive distillation products could be sent through fossil fuel pipelines.[57]

In using wood as a substitute for natural gas, engineers resort to anaerobic biologic digestion, substituting chemical catalysts for the anaerobes. (That trees contain readily available gas is easily demonstrated; for example, the jet of gas that squirts under pressure from a cut in a post oak bole can be ignited.)

Noncommercial scrub hardwood forests, as in Texas's and Oklahoma's post oak belt and cross timbers regions along with commercial pine-hardwood sites, could be designated energy forests. While lands covered with scrub broad-leaved species have relatively low rates of biomass production, their conversion to energy forest is perhaps the highest use to which they can be put. Foresters could then intensify management so that forty-year rotations—from seedling to final harvest—would be appropriate. For such stands, replanting is not necessary. New trees arise from sprouts, because the well-developed root systems of the severed stems, rich in starch and sugar, encourage rapid growth.

Silage plantations are another idea. Here, close spacing (five thousand stems per acre) of species like sycamore, cottonwood, and river birch allows prompt and maximum site utilization and harvesting at perhaps five-year intervals when the trees are less than twenty-five feet tall. With silage plantations, whole trees, including branches and leaves, are removed from the land and transported to conversion plants. This leads to a loss of soil fertility, because most of the nutrients removed from the land by forest trees are in the foliage, providing "food" for the photosynthetic process. Hence, the ash from the conversion process—and possibly commercial fertilizers—should be returned to the sites from which these fast-growing trees are cut.

Economists say that "the worth of a thing is the price it will bring." If natural gas costs one dollar per one thousand cubic feet, electricity producers could pay almost eighteen dollars for a ton of oven-dry wood. The Forest Service produced a fuel-value calculator, in the form of a circular slide rule, to enable owners and managers of southern forests to determine the usefulness of wood as a substitute for nonrenewable energy sources. Petroleum abundance in the mid-1980s negated its usefulness for both the forester and the firewood consumer of the forest.

Postscript to the Era

Toward the end of the period chronicled here as the foresters' forest—about 1975—old-timers bemoaned the transitions then occurring—the loss of the crusading spirit of Carl Schenck and Gifford Pinchot and the passing of the gung-ho attitudes that encouraged people to plant trees, manage timber, and curtail fires. One put it this way in an oral history:

> "During the fire season, foresters worked seven days a week. There was no let up. We weren't concerned about it. It was a job to do. If we had a Society [of American Foresters] meeting, everybody went to it. We shared our resources. We may have had to sleep two in a bed or four on the floor; or we may have had to eat crackers and cheese, but everybody went. Throughout the Gulf states, we knew every forester personally . . . in that era when for many acres it was appropriate to cut-out-and-get-out. We thought we were going to set the world on fire. We set our dreams high. And we did pretty well with our dreams." [58]

There is another story. While the account that follows relates to only one place in the region, the description, some will insist, applies across the South:

> Most [foresters and their kind] . . . will wax eloquent on how much
> they love the land, but for a century they have done little but abuse
> it. Millions of acres . . . have been leached out and cut over, first
> by cotton plantations, then by the timber companies, and always
> by the poor, who scratch it to survive. The land has been attacked
> with vengeance, either for one's own immediate subsistence or for
> someone else's profit. There is a love for the country . . . the love
> of hunting on it, of running dogs over it, of treeing coons, of cane-
> pole fishing, of its variety of plants and animals—but that love
> fades quickly when it comes to cutting down the forests for timber
> or flooding them with huge lakes to raise the price of land. Love, it
> seems, does not go so far as practicality.[59]

What now of the future?

CHAPTER 6

The Next Generation's Forest

HE DECADE that closes out the twentieth century and the decades that open the twenty-first are bound, I believe, to exhibit dramatic changes in the forests of the South. Confrontation among ideologies on the use of the woodlands, how best to manage them and the economic incentives for management, may hinder optimizing production of these lands for any one of their potential uses—wood, water, wildlife, recreation, and forage. Government, industrial, and small nonindustrial ownerships may suffer from the shift from fiber production to less-financially rewarding uses, reducing income from those lands for public treasuries, stockholder purses, and individual bank accounts. The foresters' oversight of Dixie's woodlands passes; decisions about how best to manage them will be made in legislative halls and courtrooms where the influence of special interest groups, financed by various publics, may prevail. No longer is the professionally educated forester entrusted with the stewardship of the South's forest. The "foresters' forest" has become only an era in resource management. I think this will be the situation whether the federal lands in the South are managed by the Forest Service in the U.S. Department of Agriculture, the Fish and Wildlife Service in the Department of the Interior, or the Tennessee Valley Authority; whether they are state lands controlled by the several forestry and parks departments or whether these lands are privately held by wood-using corporations and nonindustrial owners—farmers living on the land or entrepreneurial absentee owners. (National Park Service lands are not open for management, and the Bureau of Land Management has no timber holdings in the South.)

Some reviewers of this chapter have rightly called attention to the presentation here of positions that are inconsistent and contradictory. I have written that way intentionally. My purpose is not to dogmatically state a position but, rather, to present those issues being debated in industrial and professional journals and forums. Unavoidably, opinions—some my own, some those of others—appear as part of a prophetic statement.

The Community's Voices

Southern forests and the foresters that manage them will be paramount in numerous controversial issues as the twentieth century wanes. Even as I write, professionals gear to understand better opposing interests and to compromise strongly held opinions that are not convictions of conscience. Among issues of concern are preserving the wilderness character of the forest, using the forest for recreation, and regenerating stands of timber when they reach maturity.

Informing the public about forestry, deciding how land should be used and taxed, introducing exotic wildlife, and intensifying management to satisfy consumptive appetites for wood that will be used for construction and for paper products are matters of signal importance to certain publics and politicians. Many argue that the forests are too important to be left to the foresters. Today socioforestry takes on greater significance and competes with econoforestry for tax dollars and stockholder deposits.

In the future, the South's potential to provide wood and wood products to foreign lands as populations continue to grow suggests the possibility of dramatic changes in the region's economy, reversing the late 1980s trend of declining dependence upon its wood. Serious incursions by the wood-using industry into Canada's forests, overcutting that nation's spruce, fir, and Douglas-fir to supply wood to the United States and to Pacific Rim countries, will eventually deplete the Dominion's growing stock. Fast-growing southern species, along with remaining western conifers, can then be expected to fill resulting international vacuums. But the South's soil, climate, and species nearly guarantee a wood bin that will, in, say, fifty years, be the envy of the Northwest's forestry interests.

Radical Environmentalists versus the Foresters

Physical action too often replaces the name-calling of earlier years in disputing the use of forest lands. Where once foresters referred to park enthusiasts as sentimental and advocates of preserving the aesthetic in nature called the conservationists utilitarian, future confrontation may not be so mild. Physical abuse amounting to terrorism escalates as environmental extremists in the forest find judges less willing than previously to tolerate frivolous litigation over environmental issues. Spikes driven into trees to discourage their harvest threaten to maim or kill unwary loggers whose chain saws encounter the steel. Upon discovery of these hazards, lumbermen leave felled tree trunks in the woods to decay rather than haul them to the mill, there to risk injury to sawyers. Woods workers must use metal detectors to locate the potential missiles. Another contemporary tactic is to tie up Forest Service telephone lines with continuous calling. Important business necessary for managing the lands for goods and services goes undone as professional foresters are harnessed to their desks.

      Other antagonists, this time antihunting advocates, risk life and limb at dawn to spook game near the hunter. Rattling cans, banging on pans, and shooting off fireworks may preserve the wildlife for a season, only to have starvation or malnutrition "harvest" the game later on. Do not ask, "Who would be fool enough to anger hunters equipped with scope-sighted rifles?" For some, to save a mythical Bambi is reason enough.

      The devastating effects of southern pine beetle outbreaks in unmanaged lands set aside for wilderness preservation aggravates the situation. Presently, the insect is controlled by cutting green trees in front of the beetles' infestation point. Some wilderness groups prefer to let the trees die: the forest then remains natural.

      Dendroctonus frontalis larvae kill trees as the adults hurtle survey lines and fences, moving a few feet at a time to adjacent trees or jumping hundreds of yards to infest healthy stands ahead of their front. A neighbor's stand is then destroyed. Whether government or private land is infested, consumers suffer as higher prices for wood products compensate for the higher costs involved in more intensively managing fewer acres.

      Insecticide prohibitions, along with a lack of appropriate thinning procedures—because of their cost—suggest that a once-a-decade rampage by the southern pine beetle will continue to occur. Each outbreak will outdo its predecessor, exceeding infestations of five thousand acres at a time. Many landowners shift to more-resistant pine species, such as longleaf pine, or permit natural succession of the site to hardwood species rather than risk losses to the beetle.

      Disputation relates to whether lands covered with trees fifty years old, those stands naturally seeded-in or planted following the cut-out-and-get-out days of the 1930s, should be managed for fiber or retained only for observation and recreational pursuits. Preserved wilderness is the desire of many. (Distinctions between recreational and wilderness use of the forests may not be well understood. Recreational use is nearly synonymous with playground activity: camping, hunting, biking, fishing,

Devastating root rot fungus attacking slash pine. Tomorrow's foresters will need to deal more intensively with controlling diseases such as this one caused by *Fomes annosus,* which attacks slash pine principally in thinned stands planted on agricultural land. Remedies may affect other organisms in ways presently not understood, as when controlling red heartrot disease, caused by *Fomes pini,* in southern pines destroyed the habitat of the red-cockaded woodpecker. (Courtesy U.S. Forest Service.)

swimming, and animal stalking. Wildernesses may be utilized, with some exceptions, for these purposes, but the sites are essentially untrammelled by people or so recovered from timber harvesting that, to the average person, they may appear to be virgin lands. Their intended use is more *re-*creational than recreational—to lift the intruder's spirit. They also serve for scientific study and for posterity to view.)

Confrontation with strongly opinionated environmentalists also involves the use of prescribed fire for preparing seedbeds, controlling undesirable vegetation, and improving habitat for wildlife. Much more expensive alternatives include the use of plows, herbicides, and fertilizers, all more damaging to the environment than fire when used under carefully mandated conditions. Foresters, having learned the proper use of prescribed burning, want to use fire more, not less, to imitate nature's way of managing woodlands. In their view, it is a more economical and more ecologically responsible management method than plowing the ground and applying chemicals in order to maximize wood production.

Advocacy groups, which sprung up in the 1960s, have been joined by those caught up in the emotional climate. Well-heeled supporters often lack an understanding of the issues. Articulate speakers and persuasive writers inspire contributors to finance large salaries for the leaders of the nonconciliatory organizations. Their ability to hire top-flight lawyers has led to dozens of appeals, "paper monkey-wrenching" forest management with judicial silviculture. Reconciliation could eliminate the need for an advocacy group and its death affect employment opportunities for the organization's high-salaried leaders. One plaintiff's attorney, upon winning a case against the U.S. Forest Service regarding harvests in the red-cockaded woodpecker's habitat, submitted to the court a petition to recover over $578,000 in fees and costs for the two-year lawsuit.

I'm hopeful frivolous litigation by overly zealous groups will diminish. Trials are expensive, costing advocacy groups as well as tax-supported defendants of the public's estate. One state's attorney general, in an attempt to capitalize on the publicity just before an election, suffered adverse consequences in the end. Siding with uninformed and emotional activists, he learned how true is Alexander Pope's dictum that "a little learning is a dang'rous thing." Wearying of fighting the federal defendants in a suit over forest management methods on national forest lands, he chose not to appeal a jurist's decision that favored the professional foresters' methods for farming the forest. He failed to get reelected because enough voters perceived his tactics as self-serving.

Yet it must be said that the efforts of groups competing for public and legislative attention continue to serve the nation well. The public learns from the opposing sides the issues at stake, and state and national lawmakers are forced to reconcile the divergent viewpoints. Government leaders do this most successfully when they have the benefit of well-stated opposing opinions. Changing management procedures for the South's public and private forests over the past fifty years attest to this. By the mid-1980s, old-timers in the U.S. Forest Service were publicly urging the agency to return to less-drastic management practices than clear-cutting tracts on national forests. Many of the Service's retired and active professionals were calling for balancing stands of timber with trees of various ages and species.

Forest managers inevitably will face several dissatisfied user groups that neither approve of the judgment of the foresters nor believe they have the authority to make judgments, even for privately held lands.

Thus, the best that can be accomplished is "a state of moderate dissatisfaction among all client groups—hardly inspirational or motivating and virtually guaranteed to reinforce any latent tendency to fortress mentality." The more politically motivated among the users then take control, suing if necessary to win the day.[1]

Industry Response

To counteract the influence of radical environmentalists on the general public, its elected representatives, and the press, forest industry and related groups continue to increase efforts to head off the adversaries at the pass. At appreciable cost, Project Learning Tree (PLT) aims to enlist every schoolteacher in the country in an effort to enable them to understand the issues, both economic and ecological. The aim of PLT is to explain why foresters do what they do. Just as this intensive program is the culmination of lesser ones conducted over the past several decades, more elaborate efforts are forthcoming. While industry rightly may be accused of promotional excesses in the past in order to protect its raw material supplies, it need not have done so. Simply stating the facts to a rational audience should enable that audience to understand the need for proper management practices if adequate supplies of lumber and paper are to be produced for a growing population. To irrational antagonists, truth has little persuasive power. "I've made up my mind. Don't confuse me with facts" seems to continue to be the banner under which some march.

Land-use Planning

Reasonable preservationists commend the use of elected and appointed committees from among various publics to decide how land should be managed. These people can then recommend compromises for the aims and claims of many, often divergent, user groups in the decision-making processes. Such land-use planning for the southern forests will continue to increase the acreages retained in parklike settings while diminishing the land base designated for the production of wood. Additional watersheds in mountainous areas will be set aside for the production of clear, clean water for the manufacturing industry and for human consumption. Greater acreages will be reserved for hunting, some further allocated for specific kinds of hunting—eastern gray and western fox squirrels, American woodcock, white-tailed deer, eastern wild turkey, raccoon, bobwhite quail, and a growing catalog of other game.

In the future, I believe land-use planning will dictate diminishing the forested acreage grazed by livestock. The public's demand for high-quality beef encourages the development of improved pastures that produce nutritious herbage and support high carrying capacities.

Land-use planners designate certain tracts for multiple uses while allocating some parcels for a single purpose. Even state and national parks will be managed for more then the single recreational use for which they are now set aside in order to provide goods and other services for human populations expected to double in little more than the next generation. Demography drives land-use planning, notwithstanding the joining of cattlemen with lumbermen and other property-rights advocates to resist the encroachment of bureaucratic planners upon the South's social order.

Benefits of southern forests apart from wood products continue to attain greater importance. The use of timberlands for filtering water, for controlling erosion, and for disposing of municipal and toxic wastes, as well as for aesthetic value, may be decided by zoning boards. More woodlands, including private holdings, could be strictly designated as habitat for threatened and endangered plants and animals. Availability of privately held lands for such ventures will depend upon tax incentives and disincentives. A woodland site for filtering human waste water could become a marketable benefit, while the site set aside to preserve an insect-eating pitcher plant produces a nonmarketable benefit.

Not only nonmarketable, but immeasurable benefits, could accrue. The forest serves as an environmental sink for receiving increasing quantities of carbon monoxide (much converted to carbon dioxide) pouring into the atmosphere from humankind's activities. Forests provide great amounts of foliage (quantified as square miles of surface area in an acre of 43,560 square feet), the surfaces of which are indented with stomata. Carbon dioxide, the waste of peoples and their manufacturing, passes into these openings; out of them pours oxygen for the respiration of all life. Obviously, evergreen needles are more effective than the seasonal foliage of deciduous trees for this purpose. Thus, greater acreages of conifer woodlands will be protected as greenbelts around cities. These also serve as noise barriers and, partly because of their green color, provide some ease for emotional stress.

National Forest Planning

Major laws enacted by Congress during the waning years of the foresters' forest will have long-lasting consequences in the South. These legislative pieces—the National Forest and Rangelands Renewable Resources Planning Act (RPA) of 1974 and the National Forest Management Act (NFMA) of 1976—catapulted the U.S. Forest Service in the

South, perhaps more than elsewhere, into a new era of visibility and public involvement. The evidence: by August 1986 public administrative appeals to Forest Service plans for national forests in the region already numbered forty-nine. (By early 1991, "a thousand or so" appeals to the chief and related lawsuits had been filed nationwide.)[2] That sixteen of these involving the South had been resolved suggests the wisdom of Senator Hubert Humphrey's comment at the time the legislation was written that the Forest Service "needed not new management policy but a new resource-planning and conflict-resolution process.[3]

To satisfy the NFMA, the Forest Service must give citizens an opportunity (read *encourage citizens*)to identify issues that concern them, analyze management objectives, request studies of various resources (e.g., water, soil, wildlife) affected by management procedures, and recommend alternative methods for managing forestlands. Citizens may maintain periodic involvement over the life of the plan finally approved by the Forest Service. Citizen groups and individuals must appeal plans with which they disagree to the agency's chief within forty-five days of the release of the final plan. Unresolvable disagreement with the chief then leads to litigation in the federal courts. More suits are anticipated, thereby preventing Forest Service professional foresters from managing the forests full time. The foresters stay busy helping attorneys unknowledgeable in silviculture prepare briefs, being deposed, and testifying in court. One leader of an environmentalist group predicts the bureau will alter its stance as a timber producer as a new roster of foresters geared to multiple-use practices works its way up the professional ranks. Older foresters, however, recall that in the 1960s *socioforestry* was a prominent term in the vocabulary of the southern regional forester. Experienced foresters also view forests in terms other than timber production.

I believe below-cost, and even low-cost, timber sales on the national forests will no longer occur. Nor will management plans for these federal lands have as a principal objective, as the Congress once directed, the stabilizing of community economies. As government timber sales decline, the "peckerwood" mills—the fly-by-night operators accustomed to enduring economic stress—will disappear from the woods. Banks will no longer tide them over. The Forest Service will abandon much of its emphasis on clear-cutting and planting as silvicultural practices. Ugliness—even for a few years—and the unnatural appearance of straight rows must give way to more pleasant landscapes, though the loss of future economic benefits to the federal treasury and to local community incomes must be recognized.

The Forest Service and its adversaries' lobbyists surely will encourage Congress to fine tune the RPA and the NFMA (the latter at times considered an amendment to the former). With new legislation, policy agreement will continue to be elusive. One observer of the scene put it this way: "[The people] at best have a process for assessing conflict and making decisions. Nothing can prevent the conflict or keep it from growing as public demands proliferate and compete. To succeed, land management professionals must recognize that they are part of a confusing policy arena, increasingly politicized and uncertain. The objective must be not to seek certainty, but to live with uncertainty."[4] To this, a preacher of the Old South whose name is lost to memory might suggest the paraphrase, "The object must be not to seek one's preference solely, but to live with harmony, an offspring of compromise."

Recreation Pressures

Increasing pressure by wood-using industries to produce more wood in the South affects the national forests and, conversely, some of the public's attitudes toward greater timber production on those lands. People who want the Forest Service charter amended will be heard. Another Congress, like that of the 1960s' Great Society years, could lean toward the conversion of considerable acreages to solely recreational use. Any reduction in commercial forest acreage for timber production on federal lands will, of necessity, influence management on private lands, even though national forests in the region mainly have an impact on local economies.

The recreationists' concerns could backfire: an unsympathetic Congress and president, rather than face the enduring controversy, could opt to sell the national forests in the region. In most cases, the land would go to industry, often to the same companies that disposed of the cut-over and burned-over land to the federal government in the 1930s. (Such an attempt was made by the East Texas Chamber of Commerce for Texas's four national forests in the 1950s.) While neither economically nor politically realistic, privatization could result in more intensive management of timber on the land and, therefore, result in a greater inventory of wood for the future consumer.

Industry desires ownership of only accessible land and productive sites, though accessibility to all forestlands greatly increases as roads are built to enable better management. Because access roads encourage travel by the general public, entry is gained into less-accessible areas, often at the higher elevations, by hiking and camping recreationists.

Higher fuel costs and highway taxes cannot be expected to reduce visits to forested recreation sites. Americans readily sacrifice for psychological refreshment at fishing holes, picnic grounds, and hunting leases. They will do so even more willingly in the years that lie before them: they must escape the concrete jungles and the small town squares in order to relieve emotional stress.

Locking up federal lands for wilderness, sometimes a quasi-recreational use, will require industry and small timberland owners to produce more wood on lands not set aside for this singular use. Nonindustrial landowners will do so only if the payoff is worthwhile. If production is not increased because it is not economically worthwhile, imports of lumber, plywood, and pulping-grade material from Canada and the Southern Hemisphere will increase, thereby diminishing the market price of stumpage on nonreserved land. Presently, Louisiana, Mississippi, Alabama, and Arkansas seem destined to be the South's (and possibly the nation's) principal timber-producing states. In the balance of the region, recreational and aesthetic demands upon the forest will drive out industry; for these four states, in the absence of economic incentives for other uses of the land, employment and income will depend increasingly upon the forest-products industries.

Meanwhile, authorities reserve more streams through the forests for canoeing and rafting. To protect the stream sides, they order that trees on either side of the watercourse remain unharvested, and the banks return in a few decades to a virgin-appearing state. At the same time, allocations of additional public acreage provide for off-road vehicles that inevitably encourage soil erosion as they wreak havoc on the hillsides.

Adequate wood supplies for at least the next six decades reduce the need to drain wet sites for timber production. Some drained sites may be returned to their original condition, thereby providing wetland habitat for migratory waterfowl.[5]

Commercial forest acreage continues to decline dramatically as municipalities and industries dam new lakes for the water needs of a growing Sunbelt population. Around these lakes, middle-income and wealthy people build first and second homes. Even the 1987 revised federal tax law continues to encourage ownership of vacation homes by providing a mortgage interest income tax deduction on loans made to build recreational dwellings. Confrontation, at least in legislative halls, may end this incentive, which those of lower income cannot enjoy.

Argument is also expected to erupt over other taxes levied, or not levied, on forested land. Most notable is the use-value tax, presently levied in many states. This low-rate assessment encourages landowners to refrain from converting their woodland holdings to such higher-value uses as commercial and residential real estate. Low tax rates therefore subsidize a landowner's recreational use of his holdings, just as they sometimes do the production of wood.

Taxing Timber

Zoned land ordinarily is taxed according to its highest use. Already in many states exceptions to appraisal valuation encourage lands to be set aside as natural areas. Owners who in good faith convince the tax collector of the intent to retain land in an unmanaged condition pay substantially less than the appraisal otherwise requires. Should owners renege on the agreement, the sheriff and tax collector see that back taxes with interest are promptly paid. Authorities will expand such assessment conditions in the future.

More timberland in the South awaits taxation according to a variety of uses—like wood production or recreation—as well as to the quality of the site for growing trees. For the latter case, ad valorem taxes are certain to be assessed more definitively according to the quality of the site. These assessments will be based upon site indexes ranging widely for a single species. For loblolly pine, the South's most valuable and most ubiquitous tree, site indexes vary from less than 50 to 125.

Severance taxes continue to replace ad valorem taxes, at least in part, in the South. School boards and county governments prefer the regularity and dependability of ad valorem taxation, payments depending solely upon land (and sometimes timber) value, which varies little from year to year. Timberland owners, in contrast, dislike paying taxes for many years on property that provides income only periodically, perhaps every ten to twenty years, at the time of a timber sale. Owners pay severance taxes on the value of the timber removed and only at the time of a harvest. Assessors hire foresters to oversee this taxing effort. A combination of the two taxing methods—ad valorem and severance—is expected eventually to encompass the region.

High land taxes, however, drive people out of the timber-growing business. Both small nonindustrial forest owners and the giant corporations suffer. The only escape is to raise the price of the product—wood or paper—which ultimately the consumer then pays. Importation of Canadian wood also encourages higher ad valorem taxes because the value of standing timber diminishes with increasing competition from outside of the region. The assessor will have what he must for schools, roads, and society's protection. Dominion imports in the late 1980s made up about one-half of the lumber sold in the South's lumberyards. Whether tariffs and proposed limitations on wood volumes imported from north of forty-nine degrees north latitude will affect timber harvests (and therefore taxes) in the South is too unpredictable to suggest. At the beginning of the Bush Administration, free trade with the Canadians meant the free flow of wood.

Tax collectors and elected and appointed officials hesitate to encourage further acquisition of private lands for the public's use. Such lands are removed from tax rolls. Some government lands—for example, the national forests—return to the counties from which harvests are made 25 percent of the income from timber sales. This in-lieu-of-tax money from a timber sale (or grazing lease, special-use permit, etc.) does not go into the U.S. Treasury Department's coffers, but remains in a trust fund earmarked for schools and roads. State legislatures determine the percentage for each of these two entities. If more lands are removed from tax rolls, Congress can be expected to increase the percentage designated for the counties from which the timber is harvested. This will diminish the money from timber sales deposited in the treasury of an already seriously indebted nation. So, too, state and other governments controlling managed timberland may provide an alternative for the ad valorem tax so that school and hospital districts and county services can survive. Legislators can be expected to provide in-lieu-of-tax money even when no salable product or service from the forest is involved.

I expect gifts of scenic and biologically unusual lands to groups that agree to maintain the tracts in their natural condition and which protect the woodlands to increase. These parcels are deleted from the tax rolls. Industries and individuals who donate such forested tracts to governments or preservation associations benefit with handsome tax breaks. Justification for the deduction from the donor's debt to the people's treasury in corporate or personal income taxes, is that all the people of the nation then own and may enjoy these lands.

More or Less Public Land

The public's demand for more land freed from timber management does not abate. It will, however, lead both industry and government owners to trade land in larger and larger blocks for more efficient care. National forests in the South typically occupy one-half of the land within the purchase-unit boundary. With the federal budget and the public's attitudes discouraging further acquisition of private lands for national forests, the government's trading of land and timber with industrial and nonindustrial owners gains momentum. For more efficient management, certain lands under the care of the National Park Service, like the Big Thicket National Preserve in Texas, could have their charters altered by Congress and be transferred to nearby national forests. At the same time, less acreage of the South's national forests could be used for wood fiber production; some tracts may be transferred to the Department of Interior's national park and national wildlife refuge systems.

Meanwhile, a movement mounts to encourage privatization—the sale of federal holdings to private interests to help liquidate the national debt. Although the idea seems incredible to some, there are those who would sell federal lands to fill federal coffers. Long before former Secretary of the Department of the Interior James Watt orated on this controversial issue, chambers of commerce and other groups promoted the idea. With each American paying about two thousand dollars per year to service the nation's indebtedness (that is for interest alone; none of that money goes toward paying the principal), I think privatization warrants further consideration. However, the 11.3 million acres of national forests in the South, at a round-number average value of eight hundred dollars per acre, would gain for the Treasury but $9 billion.[6] That would pay the interest for little more than two weeks. And, too, the sudden sale of so much land would flood the market, reducing the average value below even the estimate given here for the region.

Management Matters

Diminishing Roles for Foresters

Lack of consensus over land uses, harvesting methods, taxation, and public land ownership are not alone the obstacles to forestry to be encountered in the region for the next few decades. Lack of money for intensive management by both governments and industry means fewer foresters will be hired to carry out the tasks for which young men and women are prepared. Reduced enrollments, I expect, will result in the closing of professional forestry schools. And with that loss, a cadre of experts and their academic offspring, certainly sorely to be needed in the future, pass from the classrooms, laboratories, and experimental forests.

In recent years, landscape architects replaced foresters in the national forests to accommodate the Forest Service's concept of the public's desire for aesthetically pleasing woodlands rather than well-managed tracts. So, too, entomologists, pathologists, recreationists, engineers, accountants, public relations personnel, and computer specialists each do a little of the work that foresters, as generalists, have done in the past. Already the passing of the forester from the top echelons of industrial management, to be succeeded by lawyers and accountants, affirms this prediction.

While I hear foresters told to earn master's degrees in business administration, no one tells the company executive to get a BSF, the professional forestry degree. Chief operating officers may have master's degrees in business administration, but their lack of a knowledge of silvics, silviculture, and ecology diminishes the quality of the forests in the South. In the climate of the mid-1980s' depression in the wood-using industry, the question receives no response about who—the MBAs or the foresters (both in business and government)—recommended and authorized allocations of $150 and more per acre in the 1970s to prepare sites for planting and to artificially regenerate those sites with nursery-grown stock. Stockholders and taxpayers will be paying for these practices beyond the end of the next generation's forest. Who failed to understand the compound interest formula? Or was inflation to continue at 20 percent per year?

Compound Interest Neglected

The equation $V_n = V_o(1.0p)^n$ remains a valid economic concept in forestry, as it is for any investment. Readers will recognize this as the omnibus compound interest formula. V_o is the value of an investment initially, V_n is the investment's worth after n years, when interest rates are p percent. In the 1970s, prime interest rates, and loans dependent upon them, exceeded 9.9 percent, thus necessitating in those inflationary years dropping the 0 before the p. Hence, $V_n = V_o(1p)_n$. Consequently, $150 spent in preparing and planting an acre of land becomes, at 15 percent interest compounded annually, $1,907 at a pulpwood harvest time of eighteen years; $4,938 at twenty-five years; and $40,185 for a sawlog harvest at age forty years.

Knowledgeable foresters spend twenty-five to fifty dollars per acre to naturally regenerate southern pine and hardwood forests, utilizing silvicultural systems long known to them. Seed-tree, shelterwood, and clear-cutting regeneration systems need no drastic preparation techniques if done properly. Owners may spend a little more for directly seeding cut-over lands with seeds treated with rodent and bird repellents. For forest cover types composed of shade-tolerant species, selection harvesting—requiring minimal site preparation—is an appropriate regeneration method. Even as I write, industries move rapidly to less intensive and therefore less expensive management practices.

To beat the banker's compound interest returns at high percentage rates, industrialists shorten rotation periods for the southern forests. Industrial owners of forests trim final harvest periods by 50 percent. I expect national forest rotations will be reduced by 10 to 15 percent if the courts permit: more frequent harvests than that would generate too much heat from environmentalists. Greater reductions also would necessitate more acreage needing regeneration than Congress would be willing to pay for.

Corporation plans that call for sixty-year rotations today will be changed—even at mid-cycle—to thirty years. To grow the necessary wood in these shortened time spans, industrialists will find genetically improved planting stock, commercial fertilizers, more intensive weed control, and water regulation necessary. But these procedures cost much money, thereby exacerbating the rotation age–compound interest dilemma.

I believe arguments within government agencies and private organizations will occur over low-cost natural regeneration and intensive plantation establishment using genetically superior nursery stock. Many individuals and groups with heavy investments and vested interests in tree improvement programs insist on capitalizing on that investment.

Commercial timber production, I believe, will phase out at the periphery of metropolitan areas as population pressures require more land for residential and business use and for lakes to store surface water. In contrast to this loss of timber-growing acreage, new owners—perhaps the offspring of cattle ranchers—will convert some pastureland to trees because they will have little appreciation for branding, dipping, and rounding up herds. Interests of latter-day forest landowners will lean more toward hunting, second-home siting, realty investment, and recreational aesthetics.

Ownership for timber production will play a minor role, if any, in zones surrounding large cities. As a result, markets for forest products will diminish and, with them, further interest in growing trees as a source of fiber.

Price Fluctuations

From 1955 to 1986, prices paid for hardwood stumpage of all sizes and grades and for softwood pulpwood fell when measured in 1967 dollars. Only slight increases in noninflated stumpage prices for pine sawtimber were apparent through 1980, when the market fell dramatically.[7] The market remained low but steady through the mid-1980s. Had there not been the abundance of wood at low prices, brought about by the salvage of trees killed in the outbreaks of southern pine beetle infestations at various locales in the region, the price of pine stumpage might have risen. Lumber markets that are flooded, because of timber removed from beetle-infested lands, choke out opportunities to move wood from well-managed healthy forests. The continuing low price could have a devastating effect upon the ability of the nation to provide wood for its citizens three, four, or more decades hence. Low prices for trees standing in the woods preclude the owners spending money for forest management. Minimal managerial effort for a crop that takes so long to grow may well cause a bona fide timber famine.[8]

Timberland values will continue to fall from their late 1970s values. Sixteen hundred dollars an acre for land and timber already in some areas is worth one-half that. Foresters involved in real estate transactions attribute this to several factors. The general national control over inflation in the 1980s encouraged revising the federal tax laws late in the decade. Landowners of small parcels, unable to utilize the previously enjoyed capital gains tax breaks, opted to sell. The new rules on active and passive management also play a role. To deduct management costs from the Internal Revenue Service's annual bill, the landowner is obliged to show that he and/or his spouse have spent five hundred hours in day-to-day work. Only in harvest years is this likely, leaving the interim between sales without significant deductible claims. Specifically, the rules now state that time spent by consultants and paid for by landowners automatically brings the owner under the passivity rules, allowing no deductions.

Another reason forestland values fall is the "discovery," now that inflation is past, that mills can buy stumpage from nonindustrial and government holdings cheaper than they can grow it on their own lands. As the timber-famine threat diminishes and the Forest Service moves back its date for the significant domestic shortage of wood from 2000 to 2050, industrialists not only see no need to buy land in order to assure sustained wood supplies, they put land on the market, anticipating real estate sales will provide cash flow for alternative costs, including mill modernization.

The dramatic restructuring of the pulp and paper industry occurred when many old-line companies were purchased by competitors and corporate raiders put a lot of land on the market that was considered excess to a mill's requirements. Finally, increased imports, especially from Canada, and more efficient use of wood through improved technology also reduce American mill requirements.

In all silvicultural practices, weather is a risk. High costs include the necessity to replant, reseed, or wait out the production of a new seed crop on the residual trees when drought, floods, or freezes take their toll. Hurricane Alicia, for example, not only created havoc throughout the Gulf states, but the flooding that accompanied the wind further weakened the trees and, by so doing, invited serious infestations of the notorious southern pine beetle. These situations cause timber price fluctuations.

A rule of thumb not many years past for the ratio of the num-

ber of foresters to the acreage they manage was 1:8,000. By the early
1980s, the figure was 1:25,000. With ever-larger spans of control, as one
industry manager anticipates, a forester will be allocated for every fifty to
one hundred thousand acres.[9] The price of stumpage varies in part with
the costs for managerial overseers. But as the numbers of foresters decline,
in proportion to their land-managing responsibilities, I believe silvicultural disaster for the region becomes more imminent. Subprofessional
technicians called upon to fill in the gaps, with some notable exceptions,
have inadequate preparation to carry out the tasks. When timber famine
really occurs, however, knowledgeable foresters will be able within two
decades to restore the forests to productivity and profitability. An inadequate cadre will delay that accomplishment.

Best Management Practices

Best management practices (BMPs) involve minimizing erosion and water runoff from harvested sites, improving the design of road
cuts and fills, and choosing between regeneration practices (like clear-
cutting or selection). Many such BMPs, now subjective judgments, are
beginning to be cast in concrete as new laws and regulations. What one
professional considers the presently known environmentally best practice
may be marginal to another forester or inadequate to an official charged
with ensuring the quality of water or aesthetic beauty.

Some such rules aim to preserve dwindling timber supplies,
while others diminish the supply. Regulations that reduce waste in the
woods by requiring the use of more of the tree serve to increase the inventory. Forbidding the use of herbicides for fear of harming wildflowers
cataloged on the congressionally mandated Smithsonian Institution's list
of endangered plant species operates conversely. Seed yields of superior
strains of conifers must decline if, as is likely, insecticides cannot be used
to control insects that attack strobili, cones, and seeds in conifer seed
orchards and seed-production areas.

Site productivity diminishes as heavy equipment prepares sites
for regeneration. Soil compaction and removal of surface organic matter,
along with its chemically adsorbed nutrients, necessitate soil amelioration
expenditures. Fertilizers, water controls, and even organic matter addi-
tions may be required. Prescriptions for the time that must lapse between
rains of various intensities and the resumption of logging with machinery
are certain to be set out in a future BMP regulation. Environmentalists
often emphasize watershed management in their litigation testimony.

Of particular concern where harvests are severe is the movement of nutrients to stream channels. Such chemical element flows affect

water quality and fish life. Even though the situation is self-correcting when new vegetation—herbaceous weeds and low-lying shrubs—reinvade harvested areas, I anticipate a BMP to cover the situation. Government inspectors can be expected to observe and to regulate silvicultural treatments to minimize environmental insults. Antigovernment activists see BMPs, when used as management objectives, amounting to land-use control by government.

Management Intensity Increases

Misunderstanding the relationship of *ecology* to *economics* (both terms derive from the same root, in Greek and Latin, respectively) has diminished management. Clear-cutting is, indeed, good ecology—if properly conducted. Now, to make up for the financial losses of recent decades, foresters must intensify silvicultural efforts. To encourage tree growth, for example, they use mineral and nitrogen fertilizers, carefully placing the supplemental nutrients where only the trees, and not the competing vegetation, benefit. Drainage of wet sites to (re)claim them for commercial forest production is under way. Meanwhile, estuary ecologists, supported by aquatic bird hunters, lobby for no net loss of wetlands on public and private ownerships. Indeed, surface-mined land reclamation foresters intentionally allot areas in drainage designs for swamps and sloughs. Irrigating other land—for specialty black walnut plantations, for example—is an anticipated practice.

I predict managers will seek species exotic to the region. As the poplar hybrid of eastern (U.S.) cottonwood and Europe's black cottonwood combined to produce *Populus euroamericana*, so new genetically improved crosses and hybrids show potential. Forests of the fast-growing *P. euroamericana*, developed by geneticists shortly after the Second World War so that Europeans could have houses and paper, now cover millions of acres throughout the Mediterranean area. Experience documents the problems with introducing exotic vegetation. Survival failures and insect and disease injury are not uncommon.

Foresters in the 1950s, at the urging of company executives who had witnessed the rapid growth of California's Monterey pine in Australia and New Zealand, planted that species in the Gulf South. Apparently none survived. Also unsuccessful have been the plantations of various eucalyptus species. On the other hand, the rapid growth of timber bamboo, introduced from the Orient into southeastern Georgia, and that hard fiber's potential for paper pulp may encourage further introductions in the region of this tree-size grass. A Savannah, Georgia, newspaper published an edition on newsprint made from bamboo grown nearby and

Conversion of wetlands. Vast areas of southeastern wetlands were converted from dydric forest cover types, like pondcypress, to more mesic and more economically desirable species, like loblolly pine, during the period here called the foresters' forest. (Such lands also became high-value vegetable farms.)

converted to pulp and paper at Charles Herty's research and development laboratory in that city.

Just ahead is the development of herbicide-tolerant trees. Biotechnology also focuses on trees with a tolerance to insects, fungi, and airborne chemicals. Tolerance can be achieved by inserting unique genes or by obtaining unique genetic change during reproduction of plants in tissue cultures. Simplified, as a common soil bacterium that causes crown

Low-value moist site, growing dense stands of pondcypress. Compare site with that in following photograph.

gall disease, *Agrobacterium tumefaciens*, inserts its genes into the cells of its host plant, so too may it transfer a gene that confers tolerance. Genetic engineers search for these genes, perhaps one that provides tolerance to a herbicide. Regenerated shoots from the infected plant are tested to determine whether the tolerance gene was actually implanted. The tolerant shoots are then freed of the introduced exotic organism (in this case *A. tumefaciens*) by using culture techniques and antibiotics.

In the forests of the twenty-first century, I expect managers

More merchantable species planted on the former moist sites ditched and drained. Such procedures, in common practice in the 1950s and 1960s, ceased with the growing concern for wetlands protection, a matter belatedly grasped by foresters.

may replace pond pine in undrained bay areas with Atlantic white-cedar. Fires in that event must be totally excluded, for the latter, unlike the former, has no resistance to heat. In that day, too, hybrids of pond pine and loblolly pine may be common, taking advantage of the best characteristics of each species. Pond pine's serotinous characteristic enables regeneration following fire: loblolly pine has a much superior form, desirable for poles, pilings, and plywood.

Until now "super" pine trees have been the progeny of crosses

Forest geneticists bagging both male and female flowers (for conifers more properly called "strobili"). (Courtesy U.S. Forest Service.)

from the best residual trees of a single species, the offspring of the virgin stands. Interspecific hybrids will follow. By the early 2000s, forest trees will be regenerated from seeds genetically suited to particular environments. Unfortunately, improved growth from these "supertree" selections seems to disappear after the third generation.

Pollination and parent crossing controlled. Pollen collected in the male bags is inserted through a hypodermic needle into the plastic bags covering the female flowers. Offspring of these slash pines will be tested for oleoresin yields. The best will be selected for further breeding. (Courtesy U.S. Forest Service.)

Propagules other than seeds, such as buds and vegetative reproductive tissues, will be more intensively employed in the future. Forest geneticists anticipate growing superior stock from cloned trees originating from vegetative tissue. Thus, sections of pine needles or small portions of root hairs of a rapidly growing, well-formed tree "planted" in a petri dish provide the "seed" for a whole forest of genetically identical stock. Genetically improved trees will be designed to endure preharvest shade so that, when an overstory is removed, the site already has a soil-protecting canopy of a new stand of trees. The presence of new trees, too, promptly making height growth, avoids the loss of productive use of the land for a year or two, which is what usually occurs with conventional even-aged management harvests. In addition, foresters must breed trees for higher

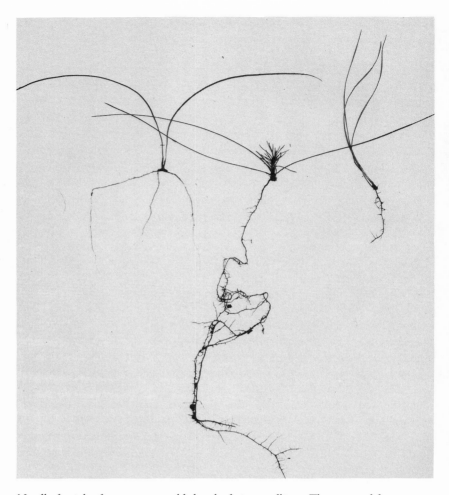

Needle fascicles from one-year-old shortleaf pine seedlings. These rooted four months after planting in a special medium. The center fascicle produced the shoot from its base after four additional months. Thus, clones of highest-quality trees can be produced from young parents in a brief time. (Photograph by Dr. B. Zak courtesy U.S. Forest Service.)

specific gravity for certain markets, like poles and pilings. This may re-quire increasing rotation ages for selected stands of these slower-growing stems.

I expect high-quality sites for hardwoods destined for furniture and paneling markets to be intensively managed within three decades. Much of the lumber from many species is sold in European markets. The

forests on the Continent and in Great Britain become increasingly depleted of commercial timbers. Meanwhile, demand grows.

Foresters know how to grow valuable furniture and panel
woods, such as black walnut, "pulling out all the stops" to do so. Strains
selected for wood quality, rather than nut production, are planted on the
best mesic sites. Preparations for future stands will include drainage in
case of flooding, irrigation in the event of drought, weed control, nutrient
fertilization, and pruning of branches to produce knot-free lumber. The
high value of the trees could necessitate fencing and other measures to
protect them from theft. Prices for the dark-colored heartwood continue
to soar as markets increase. Furniture manufacturers now seem satisfied
that southern-grown black walnut is quality wood.

Some workers in wood may still argue, however, that southern-grown black walnut is brash and the heartwood too light colored for
the furniture market. To test these criticisms, a Dixie furniture maker distributed to willing observers a dozen personally created ornamental drum
tables made from locally grown stock. Fifteen years later, the parts of the
tables remain sturdy, the grain as dark and pleasing as that of the wood
from stream sides in Indiana and Illinois, the zone claimed to be the best
habitat for producing hard, stable, dark-complexioned black walnut
wood. The light-colored sapwood is now stained to appear as heartwood,
and only an expert wood technologist is able to tell the difference.

Managing sites to produce both pines and hardwoods will
intensify as landowners realize the high cost of completely controlling
broad-leaved species. The former waste of the broad-leaved woodlands,
the typical low-grade hardwood tree, now goes into particle board and
into the shipping platforms of an ever-increasing pallet industry. Already
trees are grown specifically for this expanding market. Mixed stands also
simplify pest management: pine beetles, especially, are less apt to proliferate in forests containing a goodly number of hardwood trees. In time,
too, the hardwoods could be more valuable than the pines for certain
industrial uses. The foresters' antagonists are more forgiving where deciduous, mast-producing species improve the habitat for an assortment of
wildlife. Decaying nutrient-rich foliage also improves infiltration and
percolation of precipitation in watersheds, while autumn coloration provides more aesthetic pleasure.

Value and Volume Harvested

Just before the mid-1980s' timber recession appeared, stumpage delivered to local points of sale in the South were more than twice as
valuable as soybeans or cotton and more than three times as valuable as

tobacco, wheat, or corn. Wood in 1984, for example, was the highest value crop in six states. In Alabama, roundwood approached the value of all other farm crops together.[10]

In the mid-1970s, about 44 percent of the ten billion cubic feet of softwood trees annually harvested in the United States came from southern forests. From this region, too, came about half of the 4.2 billion cubic feet of hardwoods. A decade later, softwood removals from the South increased 17 percent and hardwood harvests 28 percent.[11] As loggers in the Pacific Northwest and northern California cut their virgin stock, these percentages will rise further. The increase, however, is expected to be limited by the unwillingness—for whatever reason—to place lands under the management of trained silviculturists. Politically inspired disincentives, like taxes and radical environmentalism, will be major reasons.

"Silviculture, I will master / I will grow trees even faster," opening lines of a ditty, depict the capacity of those with education and experience in the art of growing trees in managed stands to carry out an ecological mandate for the region. Regrettably, the economic mandate does not follow. Less than one-half of the forests receive barely adequate silvicultural treatment at stand regeneration time.[12] Economic considerations will likely preclude such treatment until well into the twenty-first century.

The South's silviculture is complex, as more than one hundred commercial tree species inhabit the region. These include many broad-leaved and needleleaf trees, whose ranges vary from the peaks of the Southern Appalachian Mountains through its Piedmont foothills to the plains of the South's Atlantic and Gulf coasts and the interruptions along those shorelines that, over time, have been channelled by streams that overflow to form bottomlands and swamps. Volumes and values of the harvests depend upon the variety of management objectives achieved for this intricate forest. Methods for determining these volumes and value continually evolve.

Measurement Methods

New technology will enhance forest inventories for relatively small parcels as well as for the nation. To count trees and to determine volumes in individual boles and stands, foresters now test with an airborne pulsed-laser profiler. This instrument replaces aerial photography, the dependable method providing pictures from low and high altitudes and in use by field foresters for fifty years. The new laser signal, returned to a satellite above the earth, enables mensurationists to obtain stand data, including the vigor of the vegetation and the form of trees on a tract of land. Helicopter-housed color-infrared video in combination with the pulsed-laser profiler is expected to provide important information at minimal cost. Meanwhile, Landsat, a National Aeronautic and Space Administration program, provides stand characteristics useful for managing large areas. These technological advances also improve assessment of influences—like fire, insects, diseases, toxic atmospheric problems, and mysterious ailments—that affect the forest.

Foresters teamed with computer programmers continue to develop methods for conveniently estimating yields of stands of timber. Such computer languages as FORTRAN are used to determine growth in plantations and natural stands by species and site class and calculate mortality rates from such phenomena as fusiform rust. Stand structure—the number of trees by size classes on an acre—is readily predicted from data collected in the field and converted to tabular form.

Smoke Management

The threatening influence upon humans of the use of prescribed fire in the forests of the South is gaining attention. Smoke-related lung problems and allergies (smoke carries carbon particulates and fungi spores) affect human health. Smoke and the smell of smoke are aesthetically bothersome. The cloud of smog often accompanying the burning operation is a potential hazard on highways, sometimes causing vehicular accidents. Fires escape to burn structures and farmers' fields. Although these hazards exist, most states now require only that state forestry agencies be informed of the intended fire so that fire-fighting crews will not be dispatched to extinguish it when it is reported from aerial surveillance, from one of the few remaining lookout towers, or by a telephone call from a passerby. States also may hold liable those conducting the fire if an accident occurs that may be attributed to reduced visibility on public roads.

Managing smoke from prescribed burning is destined to become a concern for legislatures, industries that utilize burning, and the professional foresters who identify conditions for which burning is desirable. As noted in chapter 5, foresters in the region utilize fire for preparing a site prior to planting and seeding (by workers or by natural seedfall), for controlling brownspot needle blight in longleaf pine grass-stage seedling stands, for controlling scrubby weed trees and shrubs, for improving the range for grazing cattle in the woods, for exposing seeds in bobwhite quail and eastern wild turkey management, and for reducing hazards. In the latter case, owners burn their woodlands under prescribed conditions to avoid a wildfire occurring when the weather could permit a conflagration. Burning is already prescribed in some of the region's municipal forests in order to protect urban areas from California-type holocausts.

Fires slow successional trends of southern forests. Without fire, structural-quality southern pine stands advance in ecological stages to deciduous species of lesser value. Burning a stand of timber under prescribed conditions when broad-leaved trees are young kills them, or at least sets them back without damaging the coniferous overstory. Ecological succession to the less valuable climax forest is thereby delayed.

Other, and always more expensive, procedures than prescribed burning are available. Plowing prepares sites for regeneration; fungicides protect seedlings from plant-destroying disease attacks; herbicides kill weed trees and shrubs; nutrient fertilizers and herbicides improve the range for cattle and game; and surveillance from aircraft and surface vehicles provides some protection against the dreaded blow-up fire. BMPs could well require these more expensive procedures, costing up to a hundredfold more, in order to protect the air over communities that may lie many miles from the fire. Thus, cities along the Gulf of Mexico and the southern Atlantic coasts would be spared temperature inversions that might take place when cool, smoke-laden air, driven by northern winds, meets warm Caribbean air currents immediately over the many metropolises along those shorelines.

But those opposing controlled burning need to consider the environmental insults attributable to alternative practices for prescribed burning: motor-vehicle fuels consumed by plows and chemical application equipment add carbon monoxide to the atmosphere; heavy equipment compacts soil, thus encouraging erosion; pesticides escape into air and water supplies; and fertilizers leach into streams and lakes. As management at minimal cost intensifies and a holistic view of environmental resources becomes fashionable, greater acreages may be set on fire under carefully orchestrated prescriptions.

New Uses for Land

Energy Forests

At the time of the nation's birth, wood was almost the sole source of energy for a capital-short and labor-short economy. The iron industry, *the* metal industry of the time, required charcoal for manufacturing. Heating, cooking, and lighting fuel came from wood. The exceptions were the sawmills and grinding wheels that often were turned by the push

of water current. The shift from wood to coal was encouraged by the development of transportation systems, even though wood remained the
primary fuel for trains and riverboats at least through 1850. By 1865,
however, railroads relied upon coal for 25 percent of their fuel.[13]

The early 1970s' significant rise in oil prices brought wood, as
waste in both forest and mill and in standing trees grown for the purpose,
to the fore as a principal energy source. In the future, between 5 percent
and 20 percent of the nation's forested area, set aside as energy forests,
could supply the country's electrical demand.[14] Additionally, methane gas
and methanol alcohol, the latter commercially known as wood alcohol,
are readily produced from wood, as indeed methanol once was exclusively
made.

Kinds of woodlands set aside for storing energy on the stump
include presently noncommercial scrub hardwood stands. Pine-hardwood
forests now of commercial value could be designated and their management intensified for this purpose. All principal species would be available,
but perhaps none so effectively utilized as American sycamore.

Genetically superior stock of this species, cultured as silage in
plantations, yields more than sixteen tons of dry matter per acre per
year.[15] River birch does about as well.[16] As noted earlier, in plantations of
five thousand stems per acre (at about three-by-three-foot spacing, in
contrast to a typical newly established southern pine plantation of seven
hundred stems per acre, spaced eight-by-eight-feet), harvesting takes
place at five-year intervals, when the trees are about twenty-five feet tall.
New trees arise from sprouts, making replanting or seeding unnecessary.
Well-developed roots of the severed stems, rich in starch, encourage rapid
growth of the "coppice" reproduction.

Wood adequately substitutes for nonrenewable energy resources in other ways. A cord produces the equivalent energy of almost a
ton of lignite. A steel I beam weighing 180 pounds requires 240 pounds of
coal for production in a Bessemer furnace.[17] Six cubic feet of laminated
southern pine has the equivalent supporting tensile strength of that
beam. For fabrication and packaging materials, minimal energy and
chemicals are required when wood is the raw material, in contrast to considerable volumes of gas (natural or synthetic) utilized in the production
of plastics. At the end of the Second World War, Europeans powered
their cars with wood, producing methanol in trunk-mounted burners. To
accommodate consumer demands by the twenty-first century, car manufacturers could return wood to the prominence it once enjoyed.

Further erosion of relationships with Mideast oil-producing
nations, as more radical governments seize power, is bound to cause a se-

rious oil shortage. This, in turn, may result in a lower standard of living for U.S. citizens. A public more tolerant of forest management practices that enable affordable housing and paper is then inevitable.

The federal energy administration's prediction of "potential" U.S. independence of foreign oil in the 1980s has not been attained. Nor does it appear that new applications of nuclear, geothermal, water, wind, ocean current, tidal, solar, and fossil fuel resources are forthcoming. Because it seems impractical to suggest that we will ever be free from depending upon other nations for petroleum, use of wood could help sustain us. Meanwhile, we use coal from beneath the ground for energy and, in doing so, provide another matter for future concern: land reclamation.

Land Reclamation

The rate at which coal and minerals will be removed from lands of the South continues to increase as people and their industries demand more nonrenewable natural resources for economic and social benefits. Reclamation of lands surface-mined for these amenities is expected to depend upon successful reforestation or afforestation. Compliance with the federal Surface Mining and Reclamation Act of 1977 requires each operator to establish on all areas effective and permanent vegetative cover. In Texas alone, authorities expect lignite removals to disturb over three hundred thousand surface acres by the year 2000. Eventually, such disturbed lands may total over a million acres, most of which is in the pine-hardwood and post oak regions of that state.[18]

While current trends suggest revegetating surface-mined lands with grasses and forbs for livestock grazing, forests are often more beneficial. Woodlands stabilize soil, hasten soil genesis from the inverted profiles that result when excavated earth is returned to the pit, and require less maintenance. They also are less costly to establish, nutritional amendments being the single item of appreciable expense.

Research indicates that the concentrations and combinations of macro- and micronutrients necessary for greatest survival and growth of various southern pine species are calculable. Foliar diagnosis, the Frenchmen's *foliar diagnostique*, and foliar analysis (using spectrophotometry and atomic absorption apparatuses) to ascertain nutrient deficiencies for these peculiar sites are accompanied by the use of standardized color charts. Minute changes in hues exhibited by needles and leaves tell the forester the kind and amount of fertilizer to apply to the replaced "mine spoil," those hills of earth removed and turned over in surface mining. These materials supplement the added nitrogen and phosphorus which are not infrequently found deficient in the South for maximum growth of loblolly and slash pines. Nutrient levels in the needles of loblolly pine grown on lignite spoil tally well below the optimum for needles on trees growing on adjacent unmined sites.[19]

Forests for Sewage Disposal

The twenty-first century's forest will be an important receptacle for the liquid wastes of the cities. Already trials under way in Florida's peninsula indicate the feasibility of piping processed wastes to forested sites, where trees recycle the water through evapotranspiration. A major drawback to the procedure is that toxic quantities of mineral elements build up, requiring methods yet unknown for removing them from the sludge. Organic toxic chemicals also need to be considered; but these, for the most part, break down in the soil through oxidation, reduction, hydration, and other chemical reactions. If dangerous microbes are not eliminated in the processing at sewage disposal plants, the forest may be fenced and declared off-limits to humans and large terrestrial wildlife. The long-term effects upon the biome of forestlands treated in Florida await documentation.

Hunting Increases

Following the financial successes of the game ranches in the Hill Country of Central Texas, landowners across the region are beginning to dedicate a considerable acreage of southern woodlands to the production and hunting of wildlife introduced from abroad. One might envision kangaroos from Australia added to the menu of bison, elk, and Barbados sheep already in the region's wild. Hunters pay high fees for the privilege of stalking and taking these big game animals with cameras, arrows, and rifles.

State game departments at present have no authority over hunting exotic game. Landowners assess fees and control the harvest. This is likely to change as the introduced animals compete for forage and browse with domestic big game. State agriculture departments, however, have already assumed authority, inspecting the meat of harvested animals and charging a fee for each head killed. Much of this meat goes to fancy restaurants in distant cities of the North. A New York restaurant lists on its menu such delicacies as axis venison, blackbuck antelope, and fallow deer for which diners pay well above the price of prime beef.

Most tropical exotics require little water, compared with

cattle. While cattle overgraze their water holes and then move away to destroy other rangelands, for thousands of years desert animals have lived in harmony with the lands they graze. However, exotic grazers become browsers when the range is stressed, thereupon competing with deer. Because the introduced animals have no predators in the southern woods, their numbers grow rapidly. The effect of foreign game upon domestic livestock is similar to that of a food-competing animal or a predator.

Owners expand acreages dedicated to short-term bird hunting, as the sport of shooting pheasants and doves attracts new enthusiasts. These game birds, raised in captivity and released for the day's hunt, provide income for the landowners and recreation for guests. Other put-and-take fowl include the Spanish redlegged partridge, the chukar partridge introduced from India, the Hungarian partridge from mid-continental Europe, bobwhite quail, and domestic turkey.

To the millions of acres now commercially leased for the hunting of common native game, much of the balance of the forest will be added. The fees landowners receive are far more than the taxes assessed on these lands, an amount until recently considered adequate compensation.

High costs for leases, even for indigenous game, encourage the dedication of more public hunting grounds for those unable or unwilling to pay costly fees. The South's public lands open to hunting are minimal, but legislation enables states to lease lands from industries for temporary use as wildlife refuges. Such tracts will not be open to the public in the present usual sense, for the possibility of injuring and killing other hunters is too great. Rather, hunting in these woods will be restricted, like those rules applying to a public golf course. Although anyone may use the area and fees will be charged, entry will be controlled by wardens to protect the hunters as well as the game. Access will be regulated—only a certain number of hunters allowed on the land at a time. Courses of instruction on animal habits and hunter behavior will be required before permits will be issued to enter the game "preserve." Legal hunting may become more a sport for wealthy folks. But thirty-five dollars for a permit to stalk game on these semiprivate lands contrasts with five hundred dollars per gun for some leases. Present federal law enables landowners, under the Conservation Reserve Program, to put up to 10 percent of their holdings in game food crops. This, too, encourages use of adjoining forestlands for sport wildlife production.

The country coon and cat hunter who, until now, has had free access to his neighbors' lands loses that privilege. Trees and fences display *Posted* signs, bringing regret to octogenarians whose hounds have led their masters to prey since boyhood forays into the bush. One county currently experiences serious incendiary fire as a result of doubled hunting fees on lands recently acquired by new industrial owners.

Opportunities in the South

Southern Wood Exports

The happy combination of soils, climate, and tree species in the South makes the region a potential exporter of vast amounts of wood and wood products to nations abroad as well as to other regions of the United States. As the Pacific Northwest concludes the harvest of its virgin forests, much of that region's better soils may be expected to be used for agriculture or industrial and residential development. Because the regenerated second-growth forests there are established on the lower-quality lands, enabling only slow tree growth, the United States is likely to depend in the future to a greater degree upon the South for its wood supply. Real estate developers in mountainous regions take over level, alluvial benches—also of high site quality—for home lots and shopping malls: this too leads to dependence upon the South's structural softwoods to supply the nation's needs.

(West Coast lumbermen may disagree, believing the virgin supply, accompanied by second-growth, has a longer life. They call attention to their recent efforts to recapture eastern markets lost to the South's entrepreneurs in the late 1970s. The eighteen billion board feet of federal timber returned to the inventory of standing trees when buyers, with the approval of Congress, were forced by the economic slowdown of that period to surrender their contracts lends credence to their optimism.) So, a leading southern lumberman could contend that the greatest strength of the region's wood-dependent industry is an "unfair advantage" over the West. The South is "in the enviable position of sitting right in the middle of one of the major market areas of the country," the fast-growing Sunbelt.[20]

Other nations, too, may soon depend upon the South for wood. Mainland Chinese entrepreneurs consider proposals to import round wood (unprocessed logs) to Asian ports from Gulf coastal forests. Pine chips for pulp production, woodpulp, and finished paper can be expected to be sent to citizens of the Peoples' Republic of China. This will occur with only slight improvement in that nation's economy. Meanwhile, wood chip shipments from the South to Scandinavian countries resume as prices for oil and gas, used as sources of energy for paper production, level off. Wood chips left southern ports in the holds of large tankers until rising oil prices made it unprofitable to ship them that way. Local mills then utilized this by-product from sawmills and plywood plants in fuel boilers.

On the other hand, competition with Canada's spruce and fir for paper and the Dominion's Douglas-fir, western red cedar, and Sitka spruce for lumber is expected to continue to dampen southern wood export markets. Canadian provincial and Dominion governments provide the wood for lumbermen to harvest at less than appraised value. In contrast, the South's export wood comes almost solely from privately owned lands.

I expect high-quality oaks, maple, black walnut, and wild black cherry from southern woodlands will compete more earnestly with tropical hardwoods in Europe and the Far East when North American promoters endeavor as earnestly as Oriental traders to capture these markets. Quality furniture and paneling woods move from South America, Africa, and Southeast Asia—often through Japanese and Singaporean middlemen—to supply the requirements of Europe and the United States. Yet the soils and climate of southern hardwood-producing lands—in the Mississippi Delta, other river bottomlands of the Atlantic and Gulf coasts, the Mississippi Bluff Hills, and the Appalachian Mountains—enable production of high-quality deciduous species that could well compete with tropical hardwoods for such uses. Management methods to produce these trees have long been known: economics has precluded the effort to capitalize on the opportunity.

With the export of vast quantities of raw and processed wood, I believe the demand should enable prices to rise sufficiently to warrant intensifying management two or three times present levels. Typically, the South grows about three-quarters of a cord per acre per year. More than two cords can be grown with modest additional effort and with present silvicultural knowledge. Intensive management on the best sites can double that. A genuine threat of worldwide timber famine will enable southern foresters and their employers to produce the necessary wood. It will not be cheap.

There is another side to the world trade in wood that affects the South. Already, South American timber and forest products move to American ports, replacing pulping and construction material formerly utilizing U.S. wood grown in the South. Cheap labor, cheap stumpage, cheap transportation from the woods to the dock, and cheap sea shipping from Latin lands dramatically reduce the demand in marketplaces supplied by Southern Hemisphere nations for wood that otherwise would be harvested in the southern region of the U.S. New York bankers encourage the import trend if it enables repayment of loans now jeopardized by the near disastrous economies of nations to the south of the Rio Grande.

Changing Ownerships

The commercial forestland base of the South is expected to diminish at least through 2015, continuing the decline that began in 1965. In the two decades after 1965, acreage decreased by about 12 percent, the fastest rate of loss of forest land of any region in the nation. Losses in the mid-1980s for the South amounted to about one-half million acres a year.[21] While much of the loss was in the Mississippi Delta's alluvial flood plain, this trend for that zone is expected to be reversed. Here grow not only long staple cotton and soybeans: the land has some of the best hardwood-producing climate and soil in the world.

Timberland ownership of the South's 222 million commercially forested acres in the fifteen southern states (including Delaware, Maryland, and Kentucky) at the beginning of the 1980s breaks down like this: industry, 19 percent; nonfarm private, 41 percent; national forest, 6 percent; other public, 4 percent; and farmer, 30 percent.[22] Anticipated changes involve increases in other public ownerships (states, counties, and cities) and a slight increase in industry ownership (though many exchanges between companies will be made in order for each to block in lands nearer its mills). Farmer and other nonindustrial private forest (NIPF) ownerships will diminish as these owners realize that timberland is only a good investment in the very long run and only then largely because of inflated values for land. (See Table A for early 1960s and mid-1980s ownership percentages of commercial forestland in the twelve states of the South recognized by the U.S. Forest Service as the region.)

Vast acreages of lands abandoned from agriculture returned to forest as cotton lost its kingdom in the South and wool and mutton production failed to materialize as a replacement for the fluffy white-boll agronomy. Each year the forested acreage increased until the early 1960s. Since then the amount of land in timber has steadily declined, the loss amounting to 15 million of the region's original 197 million wooded acres. Conversion of the Mississippi River Delta to soybeans accounts for about one-third of this loss.[23]

The proportion of forestland owned by farmers continues to decline as lawyers, physicians, merchants, and bankers buy agricultural tracts as investments. The U.S. Department of Agriculture's Cooperative Extension Service estimates that absentee landowners hold about 70 percent of the South's privately owned forestland.[24]

Table A. Owners of Commercial Forestland in the South

	1962 (200 million acres) (%)	1985 (182 million acres) (%)
NIPF	73	66
Industry	18	24
Public	9	10

Although these new owners, especially the absentees, depend on higher future value of the land to justify their investment, they may opt for pine plantation establishment for intermediate income or to enhance the land's value for a future sale. Their interest in ownership often contrasts sharply with that of the farmer from whom they bought the parcels. For the farmer, ownership frequently has been partially emotional ("This land was my grandad's"); for the new owner, the interest is strictly financial. Those earlier men-of-the-soil owned 60 percent of the South's commercial forestland in the mid-1950s; in contrast, they held less than 30 percent in the mid-1980s.[25] The decline continues.

Although some forestland has gone back to agricultural use, mostly improved pastures sprigged with coastal Bermuda grass, much has been reassigned to new towns, airports, shopping malls, and rights-of-way for utility lines and roads. Wilderness designation in national forests and in other federal and state ownerships locks up considerable acreage across the region. These kinds of transitions are projected to continue. The inevitable lesser land base that is now the remainder of the southern forest must require more intensive management in order to accommodate consumer demands.

Congressional allocations of money for planting trees on eroded lands expand the forest land base slightly. Converting thousands of acres of refuse land fills (formerly called garbage dumps) to woodlands also increases the forested acreage. Reclaiming mine lands stripped for minerals and coal (including lignite) for electrical energy generation both adds and subtracts some lands from the inventory. The former occurs because some mined lands once farmed are planted with trees; the latter because surface-mined lands formerly covered with trees are reclaimed for pasture. Earlier owners usually have the option to buy back the reclaimed lands that they had held before mining took place.

Table B. Percentages of Land by Forest Cover Types

	1962	1985
Bottomland hardwoods	18	16
Upland hardwoods	31	35
Natural pines	33	19
Planted pines	4	14
Oak-pine mixtures	14	16

Across the South, percentages of land classified by broad forest cover types in 1962 and 1985, respectively, are shown in Table B. The decline in acreages and volumes in natural pine and bottomland hardwood stands is expected to continue, while low-value upland hardwoods capture thousands of acres of second-growth pine stands in all provinces of the region.

Mysterious Decline and Other Threats

Foresters in the Piedmont Province and the Southern Appalachian Mountains are apprehensive over declining growth rates from conifer stands. The cause of reductions in increments of some 20 to 30 percent during the past two decades seems not to be related to a lack of thinning. Diameter growth rates for all species together in natural stands for the whole Southeast have dropped as much as 50 percent over the past three decades.

As a result, annual growth of softwood timber in the South seems to have peaked about twenty years sooner than earlier anticipated by U.S. Forest Service resource projections. The cause of the downturn, whether it is a temporary or permanent manifestation, and its effect on wood availability for industrial consumption are subjects for intense study.

Growth decreases are attributed to greater annual tree mortality, partly because of insect infestations. Reproduction following harvests is inadequate as landowners allow land to lie idle. Developers convert forests to other uses and few old-field sites remain to be reforested to conifers. Hardwood invasion competes with the pines. But the puzzle is that the reductions in rates of diameter growth and lowered stand density take place where neither pests nor human lethargy and activity can be blamed.[26] Drought and stand ages (growth begins to culminate as stands grow toward maturity) no doubt play a role. The search for the cause includes consideration of atmospheric pollutants. Many ask, Could acid rain be the culprit? That air contaminated with sulfuric and nitric acids will greatly affect southern forests is assumed.

While most of the talk about acid rain, global warming, and ozone depletion relates to the forests of the Northeast or southern California, the South has begun to study the effects of air pollutants on its pine and hardwood forests. The federal Forest Response Program, cooperatively managed by the U.S. Forest Service, the Southern Commercial Research Cooperative, and the Environmental Protection Agency has taken the lead. Forestry schools and industries also participate in the effort. It is too early to allege any detrimental effects across the South, but the great amount of industrial air effluent produced along Gulf coastal shores and carried by Gulf winds may well influence tree vigor and growth. Studies currently under way look for past effects, utilizing historical data and dendrochronology—tree ring records.

Throughout the region, researchers currently simulate air contaminants in tents in which they grow various tree species. In these plastic enclosures they attempt to isolate physiologic stresses on the vegetation. To understand the potential for volume and vigor losses, industry has funded an independent staff of researchers. It has a special interest: pulp and paper mills produce many of the contaminants that may affect the production of the raw product upon which those mills depend. The future may necessitate development of genetically improved resistant strains of various species able to endure high levels of toxic chemicals poured from industrial stacks.

Meanwhile, the effect of the southern pine beetle on timber inventories continues to mystify the keepers of timber accounts. Periodically, the small black insect has gnawed its way through stands of seemingly healthy conifers, playing havoc with volume estimates for future years. Should the beetle attacks continue unabated, lowered standing timber inventories could place the region in a serious dilemma. Had the early 1980s' recession not occurred and had the Canadians kept their wood above forty-nine degrees north latitude (by not suspending laissez faire), timber shortages could have occurred. The South's fourth forest would have been a troubled estate. Even so, many assessors of the situation consider the pine decline in the South a major threat to the nation's economic well-being.

Government Incentives

Government and industry groups believe that timber growth on seventy million southern acres could yield returns of at least 4 percent, apart from inflation or deflation. But 4 or even 5 or 6 percent is hardly a worthwhile investment when money without risks earns much more in certificates of deposit. I am aware that some economists insist that trees grow as much as 10 percent on the better sites. That is true, but to attain this rate requires the expense of highly intensive management and land with agronomic potential.[27] And therein lies the reason for lobbying by both industry and government for incentives from citizen treasuries. That effort will increase.

Past and/or present assistance has been from the Forestry Incentive Program (FIP), federal allocations for site preparation, prescribed fire, tree planting, and weed-tree control. Allocations from states and industries for similar purposes had been provided by the mid-1980s: more such grants are in the offing. While the capital gains taxation on timber harvests, which permits the paying of federal income taxes at lower than ordinary rates, went with the wind in the congressional tax legislation of late 1986, the 10 percent tax credit and amortization prerogatives continued to encourage good forestry practices. With the credit tax break, certain expenses involved with ownership and stewardship are subtracted from the tax bill. With amortization, the landowner is allowed for federal income tax purposes to spread out over seven years some of the costs of managing a forest. Congress surrendered in late 1990 to the demands that capital gains and other tax breaks were necessary if small landowners were to manage their lands so that future generations would have the wood necessary to build homes and mill paper. The new capital gains tax for timber was levied at 28 percent. Meanwhile, nonindustrial private forest landowners banded together in county committees to better understand forestry practices and to lobby legislatures to enhance their interests.

The Federal Conservation Reserve Program, enabled by the 1985 Food Security Act, could bring about conversion of considerable acreages of highly erodible cropland to third-forest plantations of conifers. By this legislation farmers are paid to take erosive lands out of crop production and to plant trees (or grass) on such sites. Congress can be expected to encourage such soil conservation measures with additional legislation as long as the nation's farmers produce more than enough food to meet domestic and export demands. The influence of the Forest Assistance Act of 1978, providing funds through Agricultural Stabilization and Conservation Service programs for silvicultural practices, likely will expand to assure adequate wood supplies.

Higher-grade hardwood logs to supply furniture and paneling mills become available as broad-leaved tree growth constantly increases, even though slowly. In contrast, pine trees of large diameter are in short supply because of the compound interest effect of silvicultural treatment and the infestations of bark beetles. Adequate supplies of softwood timbers for structural and plywood purposes, many argue, will require incentives beyond those presently envisioned.

Encouraged by industry, governments, I expect, will provide more technical assistance for both company owners and small nonindustrial landowners. More money will be spent for fire protection and suppression, for insect and disease control, and for producing genetically superior seedlings in nurseries. Container-grown seedlings, produced in tubes and cellulosic cups, help assure plantation survival, especially when droughts follow the planting season. Survival is essentially assured when tublings containing roots twenty inches long are placed in holes made with farm tractor–mounted post-hole drills. This prediction is based upon these facts: by the mid-1980s, about 3 million of the 1.5 billion southern pines planted annually were containerized. The 2.4 million acres planted annually at that time will certainly increase, even though more acreage is regenerated by natural, rather than artificial, methods.[28]

An incentive overlooked by promoters who would encourage wise management of the forest resource is a subsidy to the logger for thinning. Industry or government would be called upon to provide the fee. Loggers, if reimbursed from this fund, no longer could plead that thinning costs *them* money, thus making it impossible for landowners to locate woodsmen willing to move laborers and machinery for partial harvests. The cost per unit of wood harvested is much less for clear-cutting than for thinning a stand. Thinning, however, enhances the vigor of residual trees, salvages physiologically weak trees before they die, and speeds production of wood on the boles left to grow. To encourage thinning is to enhance the South's wood supply in both the short and long run.

If timber shortages appear likely, as many insist, state forestry agencies will join the list of activist organizations in cultivating support groups. County timber landowner associations and urban coalitions collaborate in fighting for agency budgets to improve NIPF and municipal forests, while industry supports the state bureaus because it needs them to help assure adequate inventories of standing timber. The uninterrupted flow of raw material through the tremendously expensive mills is essential to the nation's welfare.

Vandalism

The probability is high for greater vandalism in and on the forests, both public and private. Already noted is the need to protect valuable black walnut forests from thieves. As wood becomes more valuable and timbered lands grow high-quality intensively managed stands, tree theft is anticipated. Absentee landowners must provide security for their property.

Abuse of recreation areas escalates as vandals' sledgehammers break concrete furniture, wreck unattended bath houses, and sabotage water and sewer systems at remote campgrounds. Antagonists to silvicultural procedures increase their damaging practices by fouling fuel lines of heavy equipment temporarily parked at logging sites as well as by spiking trees.

Most disconcerting, however, is the booby-trapping of marijuana plots on both public and private holdings. (If the land is not owned by the drug growers and the owner is innocent of illegal use, the land cannot be confiscated by the government.) Acreage on national forest lands planted to marijuana quadrupled between 1981 and 1986. The same growth rate occurred for other holdings, both those of small absentee owners and the giant corporate organizations. An estimated 20 percent of the domestic crop is harvested from public lands. Guns, attack dogs, and land mines are placed by culprits. As I write, illegal drug growers plant appreciable acreages on national forests in North Carolina, Arkansas, Florida, and Missouri. Nationally, the Forest Service has closed a million acres in order to protect its employees, contractors, and hikers and hunters who work in, and visit, these woodlands.[29] The problem appears to be so great in the South that many acres will be closed for public use, thereby negating the efforts of wilderness enthusiasts to set lands aside in order for the public to enjoy a pristine, primeval habitat.

Manufacturing

Products made from trees will differ as the pages turn on the calendar. I predict every part of the tree will be used, including the root. What once was waste will be burned in more efficient generators for energy production. Mills will produce closer to 100 percent than the 70 percent of the electrical energy they now generate from their wastes.

Weed trees now killed with herbicides will be harvested and chipped for fuel or for paper pulp. Low-grade broad-leaved trees will soon make up about 10 percent of the chip mix for kraft paper. Already bond papers include up to 70 percent hardwood fibers.

Manufacturers have improved oriented strand boards, which today replace much of structural plywood. The reconstituted wood can be manufactured to designated densities; shaped and sized to builders' specifications; and impregnated with preservatives, fire retardants, and water repellents. With these procedures, as with flake board, low-grade trees can be used.

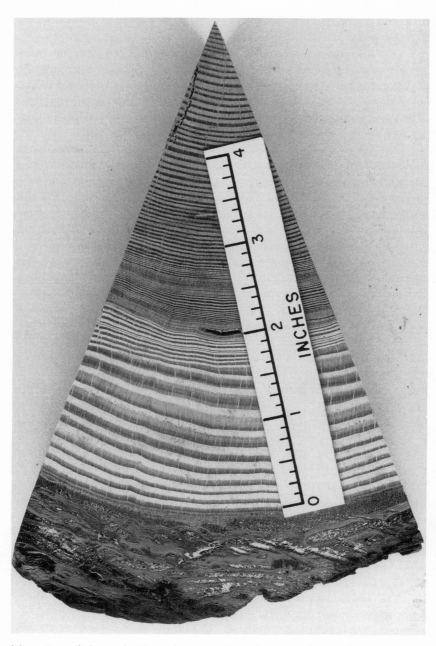

Measuring radial growth. Future foresters will need to control rates of diameter growth in order to produce lumber that will not warp or twist. Thinning and/or fertilizing sometimes results in dramatic changes in radial growth.

Lumber mills, seeing their output replaced by reconstituted wood, will improve quality control, thereby reducing the carpenter's displeasure with southern pine boards that warp and twist while stacked or when nailed in place. Considerable favor toward Canadian softwoods for construction relates to the dependability of the lumber from the North that flows to southern markets. Even high tariffs and the end of Dominion subsidization of the logging and lumbering industries will not limit Canadian imports if southern pine lumber quality does not improve.

Enabling mills to produce lumber that is stable when put in place by carpenters requires raw material that contains minimal juvenile wood (the interior core of the bole containing smaller or less structurally developed cells). Trees with much of their volume composed of this weak fiber provide products of less strength. To produce trees containing little juvenile wood, foresters must grow southern pines in stands of ten thousand stems per acre in their early years. Such high density controls the volume of juvenile wood. That silvicultural practice then calls for early precommercial thinning, and that is costly.

Juvenile wood is acceptable for newsprint and strand board manufacturing processes. Thus, merchandisers will refine the wood mix—by position in the tree as well as by species—for particular products. This means the core of sapwood, too often presently milled for lumber and which contributes greatly to the quality problems suffered over recent decades by the industry, will not be used for lumber.

Thin veneers of quality hardwoods, used in furniture and paneling, will be even thinner. Thus the available material exhibiting costly figured grains will cover more surface area.

The South's Fourth Forest

The South's virgin timber made up its first forest. The second growth that seeded in naturally following the cutting of the primeval woodlands became the second forest. In the 1960s, industry called the stands of planted trees the South's third forest.[30] Now the next generation considers the South's fourth forest, and it asks, Will it measure up?[31]

Concern for whether the next forest will measure up revolves around the supposed declining inventory of standing trees and the resulting reduced availability of wood. This, I anticipate, will cause higher prices for stumpage and wood products which, in turn, will limit lumber and paper sales. Such a situation, along with improved technology to enable consumers to have forest products at stable prices, reduces the labor force. That labor force, 10 percent of the workers in the region, now works for the South's leading employer group, the manufacturers of products made from wood. A projected loss of over one hundred thousand jobs could be a serious blow to local and state economies. Wood-using industry employees earn about 10 percent of the wages and salaries across the South and produce about 10 percent of the value added to the economy.[32]

One may argue with the premise, as I have done elsewhere in this chapter, about the relationship of stumpage availability and the price of wood. Declining timber availability results in higher prices, but the higher prices are for stumpage, not just for wood products. Stumpage costs, after all the inputs and outputs of a manufacturing process are tallied, are a wee part of the cost of the product. Stumpage prices for pulpwood, for example, could double without being noticed in the price of a ton of paper, the daily news, or this book.

More significant is this: higher stumpage prices anticipated with a rising population eventually encourage landowners to more intensively manage their forests. That overcomes the supposed threat of declining inventories, a situation that prevails for both coniferous softwoods and broad-leaved hardwoods.

Some authorities, however, do not envision stumpage in the next couple of decades reaching its late-1970s' price pinnacle. Such high stumpage prices are far-distant in time. As I write, oligopsony takes its toll upon the small landowner's purse, as a few buyers (the wood-using industry) control the demand from a large number of sellers (the nonindustrial landowners). Sawlogs in the ten- and twelve-inch class, until now sold for lumber production, are bought at pulpwood prices. Even then, these low-quality trees may be utilized in chip-and-saw mills or the whole log be simply ground into chips for particle board. Stumpage prices deteriorate as log product values diminish.

The idea of declining inventory could be a bugaboo quite unrelated to the price of wood products. The South's annual timber removal has not exceeded growth since the late 1930s. The threat that the growth-drain (G/D) ratio would be less than 1 by 1990 was valid in the late 1970s. But long before the 1990s, economic recession dynamited the industry. New home construction, to which about one-half of America's wood was destined, dramatically diminished. Warehouses across the region bulged with manufactured wood, both lumber and plywood, for which sales were not imminent. Stumpage purchases remained uncut in the woods, some acquired timber reverting to the landowners because the contract harvest date had not been met. Industry and landowners are not likely to again get caught in this warehouse- and stumpage-inventory trap.

To add to the calamitous situation, Canadians, as I have repeatedly noted, caught on to the opportunities to market throughout the

United States wood grown in Dominion and provincial forests. By the mid-1980s, over one-half of the lumber utilized in the southern states was sawn in Canada from Douglas-fir and similar softwoods. The Canadian government provided stumpage at near zero costs for its pulping plants, the wood coming from its publicly owned lands. Canadians captured paper markets that for decades had been the customers of southern kraft and newsprint mills. One daily journal in Houston, its presses but a few miles from a newsprint mill, publishes its news, its gossip, and its ads on paper shipped from a thousand miles to the north.

A report by the Forest Service entitled *The South's Fourth Forest: Alternatives for the Future*, released in 1988, again warns (or continues to warn) about declining softwood inventories and the potential for a hardwood decline after 2000. Here are the reasons given: lack of regeneration following harvest on much privately held land, increased mortality due to insects and disease, diminishing diameter growth (cited previously in this chapter), and the conversion of timberland to higher-value uses.[33] One might add to this the U.S. Department of Commerce's report that 1986 was a record year for southern pine lumber production. Not since 1925 had production exceeded 11.8 billion board feet.[34] Insect salvage of stumpage at extraordinarily low prices accounts for some of this harvest.

Many broad-leaved species in the South once considered undesirable or now considered weed trees find commercial use. When several "useless" hill hickory species dominated many forests in the 1950s, researchers discovered ways to utilize these members of the genus *Carya*. Furniture and paneling, some labeled *pecan*, went on the market. Other species (oaks, maples, beech, sycamore, and birches), killed with herbicides in the 1940s to 1960s, now provide parts for upholstered furniture, decorative flooring, and paneling. Even the obnoxious leguminous mesquite, introduced by cattle drives from South Texas to the state's northern boundary and into Oklahoma in bovine droppings, is an attractive parquet flooring and gun stock material. This occurs just as a major chemical manufacturer prepares to market, after tremendous research and testing expense, a herbicide to wage war against the Northern Hemisphere's "tropical" hardwood.

To conclude that the present use of the South's forest will lead either to timber famine or to extravagant abundance would be to ignore Sir Walter Scott's admonition:

> That man may safely venture
> on his way,
> Who is so guided that he
> cannot stray.

We cannot know how forestry shall go. In 1928, for example, a rural Georgia newspaper, probably cued by Forest Service rhetoric about the exhaustion of spruce from North America's timberlands, editorialized: "Thirty-five years ago yellow pine lands in South Georgia were selling for $2 per acre; such of them as are now left are selling for $50 per acre upward.

"Within about six years the consumption of Southern yellow pine in making paper has increased more than one thousand percent, and the mills are fast multiplying. It requires only about one-half the time to grow a yellow pine to a commercial size as is required for Northern spruce.

"*A famine in forestry is near.*"[35] Is such again a threat?

A Final Word

This chapter only touches upon forest management technology anticipated for the future. For now, however, one final prophecy: No new mills will be built in the region if they may more than minimally pollute the air or the waters (surface or subsurface). Nor will water be allocated by state authorities for any appreciable number of new wood-using industries. Additionally, the region is expected to lose two hundred thousand forested acres between 1982 and 2000.[36]

At both federal and state levels, the people have spoken: if it is a choice between jobs and a clean environment, for now they choose the latter, even if trees grow beyond economic maturity and are left to rot in the woods. Only hunger for food—and thus for jobs—and a shortage of wood at the local lumberyard will change that attitude.

Afterword

HESE PAGES have attempted to describe the forests of the South as they once were, as they are today, and as they may be in the future. For some lands, human history has altered the course of ecological transition, and this has been noted. Never has land been affected so much in so little time by humankind as within the past century. As the story of *Homo sapiens* continues to be written, so too will be observed and recorded the changes that take place in land use and in the nature of the South's forests. Use of the land and its resources by people often sets in motion natural processes that cause permanent change. Frequently the results are destructive; sometimes they are catastrophic. Erosion from cleared slopes removes topsoil developed over thousands of years, and gullies from poorly engineered roads lower the moisture regime of the soil and, thereby, degrade forest sites. Although the forests of the South have shown remarkable ability to reoccupy lands clear-cut for their timber, burned, or cleared for agriculture, new stands are often of species other than those that covered the land under virgin conditions. Pines, sweetgum, yellow-poplar, or scrub oaks may now dominate rehabilitated sites where once-vigorous beech-birch-maple, chestnut, or oak-hickory-pine stands covered the land. Hence, the forests in much of the region have been modified more or less severely by previous land use or abuse.

Forestry practices, as well as the vegetative composition of the forest, will continue to be affected by land-use transition. Conversion of timber-producing forestlands to residential communities, factories, and reservoirs or withdrawal of forests from commercial lumbering for watershed protection, game preserves, parks, and scientific studies of the environment will necessitate intensifying practices on remaining lands to supply the nation's fiber needs. The necessity for high rates of wood production will rarely permit reversion to original timber types. These managed forests will, however, be subjected to the same geographic and biotic influences as their predecessors. Foresters who manage them will be most successful when they are guided by wise consideration of the ways the factors of site—edaphic, physiographic, climatic, and biotic—are expressed by the native forest types.

Environmentalists make much of the term *ecology,* a word common in the forester's vocabulary a century ago. *Ecology* is derived from the Greek word *oik[c]os,* meaning house. Ecology deals with care of the habitat, the whole of the earth, the home of humankind and subordinate life. But little is said by modern-day conservationists of the translation of *oik[c]os* into its Latin equivalent and the English word derived from the ancient languages. *I[e]conaea* is the word and *economics* is of course its offspring. Even less debate hovers around the word which King James's scholars employed in translating Holy Scripture from its original Greek and the fourth-century Latin vulgate—or commoner's—Bible into the authorized version of 1611. *Oikos* and *iconaea* became *steward* and *stewardship* in the Anglo-Saxon tongue. Anglicizing the Greek has altered the spelling slightly, but foresters of forty years' service recall the definition of *oecology* as the study of the relationship of living things to each other and to their environment.

Ecology and economics come together in stewardship. Thus the manager of the southern forest is the caretaker of the household, the overseer of the estate, and the keeper of the accounts. Men and women challenged with this responsibility take on the mantle of faithful stewardship. That mantle, to use the Genesis admonition to "replenish and subdue the earth," requires restoration of exploited sites and the ongoing care of lands utilized to provide for the physical and spiritual needs of people. Sustained yields of goods and services until the end of time must come from this wildland estate. Such stewardship should not be confused with *biophilia,*[1] which implies a fondness for all living things, if that fondness makes the observer a worshiper of trees rather than a provider for people.

Dwindling reserves of the world's renewable and nonrenewable resources heighten the need for increased productivity in the nation's southern wood bin. These lands, as they now are, will play an important role in meeting the demands of the country's citizens well into the next century. The inherent time lag between the initiation of forestry measures and the marketability of wood products resulting from those measures calls for prompt action.

Many contemporary residents of the region, however, find it difficult to support the effort, neglecting to realize that all of us use forest

A typical second-growth stand of loblolly and shortleaf pines in the Georgia Piedmont. Note the absence of an understory of progeny pines and an abundance of
shade-tolerant broad-leaved shrubs. The abundance of hardwoods in a young pine
stand indicates that the pines seeded in on cut-over land, not on an abandoned
cotton field. By the time the conifers reach this age—forty-five years—wildlife,
wind, and water will have transported many seeds from which the broad-leaved
species arise. On freshly cut-over lands, hardwoods arise quickly from root suckers,
directly competing with the young pines, as well as from seeds. Merging ecology
with economics becomes ever more important.

resources. Those who live in houses, read books, wear clothes, and stay
warm or cool may be unaware that, as consumers, they indirectly force
environmental insults upon the land. Like the rest of us, they have a
choice: to endorse policies that will ensure increased and efficient wood
production from the best forest sites and accept minimal reductions in
other amenities; or, the alternative, to support antiutilitarian philoso-
phies that divert the commercial forest from its function of efficiently producing wood. The latter will be costly in dollars and in energy resources
spent in utilizing substitutes from ever-rarer nonrenewable raw materials.
The southern forest has only begun to make its contributions. Those contributions must be in amenities, like pristine landscapes, as well as in
water, wildlife, and wood.[2]

Ancient Chinese philosophers classified nature into five elements of the universe. For them the world consisted of wood, fire, earth (soil), water, and metal. Forestland exemplifies all but the last. The forest produces wood; is destroyed, regenerated, and sustained by fire; grows in and creates soil; and utilizes water while protecting aquifers.

Early Romans, on the other hand, seemed to appreciate little the resources of the universe. Cicero, as a royal consul, is said to have had utilitarian attitudes toward the crown's raw materials. The Empire's fall has been attributed to the reckless cutting of its forests and the abuse of its watersheds, along with the exploitation of its minerals. But some concern was evidenced, for the desolation was so prevalent in the fourth century B.C. that a governmental decree established a forest policy.[3] This, however, did not inspire an ecological conscience, nor did it encourage people of the era to observe nature in order to discover its ways. That was left to the followers of Francis Bacon who, during the Scientific Revolution, began to recognize that to have dominion over nature, one must subscribe to nature's principles. Thus, by observing, we can understand the behavior of the world around us. Therein lies the need to understand ecological relationships.[4] C. S. Lewis's oft-quoted remark about the continuing struggle between people and nature—for example, forest managers and the insects that infest the timber—bears stating once again: "Man's conquest of Nature turns out, in the moment of its consummation to be Nature's conquest of Man."[5] The Cambridge don implied that we cannot win, but comprehending ecological relationships and their restraints helps us to manage the woodland estate for its economic and other social benefits.

The southern forest must be tamed and used. Its taming was described by Walt Whitman, though a poet not of the South, in the *Song of the Broad Axe*. The ax "leaps," and from the forest come shingle, rail, sash, and floor. And more. When Whitman wrote in the nineteenth century, civilized people depended on wood for almost every part of the house, for fuel for trains and ships as well as for hearths, for structures, woodenware, and chemicals.

Nature, because of use and abuse by people for their needs, may be *awfully* ugly or *awe-full-ly* beautiful. We have seen it in the South. Ugliness need not again occur. The cut-out-and-get-out experiences of the South's timber barons is behind us. Likely past, too, are the land management excesses of the industrialists who assembled into giant holdings the lands of lesser companies. But out in front are the environmental extremists. Their romanticism and industry's contrasting utilitarianism must be wed by compromises in resource management. That kind of taming of the southern forest calls for stewardship—an old term related to the word *conservation*—the wise use of resources.

Two Hundred Men and Women of the Southern Forest

Albright, Horace (1890–1987). Second National Park Service director. The Great Smoky Mountains National Park in Tennessee and North Carolina was established during his tenure.

Ambler, Chase P. Promoter in early 1900s of the Appalachian National Park. Land designated for it was eventually purchased by Congress and became the Great Smoky Mountains National Park.

Andrews, A. Felton. President of the Forest Farmers Association 1976–77, an organization of private industrial and nonindustrial landowners in the South.

Anthony, Bruce W. President of the Southern Forest Products Association, 1971–72.

Ashe, W. W. Early-day U.S. Department of Agriculture Forest Service botanist-forester who cataloged the species of the Southern Appalachian Mountains, who promoted passage of the Weeks Act in 1911, and for whom the federal tree nursery in Louisiana is named.

Baggenstoss, Herman E. President of the Forest Farmers Association 1960–62.

Bailey, Kenneth D. President of the Forest Farmers Association 1986–87.

Barber, John C. Ninth director of the Southern Forest Experiment Station 1972–76.

Portions of this biographic material have been gleaned from the *Encyclopedia of American Forest and Conservation History*, 2 vols., ed. Richard C. Davis (New York: Macmillan, 1983) and from H. R. Josephson's "A History of Forestry Research in the Southern United States" (Washington, D.C.: U.S. Department of Agriculture Forest Service, unpublished manuscript, 1985).

Bartram, John (1699–1777). First North American–born naturalist. He made plant collection expeditions into Georgia and Florida in the mid-1760s.

Bartram, William (1739–1823). Son of John Bartram and also a naturalist who made botanical trips into the Southeast to collect specimens 1765–66, 1773, and 1778. He drew pictures of trees, flowers, and animals of the region for the financial supporters of his work.

Batemen, F. O. Chief ranger of the Great Southern Lumber Company at Bogalusa, Louisiana, who developed what has been called one of the most comprehensive and successful tree-planting and natural regeneration programs of all time.

Batson, John O. President of the Southern Forest Products Association 1979–80 and Louisiana industrialist.

Bell, Victor. Joined with Robert Long to form the Long-Bell Lumber Company, with headquarters in Kansas City, Kansas. By 1918 they held 600,000 acres and operated a dozen mills and 118 retail lumber yards. Their operation moved to the West Coast following the cut-out in the South.

Bemis, J. R. President of the Southern Pine Association 1952–54.

Bennett, Frank W. President of the Forest Farmers Association 1966–68.

Bennett, Hugh (1881–1960). North Carolinian who served as first head of the U.S. Department of the Interior Soil Erosion Service (1933) and first chief of the U.S. Department of Agriculture Soil Conservation Service (1934–51).

Bibler, James. President of the Southern Forest Products Association 1983–84 and Arkansas lumberman.

Bloomer, P. A. President of the Southern Pine Association 1939–41.

Bond, W. E. In the 1930s, with associates, issued the first in a series of reports on the costs and returns of sustained yield forestry in southern pine types.

Bowen, Dr. John H. President of the Forest Farmers Association 1985–86.

Boyce, S. G. Ninth director of the Southeastern Forest Experiment Station 1970–73.

Bragg, Braxton. Civil War general and sawmiller who, upon abandoning Pensacola, Florida, burned its mill and railroad trestles. Alerted to the South's timbering opportunities, he saw the freeing of the slaves as a setback to industrializing the South's forests.

Bray, William L. Director of the Bureau of Forestry Timber Survey in the South in the early 1900s.

Briegleb, Philip A. Fifth director of the Southern Forest Experiment Station (1954–63).

Brown, Andrew A. A Scot who in 1828 first used a fifty-inch circular saw blade to mill baldcypress at Natchez, Mississippi.

Brown, E. Lucy. Author of the ecology classic *Deciduous Forests of Eastern North America* (1950), which documented distribution patterns for forest trees. Her work was especially important in the classification of broadleaf timber types in the Southern Appalachian region.

Bruce, Donald. U.S. Department of Agriculture Forest Service researcher who provided technical guidance for the development of normal yield tables for unmanaged southern pine stands, released as the well-known and time-honored Miscellaneous Publication 50.

Camp, John M. President of the Southern Forest Products Association 1972–73 and an executive of Union-Camp Corporation.

Campbell, William. U.S. Department of Agriculture Forest Service pathologist in the 1950s, largely responsible for solving the riddle of the littleleaf disease of shortleaf pine in the Piedmont Province.

Carter, Thomas L. President of the Southern Pine Association 1963–64.

Cary, Austin (1865–1936). U.S. Department of Agriculture Forest Service roving forester who traveled the South in the 1930s to encourage sustained yield management and to promote other good forestry practices on private land. Sometimes called the Father of Southern Forestry.

Catesby, Mark. In 1737 published *Hortus Britanno-Americanus,* earliest volume in English devoted exclusively to North American trees, which described eighty-five species of the southern forest.

Chaiken, L. E. Forest Service researcher in the Southeast who showed in the 1940s how to use fire effectively to control weed broad-leaved trees in pine stands.

Chapman, H. H. (1874–1963). Yale forestry professor and textbook author whose field instruction and observations in Louisiana, beginning in 1917 at Urania, encouraged his advocacy of prescribed fire and other silvicultural practices for the southern pines.

Clancy, Leon. President of the Southern Pine Association 1956–57.

Clark, A. L. President of the Southern Pine Association 1919–20.

Cliff, Edward (1906–87). U.S. Department of Agriculture Forest Service chief (1962–77) who advocated clear-cutting but who also was responsible for many environmental enhancement programs that had an impact on forestry in the South.

Clutter, J. L. University of Georgia professor who, with others, developed data on stand structure and yields of loblolly pine plantations in the lower Atlantic coastal plain.

Coile, Theodore. Duke University professor who, with his students in the 1950s, developed soil-site tables for determining site index on lands where trees are absent.

Connaughton, Charles A. Third director of the Southern Forest Experiment Station (1944–51).

Copeland, Royal. U.S. senator who introduced a resolution to provide a national plan for American forestry. Published in 1933, the report, *A National Plan for American Forestry* (commonly called the Copeland Report), documented the forestry situation in the South and recommended federal regulation of logging on private lands.

Coulter, C. Huxley. Canadian-born forester, director (1945–58) of the Florida Forest Service, and innovator of fire protection techniques.

Croker, Thomas. Research forester in Alabama who, from the 1950s through the 1980s, developed systems for regenerating longleaf pine stands.

Crosby, L. O. President of the Southern Pine Association 1933–34.

Damtoft, Walter. First full-time industrial forester in the South, employed by Champion Fibre Company of Canton, N.C., in 1920; previously an acquisitions forester for Weeks Law purchases for national forests in the Southern Appalachian Mountains.

Demmon, Elwood L. Second director of the Southern Forest Experiment Station (1927–44) and fifth director of the Southeastern Forest Experiment Station (1951–56).

Denman, J. C., Jr. President of the Southern Pine Association 1969–70 and executive of Temple-Inland Corporation in Texas.

DeVall, Wilbur B. President of the Forest Farmers Association (1974–75), an organization of private industrial and nonindustrial landowners in the South.

Dierks, D. V. Arkansas lumberman whose family became the largest landowner in that state. Mills and lands were sold to the Weyerhaeuser Company in the 1970s.

Douglas, William O. U.S. Supreme Court Justice who promoted the establishment of the Big Thicket National Preserve with his book *Farewell to Texas.*

Doxey, Walter. Coauthor, with George Norris, in the U.S. Congress of the Co-operative Farm Forestry Act of 1937.

Driver, Charles. International Paper Company research forester who, at Bainbridge, Georgia, carried out studies in the 1950s on tree diseases and prescribed burning.

Earle, T. W., Sr. President of the Forest Farmers Association (1964–66).

Edgar, R. R. Chairman of the American Pulpwood Association (1968–70) and an executive of Hiawassee Land Co.

Edwards, Acie C. President of the Forest Farmers Association (1982–83), an organization of private industrial and nonindustrial landowners in the South.

Eldridge, "Captain" I. F. Graduate of the Biltmore Forest School in 1909 who later directed the federal forest survey for the South. As early as 1911 he recommended the use of fire to reduce hazardous fuels in longleaf pine stands.

Ellis, Thomas H. Eleventh director of the Southern Forest Experiment Station (beginning in 1984).

Ernest, Albert, Jr. President of the Forest Farmers Association (1970–72).

Flint, Rev. Timothy. Congregational clergyman of the mid-1800s who criticized the girdling of trees before cultivating the land, a practice then widely utilized in the South.

Folweiler, A. D. With A. A. Brown in 1939 published the initial text on forest fire control; later became director of the Texas Forest Service.

Forbes, Reginald D. First professional state forester for Louisiana and first director of the Southern Forest Experiment Station (1921–27).

Forsling, C. L. Second director of the Southeastern Forest Experiment Station (1934–38).

Foster, A. A. Nursery researcher who in the 1950s and 1960s showed the use of chemical pesticides for protecting seedlings.

Frankfort, Philip E. President of the Southern Pine Association (1960–61).

Frost, Edwin A. President of the Southern Pine Association (1924–25).

Frothingham, E. H. First director of the Southeastern Forest Experiment Station (1921–34).

Gardiner, Philip S. President of the Southern Pine Association (1921–22).

Gates, E. C. President of the Southern Pine Association (1959–60).

Gerry, Dr. Eloise. U.S. Department of Agriculture Forest Products Laboratory chemist who worked with Austin Cary in the South to improve gum naval stores extraction.

Gillett, Charles. First Arkansas state extension forester and later first state forester in Arkansas, in the 1930s, who championed industry stewardship of forests; subsequently chief forester for the industrial association that sponsored the American Tree Farm System.

Goodyear, A. C. One of two brothers who moved from Pennsylvania to Louisiana to establish the Great Southern Lumber Co. at Bogalusa.

Gragg, Fred C. President of the Forest Farmers Association (1981–82), an organization of private industrial and nonindustrial landowners in the South.

Gray, John. North Carolina extension forester, Florida forestry school director, and director of the Pinchot Institute.

Grosenbaugh, L. R. Scientist at the Southern Forest Experiment Station from the 1950s through the 1970s who led in the development of procedures for variable plot radius sampling and other techniques that helped increase timber inventory efficiency.

Haig, I. T. Fourth director of the Southeastern Forest Experiment Station 1944–51.

Halls, Lowell. Forest researcher from the 1940s through the 1980s on grazing of livestock and wildlife habitat; author of the monograph *The White-Tailed Deer*; adjunct professor at Stephen F. Austin State University.

Hardtner, Henry E. Urania, La., lumberman who was among the first in the South to practice silviculture, including prescribed fire. Yale Forest School summer classes were held on his land in the 1930s. He encouraged forestry legislation in the state legislature, including the forest renewal tax of 1912, a tax-deferral law that fixed the annual tax rate for twenty years, at which time a severance tax would apply.

Hardtner, Quincy T. President of the Southern Pine Association 1946–48 and an executive of the Urania Lumber Co. in Louisiana.

Hardtner, Quincy T., Jr. President of the Southern Pine Association 1957–58 and an executive of the Urania Lumber Co. in Louisiana.

Hargreaves, Leon, Jr. From the 1950s through the 1980s, leader of taxation proposals for the southern states and later dean of the University of Georgia School of Forest Resources.

Harper, Verne. Manager of U.S. Department of Agriculture Forest Service research at Lake City, Fla., who showed the effect of fire on gum naval stores production and who became Forest Service assistant chief for research in 1951.

Harrigan, Dwight. President of the Southern Forest Products Association 1985–86 and an Alabama lumberman.

Harrigan, W. D. President of the Southern Pine Association 1964–65.

Harris, T. G., Sr. Chairman of the American Pulpwood Association 1974–76 and an executive of Chesapeake Corp.

Hepting, George H. Tree pathologist in the 1940s through 1960s who demonstrated that decay is attributable to fire.

Herbst, Walter W. President of the Forest Farmers Association 1983–84.

Hermelink, Herman M. President of the Forest Farmers Association 1977–78.

Herty, Charles H. (1867–1938). Chemical engineer who between 1900 and 1910 perfected the cup-and-gutter system to gather pine sap from trees for the gum naval stores industry; in 1933, he successfully produced a good grade of newsprint from southern pine; and in 1936 showed that sulfite pulp from southern pine could be used for rayon manufacture. He did not live to see the opening in 1940 of the first newsprint mill in the South at Herty, now part of Lufkin, Tex.

Heyward, Frank. Great Southern Lumber Company (Bogalusa, La.) forester whose 1958 soliloquy moved politicians and industrialists to regenerate the region's cut-over lands: "millions of acres of bleak cutover land, apparently useful for no gainful purpose, cursed and shamed every State in the South. Instead of attracting people, the sawmills left 'ghost towns,' equalled in their bleakness and spirit of desolation only by the surrounding expanse of sun-baked land. People simply moved out, fading away with the lonely wails of the mill whistles which echoed for the last time over the endless land of stumps" (quoted in Henry Clepper, *Crusade for Conservation* [Washington, D.C.: American Forestry Association, 1975]). Heyward was also among the first to do research in the South in forest soil fertility. He served as the first manager of the Southern Pulpwood Association.

Hilmon, J. B. Tenth director of the Southeastern Forest Experiment Station (1973–79).

Hine, W. R. U.S. Department of Agriculture Forest Service investigator who initiated research in the 1920s on the lands of the Urania Lumber Company in Louisiana on thinning loblolly and shortleaf pines.

Holmes, Joseph A. Early-day North Carolina geologist involved with water resources who favored national forests rather than parks in the Southern Appalachian Mountains.

Hosner, John F. President of the Forest Farmers Association 1987–88.

Hudson, S. K. Chairman of the American Pulpwood Association 1978–80 and an executive of South Carolina Industries.

Hunt, A. T. President of the Southern Pine Association 1961–62.

Hunt, Davis. President of the Southern Forest Products Association 1973–74.

Hyde, Joseph. North Carolinian, first president of the Southern Forest Congress (1916), and a crusader for managing the southern pines.

Jessup, J. C., Jr. President of the Southern Forest Products Association 1986–87 and an executive of the Weyerhaeuser Company in North Carolina.

Jones, W. Goodrich (1860–1950). Called the Father of Texas Forestry. Jones, a banker, was the principal organizer of the Texas Forestry Association and the main lobbyist for establishment of the Texas Forest Service.

Kalmar, L. F. President of the Forest Farmers Association (1972–73), an organization of private industrial and nonindustrial landowners in the South.

Keith, Charles S. Founding president of the Southern Pine Association (1915–18).

Kirby, John Henry (1860–1940). Early Texas lumberman. Acquiring land in Texas, beginning in the 1880s, the Kirby Lumber Company eventually operated fourteen sawmills and more than twelve logging camps or company towns. Kirby served as World War I lumber administrator for the South of the U.S. Shipping Board's Emergency Fleet Corporation. He was president of the Southern Pine Association 1922–23.

Knox, Lilian M. (ca. 1895–1930). "Lady Bountiful of the Piney Woods." Knox managed the Knox lumber empire from Hemphill, Tex., until arrested in 1926 for allegedly murdering her husband. No-billed, she died destitute.

Koch, Peter. Senior scientist of the Southern Forest Experiment Station from the 1960s to the 1980s who developed harvesting methods and equipment and who authored the two-volume definitive work *Utilization of the Southern Pines.*

Korstian, Clarence F. Duke University School of Forestry dean who in 1944 published a study advocating government control of cutting practices on private forestlands.

Kurth, E. L., Sr. President of the Southern Pine Association 1935–37 and Texas lumberman who became intrigued with the potential for making newsprint from southern pine, building the first mill for such a purpose at Lufkin, Texas. It began making paper in 1941.

Lacy, John F. (1840–1913). An Iowa congressman known as the Father of Federal Game Legislation. His name is given to the 1900 congressional act that protected game (especially important in Florida) and the 1906 Antiquities Act, under which national monuments are established.

Langdale, Harley, Jr. President of the Forest Farmers Association 1958–60, president of the Southern Pine Association 1966–67; and gum naval stores producer in Georgia.

Lassen, Laurence E. Tenth director of the Southern Forest Experiment Station (1976–83).

Law, Ralph W. President of the Forest Farmers Association 1978–79.

Lawson, John. English naturalist-colonist who in 1709 wrote *New Voyage to Carolina,* in which he described the forest vegetation of the region.

Lay, Dan. Wildlife researcher in Texas who with others established the relationship between the demise of the red cockaded woodpecker and the absence of southern pines with red heartrot disease.

Learned, R. F. Lumberman who began operation of a sawmill at Natchez, Mississippi, in 1824.

Lightsey, E. Oswald. President of the Southern Pine Association 1950–52.

Long, Robert. *See* Victor Bell.

McArdle, R. E. Third director of the Southeastern Forest Experiment Station (1938–44); later U.S. Department of Agriculture Forest Service chief.

McGowen, Earl M. President of the Southern Pine Association 1941–43 and an Alabama lumberman.

MacKaye, Benton (1879–1975). Harvard forester who became an early-day land-use planner, making significant contributions to the establishment of the Appalachian Trail, the Tennessee Valley Authority, and wilderness set-asides.

McKnight, J. S. Forest Service researcher who with others developed guidelines for regenerating high-quality hardwood species in southern bottomlands; also editor of the *Journal of Applied Southern Forestry*.

McLintock, T. F. Seventh director of the Southeastern Forest Experiment Station (1962–66).

McNary, Charles (1874–1944). U.S. Senator from Oregon who sponsored legislation enabling the federal government to purchase lands for wood production and thereby authorizing many national forests in the South; also sponsored legislation that funded federal forest research in the South.

NcNeal, W. B. President of the Southern Pine Association 1944–46.

McSweeney, John. Congressman from Ohio who cosponsored an act to encourage forest research that eventually resulted in two experiment stations, each with many research centers, in the South.

Maddox, R. S. First Tennessee state forester, employed in 1921 to head a new Bureau of Forestry.

Malsberger, Henry. Manager in the 1950s and 1960s of the Southern Pulpwood Association, a pulpwood industry–sponsored organization to educate small woodlot owners.

Mann, William. Developed the program in the 1960s at Alexandria, Louisiana, to naturally regenerate longleaf pines by direct seeding.

Martin, C. H., Jr. Chairman of the American Pulpwood Association 1980–84 and an executive of Brunswick Pulp and Paper Company.

Marx, Donald H. University of Georgia scientist who with B. Zak demonstrated the effect of mycorrhizal fungi on southern pine tree growth.

Mason, William (1877–1940). Inventor of Masonite, a fiberboard fabricated from steam-treated wood fibers, and perfecter of a method for extracting naval stores from yellow pine lumber by using steam.

Mattoon, Wilbur R. U.S. Department of Agriculture Forest Service extension forester in charge of federal education work in the South; prolific popular writer and speaker on southern pine and baldcypress management.

Mesavage, Clement. U.S. Department of Agriculture Forest Service forester who (with J. W. Girard) published the monumental *Tables for Estimating Board-Foot Volume of Timber.*

Michaux, Andre (1746–1802). Father of François Andre Michaux (1770–1855) who, with his son, was a botanical collector for the French government, sending to France seeds and seedlings from the Southern Appalachian Mountains and from Florida.

Mitchell, Harold L. Fourth director of the Southern Forest Experiment Station (1951–53).

Mohr, Charles. Botanist from Mobile, Alabama, responsible for the 1880 forestry census (the first such) of the South published in 1886 and author of *The Timber Pines of the Southern United States* published in 1897. This 1897 report estimated nine thousand square miles of longleaf pine in Mississippi alone. For the South, the tally was 230,000 square miles of timberland containing 90 million acres with 170 billion board feet.

Molpus, Richard. President of the Southern Forest Products Association 1978–79 and Mississippi lumberman.

Moore, Alyse. Believed to be the first female graduate of a southern forestry school. Moore earned the B.S. degree in May 1970 from Stephen F. Austin State University in Nacogdoches, Tex.

Mordecai, C. R. Chairman of the American Pulpwood Association 1986–88 and an executive of Union Camp Corporation.

Morrow, Wm. I. President of the Southern Forest Products Association 1982–83 and an executive of the Manville Forest Products Corporation in Louisiana.

Myers, J. Walter, Jr. (b. 1919). Executive vice president of the Forest Farmers Association and editor of *Forest Farmer* magazine 1951–82; president of the Society of American Foresters 1987–88; and secretary to the Southern Forest Resource Analysis Committee, which wrote *The South's Third Forest,* 1966–69.

Neal, W. T. President of the Southern Pine Association 1938–39 and an Alabama lumberman.

Nelson, Thomas C. Seventh director of the Southern Forest Experiment Station (1966–70); later deputy chief of the U.S. Department of Agriculture Forest Service.

Norris, George. Coauthor with Walter Doxey in the U.S. Congress of the Cooperative Farm Forestry Act of 1937.

Nuttall, Thomas (1786–1859). English printer-turned-naturalist whose accounts of the western South are recorded in the *Journals of Travels into the Arkansas Territory during the Year 1819.*

Oettmeier, W. M., Sr. Founding president of the Forest Farmers Association (1941–52).

Oettmeier, William M., Jr. President of the Forest Farmers Association 1979–80 and 1984–85.

Patterson, A. B. Early-day consulting forester from Baltimore employed to cruise the Kentucky mountain region.

Peabody, George E. Philanthropist who funded the University of Georgia School of Forestry in 1906, the first public professional forestry school in the South.

Peavy, A. J. President of the Southern Pine Association 1926–27.

Pechanec, J. R. Sixth director of the Southeastern Forest Experiment Station 1956–62.

Peterson, Ralph Max (b. 1927) U.S. Department of Agriculture Forest Service southern regional forester 1972–74 and chief of the Forest Service 1979–86.

Pinchot, Gifford (1865–1946). First U.S. Department of Agriculture Forest Service head. Prior to entering government service he was a consulting forester for the George W. Vanderbilt family's Biltmore Forest in North Carolina.

Putman, John. Long-time leader (1940s through 1960s) of the U.S. Department of Agriculture Forest Service bottomland hardwood research program in the Mississippi Delta.

Rawls, Marcus G. President of the Forest Farmers Association 1973–74.

Reimers, F. W. President of the Southern Pine Association 1928–29.

Reynolds, Russell. Scientist at the Crossett Experimental Forest in Arkansas who, as early as the 1930s, issued bulletins on both silviculture and financial aspects of southern pine management.

Ross, E. W. Eleventh director of the Southeastern Forest Experiment Station (1979–85).

Ruark, R. Ed. Director of the Georgia Forest Research Council, catalyst organization for scientific investigations throughout the region.

Sanders, H. E. President of the Southern Forest Products Association 1970–71.

Sanderson, P. T. President of the Southern Pine Association 1943–44.

Schenck, Carl Alwin (1868–1955). German-born and educated forester. He was hired by George W. Vanderbilt to be resident manager of the 100,000-acre Biltmore estate in the Southern Appalachian Mountains from 1895 until 1909. The first forestry school in the U.S. began there under his tutelage in 1898.

Schumacher, F. X. Duke University professor who in the 1940s developed sampling methods for forest and range management.

Seaman, H. M. President of the Southern Pine Association 1948–50.

Sesco, J. A. Twelfth director of Southeastern Forest Experiment Station (1985 to present).

Shephard, W. Scott. President of the Southern Pine Association 1962–63.

Sheppard, C. C. President of the Southern Pine Association 1930–32.

Siegel, W. C. Among the first forester-lawyers in the South, specializing in taxation and related subjects; member of the staff of the U.S. Department of Agriculture Southern Forest Experiment Station.

Sieke, E. O. Associate of Gifford Pinchot who was state forester of Texas 1918–1942.

Siggers, Paul. U.S. Department of Agriculture Forest Service researcher in the 1920s and 1930s who demonstrated, with others, that fire retards brown spot needle blight.

Silcox, Ferdinand A. (1882–1939). Georgia-born U.S. Department of Agriculture Forest Service chief (1933–1939) when the following efforts affecting southern forestry took place: McSweeney-McNary forest research act passed; Knutson-Vandenburg stand improvement act passed; natural areas regulations passed; *A National Plan for American Forestry* (The Copeland Report) published; and the Civilian Conservation Corps established.

Sisley, John F. President of the Forest Farmers Association 1975–76.

Sizemore, Mary. Legal partner in Sizemore and Sizemore, a leading forestry consulting firm, headquartered in Alabama, specializing in timberland law throughout the region from the late 1950s on.

Smith, M. White, Jr. President of the Southern Pine Association 1958–59.

Spessard, R. H. Chairman of the American Pulpwood Association 1936–41 and an executive of N. E. Spessard & Sons.

Squires, John W. President of the Forest Farmers Association 1962–64.

Stevens, J. E. President of the Southern Forest Products Association 1984–85 and an executive of Kirby Forest Industries.

Stimpson, William H. President of the Southern Forest Products Association 1976–77 and an executive of the Gulf Lumber Company in Alabama.

Stoddard, H. L. Biologist who studied bobwhite quail. In 1931, while working with the U.S. Biological Survey, he showed the value of controlled burning in bobwhite quail habitat management. His notable 559-page *Bobwhite Quail*, published in 1931, summarized his life's work with this game bird.

Sullivan, William H. Great Southern Lumber Company, Bogalusa, Louisiana, general superintendent who designed one of the largest mills in the world, at the time producing 1 million board feet a day. He innovatively initiated using sawmill waste for paper manufacture, wood naval stores, fuel, and minor products (i.e., lath).

Swift, G. R. President of the Southern Pine Association 1954–55 and Alabama lumberman.

Swift, G. R., Jr. President of the Southern Forest Products Association in 1981 and an Alabama industrialist.

Temple, Arthur, Jr. President of the Southern Pine Association 1955–56 and an executive of Temple-Inland Company in Texas.

Tolleson, J. M., Jr. President of the Southern Forest Products Association 1974–75 and Georgia lumberman.

Traczewitz, O. G. President of the Forest Farmers Association 1968–70.

Van Cleave, Noll A. President of the Forest Farmers Association 1980–81.

Verrall, Arthur. U.S. Department of Agriculture Forest Service scientist who worked on developing decay-resistant wood and on diseases of living trees; also later a professor at Stephen F. Austin State University, Nacogdoches, Texas.

Wahlenberg, W. G. Southern forest research scientist who worked on range management and silviculture relationships. He authored the definitive monographs *Longleaf Pine* (1946) and *Loblolly pine* (1953).

Wakeley, Phil. U.S. Department of Agriculture Forest Service research worker whose pine regeneration studies were summarized in the monograph entitled *Planting the Southern Pines.*

Walker, C. O. President of the Southern Pine Association 1965–66.

Wallinger, R. S. Chairman of the American Pulpwood Association 1984–86 and an executive of Westvaco (West Virginia Pulp and Paper Company) in South Carolina.

Warner, R. V. President of the Southern Forest Products Association 1977–78 and an executive of the Potlatch Corporation in Arkansas.

Weeks, John W. (1860–1926). Massachusetts congressman. In 1911, he authored the law to enable the federal government to purchase lands to protect stream navigability. Most national forest land in the South is attributed to this law or to its amendment, the Clark-McNary Act of 1924.

Wheeler, Phillip A. Southern forest survey leader from the 1940s through 1970s. He invented the Wheelerscope, an instrument to improve the efficiency of timber inventories.

Whitfield, J. Vivian. President of the Forest Farmers Association 1952–58.

Whittle, L. A. Chairman of the American Pulpwood Association 1956–58 and an executive of Brunswick Pulp and Paper Company.

Williams, Harry N. President of the Southern Forest Products Association 1981–82 and Texas lumberman.

Wilson, Herman L. President of the Southern Forest Products Association 1975–76 and Arkansas lumberman.

Wyman, Lenthal. Naval stores research worker in the 1920s at Starke, Florida.

Youngs, Robert L. Eighth director of the Southern Forest Experiment Station (1970–72).

Zillgitt, Walter M. Sixth director of the Southern Forest Experiment Station (1963–66) and eighth director of the Southeastern Forest Experiment Station (1966–70).

Zobel, Bruce. Initiated in the 1950s forest tree genetics studies in the South, in Texas and subsequently at the University of North Carolina, out of which has come "super" trees, seed orchards, and seed-production areas.

Scientific Names of Trees and Plants Mentioned

Acacia	*Acacia* spp.
American beech	*Fagus grandifolia*
American chestnut	*Castanea dentata*
Arundo grass	*Arundonaria gigantea*
Ash	*Fraxinus* spp.
Ashe juniper	*Juniperus asheii*
Aspen	*Populus tremuloides*
Atlantic white-cedar	*Chamaecyparis thyoides*
Baldcypress	*Taxodium distichum*
Balsam fir	*Abies balsamea*
Bamboo	*Bambusa* spp.
Basswood	*Tilia americana*
Bay	*Gordonia lasianthus*
Bay magnolia	*Magnolia sp.*
Bear oak	*Quercus ilicifolia*
Beech	*Fagus* spp.
Bigleaf magnolia	*Magnolia macrophylla*
Birch	*Betula* spp.
Bitter pecan	*Carya sp.*
Black birch	*Betula lenta*
Black hickory	*Carya texana*
Backjack oak	*Quercus marilandica*
Black locust	*Robinia pseudoacacia*
Black oak	*Quercus velutina*
Black walnut	*Juglans nigra*
Black willow	*Salix nigra*
Boxelder	*Acer negundo*
Buckeye	*Aesculus* spp.
Bunch grass	*Festuca sp.*
Cabbage palmetto	*Sabal palmetto*

Carolina cherry	*Prunus caroliniana*
Catalpa	*Catalpa speciosa*
Cedar	*Juniperus* spp.
	Cedrus libani
Chapman oak	*Quercus chapmanii*
Cherry laurel	*Prunus caroliniana*
Chestnut oak	*Quercus prinus*
Chickasaw plum	*Prunus angustifolia*
Chinkapin	*Castanea* spp.
Choke cherry	*Prunus virginiana*
Coffee bean (Coffeetree?)	*Gymnocladus dioicus*
Cottonwood	*Populus deltoides*
Cross vine	*Bignonia capreolate*
	Bignonia bracteate
Cypress	*Taxodium* spp.
Dogwood	*Cornus* spp.
Douglas-fir	*Pseudotsuga menziesii*
Eastern cottonwood	*Populus deltoides*
Eastern hemlock	*Tsuga canadensis*
Eastern redbud	*Cercis canadensis*
Eastern redcedar	*Juniperus virginiana*
Eastern white pine	*Pinus strobus*
Elm	*Ulmus* spp.
English holly	*Ilex aquifolium*
Farkleberry	*Vaccinium arboreum*
Fir	*Abies* spp.
Flowering dogwood	*Cornus florida*
Franklinia	*Franklinia alatamaha*
Fraser fir	*Abies fraseri*
Genseng	*Panax quinquefolius*
Gordonia	*Gordonia alatamaha*
Gray birch	*Betula populifolia*
Greenbrier	*Smilax* spp.
Green ash	*Fraxinus pennsylvanica*
Hackberry	*Celtis occidentalis*
Hard maple	*Acer saccharum*
Hawthorn (Haw)	*Crataegus* spp.
Hemlock	*Tsuga* spp.
Hercules'-club	*Aralia spinosa*
Hickory	*Carya* spp.
Hickory pine	*Pinus pungens*
Holly	*Ilex* spp.
Honey locust	*Gleditsia triacanthos*
Horsetail	*Equisetum* spp.
Indian olive	*Fraxinus* sp.
Juniper	*Juniperus* spp.

Laurel	*Persea* spp.
Leatherwood	*Acer pensylvanicum*
Liquid amber	*Liquidambar styraciflua*
Live oak	*Quercus virginiana*
Loblolly pine	*Pinus taeda*
Longleaf pine	*Pinus palustris*
Magnolia	*Magnolia* sp.
Maple	*Acer* spp.
Mesquite	*Prosopis juliflora*
Mimosa	*Acacia* sp.
	Albizia julibrissin
Moose wood	*Acer pensylvanicum*
Mountain ash	*Sorbus americana*
Mountain laurel	*Kalmia latifolia*
Mulberry	*Morus* spp.
Myrtle oak	*Quercus myrtifolia*
Nettle tree	*Celtis* sp.
Northern red oak	*Quercus borealis*
Nuttall's oak	*Quercus nuttallii*
Oak	*Quercus* spp.
Osage-orange	*Maclura pomifera*
Overcup oak	*Quercus lyrata*
Palm	*Sabal palmetto*
Partridgeberry	*Mitchella repens*
Pecan	*Carya pecan*
	Carya illinoiensis
Persimmon	*Diospyros virginiana*
Pinchot juniper	*Juniperus pinchotii*
Pitch pine	*Pinus rigida*
Plum	*Prunus* spp.
Poa grass	*Poa* spp.
Poison ivy	*Rhus toxicodendron*
	Rhus radicans
Poison oak	*Rhus radicans*
Pondcypress	*Taxodium distichum* var. *ascendens*
Pond pine	*Pinus serotina*
Post oak	*Quercus stellata*
Poverty grass	*Aristata dichotoma*
	Danthonia spicata
Red azalea	*Rhododendron* sp.
Redbud	*Cercis canadensis*
Red maple	*Acer rubra*
Red oak	*Quercus rubra*
Red pine	*Pinus resinosa*
Red spruce	*Picea rubra (rubens)*
Redwood	*Sequoia sempervirens*

Rhododendron	*Rhododendron maxima*
Rivercane	*Arundinaria* spp.
Round-leaf birch	*Betula* sp.
Royal palmetto	*Roystonea elata*
Sand live oak	*Quercus virginiana* var. *germinata*
Sand pine	*Pinus clausa*
Sassafras	*Sassafras albidum*
Scarlet oak	*Quercus coccinea*
Scotch (Scot's) pine	*Pinus sylvestris*
Scrub hickory	*Carya floridana*
Scrub oak	*Quercus* spp.
Scrub pine	*Pinus virginiana*
Shellbark hickory	*Carya laciniosa*
Shortleaf pine	*Pinus echinata*
Shumard oak	*Quercus falcata* var. *leucophylla*
Slash pine	*Pinus elliottii*
Slippery elm	*Ulmus rubra*
Soft maple	*Acer rubrum*
	Acer saccharinum
Sonderegger pine	*Pinus sondereggeri*
Sourwood	*Oxydendron arboreum*
Southern baldcypress	*Taxodium distichum*
Southern magnolia	*Magnolia grandiflora*
Southern redcedar	*Juniperus silicicola*
Southern red oak	*Quercus falcata*
South Florida slash pine	*Pinus elliottii* var. *densa*
Sparkleberry	*Vaccinium arboreum*
Spruce	*Picea* spp.
Spruce pine	*Pinus glabra*
Sugarberry	*Celtis laevigata*
Sugar maple	*Acer saccharum*
Sumac	*Rhus* spp.
Swamp ironwood	*Cyrilla racemiflora*
Swamp tupelo	*Nyssa sylvatica* var. biflora
Sweetbay	*Magnolia virginiana*
Sweetgum	*Liquidambar styraciflua*
Sycamore	*Platanus occidentalis*
Table-mountain pine	*Pinus pungens*
Toothache tree	*Zanthoxylum clava-herculis*
Trumpet creeper	*Bignoniaceae* family
Tuliptree	*Liriodendron tulipifera*
Tupelo gum	*Nyssa sylvatica*
Turkey oak	*Quercus laevis*
Virginia pine	*Pinus virginiana*
Walnut	*Juglans* spp.
Water hickory	*Carya aquatica*

Water oak	*Quercus nigra*
Water tupelo	*Nyssa aquatica*
Waxmyrtle	*Myrica cerifera*
White ash	*Fraxinus americana*
White-cedar	*Chamaecyparis thyoides*
White oak	*Quercus alba*
White pine	*Pinus strobus*
White walnut	*Juglans cinnerea*
Wild black cherry	*Prunus serotina*
Willow	*Salix* spp.
Willow oak	*Quercus phellos*
Wisteria	*Wisteria macrostachya*
Witch hazel	*Hamamelis virginiana*
Yaupon	*Ilex vomitoria*
Yellow birch	*Betula lutea*
Yellow pine	*Pinus* spp.
Yellow-poplar	*Liriodendron tulipifera*

Notes

1. The Explorers' Forest

1. Quoted in U.S. Department of Agriculture Forest Products Laboratory, *Wood in American Life* (Madison, Wis.: U.S. Department of Agriculture Forest Products Laboratory, 1976), 4.

2. Peter Martyr, *First Three English Books on America*, trans. Rycharde Eden (n.p., n.d.; Chicago: Library Resources, 1970, microfiche), 135.

3. Ibid.

4. Edward Gaylord Bourne, ed., *Narratives of the Career of Hernando de Soto*, trans. Buckingham Smith (New York: Alterton Book Co., 1922; Chicago: Library Resources, 1970, microfiche).

5. Albert E. Cowdry, *This Land, This South* (Lexington: University Press of Kentucky, 1983), 16.

6. Ibid.

7. In my early years as a forester in Texas, a timber marker on a national forest crew ran up excitedly to ask, "Mr. Ranger, what is this tree?" Unknown and uncharted in those woods, the tree was identified in the books as spruce pine. Did a plane, a bird, or a wayfarer drop the seed that gave rise to this intruder so far from its native habitat?

8. Mark van Doren, ed., *The Travels of William Bartram* (New York: Dover, 1928), 102, 103. See also Francis Harper, ed., *Bartram's Travels* (New Haven: Yale University Press, 1958).

9. Van Doren, *Travels*, 34.

10. C. S. Sargent, *Manual of the Trees of North America* (1884; reprint, New York: Dover, 1961).

11. The description of this rare tree was first published by a cousin of William Bartram, who, however, acknowledged its listing in the *Catalog of Horticulture* authored by Bartram, thus properly crediting him with its discovery. Moses Marshall saw the tree in 1790 and John Lyons saw it in 1802 (Harper, *Bartram's Travels*). It is often confused with the small tree of the genus *Gordonia*, but the

flowering periods aid identification: for *Gordonia,* it is April usually; for *Franklinia,* it is summer.

12. Marjorie B. Sawyer, *Billy Bartram* (New York: Farrar, Straus, & Giroux, 1972).

13. E. S. Ayensu and R. A. DeFillipps, *Endangered and Threatened Plants of the United States* (Washington, D.C.: Smithsonian Institution, 1978).

14. Ibid.

15. B. J. Healey, *The Plant Hunters* (New York: Scribners, 1975), 63.

16. Harper, *Bartram's Travels,* 377.

17. Unless the father, John, is noted, or the plural is used, son William is referred to as Bartram.

18. Harper, *Bartram's Travels.*

19. Ibid., 58, 414.

20. Ibid., 91.

21. Ibid., 18, 339.

22. Van Doren, 51.

23. M. L. Fernald, ed., *Gray's Manual of Botany,* 8th ed. (New York: American Book Co., 1950).

24. E. Lawson, *The Discovery of Florida* (St. Augustine: E. Larson, 1946).

25. *Bulletin American Geographical Society* 45 (October 1913): 721.

26. Harper, *Bartram's Travels,* 90.

27. Ibid., 73.

28. Fernald, *Gray's Manual.*

29. Harper, *Bartram's Travels,* 83.

30. Ibid., 93.

31. Ibid., 81.

32. Fernald, *Gray's Manual.*

33. Harper, *Bartram's Travels,* 75–76.

34. Ibid., 177–178.

35. Ibid., 566.

36. Ibid., 52–53.

37. Ibid., 23.

38. Ibid., 399.

39. Ibid., 23.

40. Ibid., 24.

41. Ibid., 21–22.

42. Ibid., 25–26.

43. Ibid., 471–472.

44. Ibid., 59.

45. Ibid., 204–205.

46. Ibid., 31.

47. Don Fernando de Soto, *The Discovery and Conquest of Terra Florida,* ed. William B. Rye (New York, 1966), 92, quoted by Cowdrey, *This Land,* 17.

48. Cowdrey, *This Land,* 17.

49. M. M. McClung, *Caddo Lake—Mysterious Swampland* (Texarkana:

Southeast Printers and Publishers, 1974), and A. McKay and H. A. Spellings, *A History of Jefferson*, 5th ed. (Jefferson, Texas: n.p., n.d.).

50. Ibid.

51. Robert S. Maxwell and Robert D. Baker, *Sawdust Empire* (College Station: Texas A&M University Press, 1983), 5.

52. R. R. Hicks, Jr., and G. K. Stephenson, *Woody Plants of the Western Gulf Region* (Dubuque: Kendall/Hunt, 1978), 166.

53. Ibid., 268.

54. Ibid., 66, 122, 151, 243.

55. Ibid., 80, 219.

56. Martyr, *First Three English Books.*

57. Marion Clawson, "Forests in the Long Sweep of American History," *Science* 204 (1979): 1168–1174.

58. R. C. Lillard, *The Great Forest* (New York: Knopf, 1947), 184.

2. The Pioneers' Forest

1. This is the date historians use. Foresters consider "in earnest" more likely to be 1760.

2. Thomas D. Clark, *The Greening of the South* (Lexington: The University Press of Kentucky, 1984), 5.

3. Albert E. Cowdrey, *This Land, This South* (Lexington: The University Press of Kentucky, 1983), 60.

4. A. J. Morrison, "The Ohio Prospectus for the Year 1775," *Ohio Archaeology and Historical Society* 23 (19): 232–235.

5. A. B. Hulbert, *Soil: Its Influence on the History of the United States* (New Haven, Conn.: Yale University Press, 1930), 71.

6. Cowdrey, *This Land,* 29.

7. James Russell Lowell's characterization of the Republic's founders in "The Present Crisis" (*Harvard Classics,* vol. 42 [New York: P. F. Collier & Son], 1451).

8. R. C. Davis, ed., *Encyclopedia of American Forest and Conservation History* (New York: Macmillan, 1983), 225.

9. Ibid., 649.

10. Species of trees and wildlife in the forests of the early South are suggested by Mark Catesby in *The Natural History of North Carolina, Florida, and the Bahama Islands,* 2 vols. (London: Benjamin White, 1771); by Thomas Nuttall in *The Genera of North American Plants* (New York: D. Heartt, 1818); by F. A. Michaux in *North American Sylva,* 5 vols. (Philadelphia: Rice, Rutter & Co., 1865); and by Sir Charles Lyell in *Travels in North America in the Years 1841–2* (New York: Wiley and Putnam, 1845) and *A Second Visit to the United States of North America* (New York: Harper & Bros., 1849).

Chapter 1 mentioned the small flowering tree *Franklinia.* First called a *Gordonia,* it was stumbled upon on two occasions, some ten or twelve years apart, by the Bartrams. Neither the Bartrams nor others had ever recognized the species elsewhere except in gardens in which, in the interim, horticulturalists had planted its seeds. And in the Georgia locale, they concluded, its range extended over only several acres (Mark van Doren, ed., *The Travels of William Bartram* [New York: Dover 1928], 369). Lyell, having read William Bartram's works, was anxious to tread some of the ground Bartram roamed in the southeastern states. On his second trip, the geologist found the *Franklinia* tree, noted its similarity to the loblolly bay *Gordonia,* both being beautiful camellialike evergreens. He pegged the area in which *Franklinia* could be found at twenty miles in its greatest length.

11. Charles Lyell, *A Second Visit.*

12. Ibid.

13. Ibid.

14. Francis Harper, ed., *Bartram's Travels* (New Haven: Yale University Press, 1958).

15. Harper, *Bartram's Travels,* 16.

16. Lyell, *A Second Visit.*

17. Ibid.

18. Harper, *Bartram's Travels.*

19. Lyell, *A Second Visit.*

20. Laurence C. Walker, "Natural Areas of the Southeast," *Journal of Forestry* 61 (1963):670–673. Most of the following section describing natural areas is from this report prepared for the Society of American Foresters.

21. The forest must have been picturesque even before the Civil War. A spring-fed swimming pool, constructed of concrete sometime before the hostilities, still was used in 1963 by children from the nearby community.

22. Under the pines, a mull humus layer covers the soil of well-developed horizons. It is a well-drained site except along stream courses where six inches of alluvium has washed from nearby fields to hide black muck. Except for the Japanese honeysuckle, which has escaped to invade these woods, the stand is believed to be in its natural, unimpaired condition.

23. The rolling site, underlain by insoluble chert, is relatively dry, except in the coves. Elevation ranges from 500 to 750 feet. Dr. Lewis Lipps, professor of biology at Georgia's Shorter College, introduced me to this tract of unique old-growth forest.

24. The soil, derived from Coastal Plain marine deposits, is three inches of loamy sand over a sandy loam. Below fifteen inches is a reddish yellow sandy clay loam. Site index appears to be about 60 for this rolling upland. The stand will certainly be saved for the lifetime of the owner, but its permanence is not legally secured.

25. Lyell, *Travels.*

26. Ibid.

27. Lyell, *A Second Visit.*

28. Ibid.

29. Walker, "Natural Areas," 671.

30. A Seminole Indian reared on a Florida reservation insisted to me that Okefenokee means "land of trembling water" rather than "land of trembling earth"; however, the swamp's water certainly has no wave action.

31. Hardwoods intermingled with the principal cover in the Corkscrew Swamp include black willow, red maple, persimmon, and water hickory. Saw palmetto, red maple, various species of bay, and myrtle accompany the open-growing pines that averaged seventy feet in height and ranged from six to twenty inches d.b.h. A saw grass marsh exceeding a thousand acres lies adjacent to the forest. The level sands of this swamp site, fifteen to twenty feet above sea level, lie over marl and limestone deposits.

32. Harper, *Bartram's Travels.*

33. Lyell, *A Second Visit.*

34. Quoted in Cowdrey, *This Land,* 27.

35. Cowdrey, *This Land,* 4.

36. Ibid.

37. Harper, *Bartram's Travels,* 201–202.

38. Ibid.

39. Ibid., 204–205.

40. Ibid., 198.

41. Walker, "Natural Areas," 673.

42. Marjory B. Sawyer, *Billy Bartram* (New York: Farrar, Straus & Giroux, 1972).

43. C. A. Doggett, "The Moravian Foresters," *Journal of Forest History* 31(1987): 19–25. So, too, the balance of this section is attributed.

44. Harper, *Bartram's Travels,* 221.

45. Ibid., 230.

46. Ibid., 213.

47. Ibid., 216.

48. Frederick Law Olmsted, *A Journey in the Back Country, 1860,* vol. 1 (1907: reprint, New York: Knickerbocker Press, 1907), 261.

49. Walker, "Natural Areas," 671–672.

50. Harper, *Bartram's Travels,* 252–253.

51. Ibid., 253–254.

52. Ibid., 253, 255.

53. Ibid., 255.

54. Lyell, *Travels.*

55. Peter Hamilton, *Colonial Mobile* (1897) quoted in Harper, *Bartram's Travels,* 404.

56. Redcedar provides an example of word evolution. Two words in most literature sixty years ago, it became a hyphenated name in technical literature because the juniper is not a true cedar. Today forestry authorities eliminate the hyphen for the same reason.

57. Harper, *Bartram's Travels,* 271.

58. Olmsted, *Journey* 1:111.

59. Ibid., 1:20.

60. Ibid., 1:31.

61. M. L. Fernald, *Gray's Manual of Botany,* 8th ed. (New York: American Book Co., 1950).

62. Thomas Nuttall, *Journal of Travels into the Arkansa Territory* (New York: Arthur H. Clark, 1905, microfiche).

63. Ibid.

64. Ibid.

65. *Gleditsia brachycarpa* and *G. monosperma*: short-podded and one-seeded honey locusts, respectively.

66. Nuttall called it *Celtis integrifolia*, not now so classified.

67. Authors of Latin binomials follow the genus and species names in many scientific texts and in all manuals of taxonomy; for example, *Nutt.* is an abbreviation for Nuttall; *L.* is for Linnaeus; *L.f.* for the son of Linaeus. Authorships are omitted in this book.

68. L. C. Walker, *Trees* (Englewood Cliffs, N.J.: Prentice-Hall, 1984).

69. Richard Preston, *North American Trees*, 3d ed. (Cambridge: MIT Press, 1976), 327, lists a *Nyssa ogeche* in the Coastal Plain of South Carolina and Florida.

70. Nuttall, *Journal.*

71. Ibid.

72. Robert S. Maxwell and Robert D. Baker, *Sawdust Empire* (College Station: Texas A&M University Press, 1983), 18. These writers note saw kerfs at the crude mills were so wide that "some sawmills produced some lumber as a by-product of sawdust" (p. 19).

73. Ibid., 10.

74. This is difficult to comprehend, for trees two hundred years old would have had to have been germinated in deep water—an unlikely happening—and the species under such a circumstance would be different from those now on the site.

75. Laurence C. Walker, "A Slice of Wilderness," *Texas Parks and Wildlife* 41, no. 2 (1983):6–11. The narrative on Caddo Lake is also from the following sources: O. D. Bailey, "Caddo Lake Region" (typescript, n.d.), Special Collections, Ralph Steen Library, Stephen F. Austin State University; T. G. Jordan and M. C. Wier, *Deep East Texas Folk* (Dallas: SMU Printing Department, 1969); M. M. McClung, *Caddo Lake—Mysterious Swampland* (Texarkana: Southeast Printers and Publishers, 1974); A. McKay and H. A. Spellings, *A History of Jefferson*, 5th ed. (Jefferson, Texas: n.p., n.d.), Special Collections, Ralph Steen Library, Stephen F. Austin State University; Wright Patman, *A History of Post Offices and Communities—Harrison County* (Texarkana, Tex.: mimeograph, 1968), Special Collections, Ralph Steen Library, Stephen F. Austin State University; Tralor Russell, *Carpetbaggers, Scalawags, and Others* (Waco: Texian Press, 1973); and C. Van Duyne and W. C. Byers, "Soil Survey of Harrison County, Texas," in *Field Operations of the Bureau of Soils, 1912* (Washington, D.C.: Government Printing Office, 1915).

76. Quoted in Russell, *Carpetbaggers.*

77. Cowdrey, *This Land*, 23.

78. Thomas R. Cox, Robert S. Maxwell, Phillip D. Thomas, and Joseph J. Malone, *This Well-wooded Land* (Lincoln: University of Nebraska Press, 1985), 42, 96, 98.

79. G. M. Herndon, "Forest Products of Colonial Georgia," *Journal of Forest History* 23, no. 3 (1979):130–135.

80. Cox et al., *This Well-wooded Land,* 19.

81. U.S. Department of Agriculture Forest Products Laboratory, *Wood in American Life* (Madison, Wis.: U.S. Department of Agriculture Forest Products Laboratory, 1976), 28.

82. Herndon, "Forest Products."

83. Cox et al., *This Well-wooded Land,* 95.

84. Many of the plant uses noted herein are from R. R. Hicks, Jr., and G. K. Stephenson, *Woody Plants of the Western Gulf Region* (Dubuque: Kendall/Hunt, 1978), 148, 304; Eric Sloan, *Reverence for Wood* (New York: Funk, 1965); and Francis P. Porcher, *Resources of the Southern Fields and Forests* (1863; reprint, New York: Arno and New York Times, 1970).

85. Virginia Steele Wood, *Live Oaking* (Boston: Northeastern University Press, 1981), 4, 8.

86. Herndon, "Forest Products."

87. R. G. Lillard, *The Great Forest* (New York: Knopf, 1947), and Porcher, *Resources.*

88. Cox et al., *This Well-wooded Land,* 164.

89. Porcher, *Resources.*

90. This by today's terminology is poison ivy, poison oak being a West Coast plant of another species name. Poison ivy is now classified as *Toxicodendron radicans.*

91. USDA Forest Products Laboratory, *Wood in American Life,* 11.

92. Thomas D. Clark, *The Greening of the South* (Lexington: The University Press of Kentucky, 1984), 12.

93. T. C. Croker, *Story of a Forest* (Atlanta: U.S. Department of Agriculture Forest Service, 1988).

94. J. M. Collier, *The First Fifty Years of the Southern Pine Association* (New Orleans: Southern Pine Association, 1965), 6, 7, 9, 10.

95. Croker, *Story of a Forest.*

96. Collier, *The First Fifty Years,* 7.

97. Harper, *Bartram's Travels,* 175.

98. Abernathy, *Tales of the Big Thicket,* 6.

99. Clark, *Greening of the South,* 9–10.

100. Porcher, *Resources.*

3. The Lumbermen's Forest

I am indebted to my longtime colleagues, Regents' Professor Robert S. Maxwell and Professor Robert D. Baker, for much of the unattributed material in this chapter. Their *Sawdust Empire* (College Station: Texas A&M University Press, 1983), while specifically concerning the lumbermen's harvest of the Texas pine and hardwood region, provided a vantage point from which to view the rest of the South.

1. Albert E. Cowdrey, *This Land, This South* (Lexington: The University

Press of Kentucky, 1983), 103. As one migrating lumberman touring the South put it, "The woods are full of Michigan men bent on the same errand as myself" (p. 112).

2. J. M. Collier, *The First Fifty Years of the Southern Pine Association* (New Orleans: Southern Pine Association, 1965), 26.

3. Collier, *The First Fifty Years,* 19, 21.

4. Thomas D. Clark, *The Greening of the South* (Lexington: The University Press of Kentucky, 1984), 4. Clark put it this way: "No doubt the loblolly pine was God's atonement to the South for the southerners' wanton abuse of their land and natural resources. Like the mule, the scrawny striped sinewy steer, the razor-back hog, the goat, and the hound dog, the loblolly pine was capable of raising its head afresh, no matter how harshly abused. The tree can restore itself and even thrive on man's wasted acres" (p. 4).

5. Lumber production for the Southern Appalachians peaked between 1880 and 1890. In 1900, the South's production of lumber amounted to 32 percent of the total U.S. harvest. The Lake States cut in that year was 25 percent of the total. The South's zenith, when the mills cut 16 billion board feet, was 1909.

6. Thomas R. Cox, Robert S. Maxwell, Phillip D. Thomas, and Joseph J. Malone, *This Well-wooded Land* (Lincoln: University of Nebraska Press, 1985).

7. B. L. Pierce, *A History of Chicago,* vol. 3 (Chicago: University of Chicago Press, 1957), 96.

8. Ibid., 102.

9. W. W. Ashe, *Forest Fires: Their Destructive Work, Causes and Prevention* (Raleigh: North Carolina Geological Survey Bulletin 7, 1895), 37.

10. "A Look at the Past," *American Lumberman* (Jan. 18, 1908) quoted in L. C. Walker, *Axes, Oxen, and Men* (Diboll, Tex.: Free Press, 1975), 3.

11. Lyle McCann, *Early Days and Early Ways* (Kalkaska, Mich.: Lyle McCann, 1972).

12. W. G. Robbins, *American Forestry* (Lincoln: University of Nebraska Press, 1985), 22, 31, 38, 39, 62.

13. I. F. Eldredge, *The Four Forests and the Future of the South* (Washington: The Charles Lathrop Pack Forestry Foundation, 1947).

14. This was the theme of a speech by Dr. Schenck I heard in 1952 or 1953 at the New York State College of Forestry at Syracuse University.

15. Robert S. Maxwell and Robert D. Baker, *Sawdust Empire* (College Station: Texas A&M University Press, 1983), 35–38, 46.

16. Walker, *Axes, Oxen, and Men.*

17. Ibid., 37.

18. L. C. Walker, "Caton Carter," *Texas Forestry* 27, no. 6 (June 1986):8.

19. Nostalgia buffs should see Michael Koch, *The Shay Locomotive* (Denver: World Press, 1971). The last Shay, built in 1945 in Lima, Ohio, made a grand total of 2,770 used throughout the world.

20. T. G. Tilford, "Out of My Mind," *Daily Sentinel,* Nacogdoches, Tex., 18 May 1980, 9B.

21. Ibid.

22. Ibid.

23. Ruth Allen, *East Texas Lumber Workers* (Austin: University of Texas Press, 1961), 140.

24. L. C. Walker, "Hursey, First Industry Forester in Texas (an Oral History)," *Texas Forestry* 22, no. 4 (April 1981):12.

25. Many of the photographs are included in L. C. Walker, *Axes, Oxen, and Men* (Diboll: Free Press, 1975), 1.

26. "A Look at the Past," quoted in Walker, *Axes, Oxen, and Men*.

27. Ibid., p. 17.

28. Walker, *Axes, Oxen, and Men*, 19.

29. T. N. Tranton, *Lumber Company Store Tokens* (Ellensburg, Washington: T. N. Tranton, 1978), ix, x.

30. Allen, *East Texas Lumber Workers*, 147–149.

31. L. C. Walker, "Prud'homme Tells of Early Days (an Oral History)," *Texas Forestry* 25, no. 3 (March 1984):9.

32. Walker, "Hursey", 9; Donald Davis, "Logging Canals: A Distinct Pattern of the Swamp Landscape of South Louisiana," *Forest and People* 25 (1975):14; and Ervin Mancil, "Pullboat Logging," *Journal of Forest History* 24, no. 3 (1980):135–141.

33. Amy Bean, "The Great Swamp Timber Harvest," *Georgia Forestry* (December 1986):5–7.

34. T. C. Croker, Jr., "Longleaf Pine," *Journal of Forest History* 63, no. 1 (1979).

35. Ibid.

36. "A Look at the Past," quoted in Walker, *Axes, Oxen, and Men*, 9.

37. Cox et al., *This Well-wooded Land*.

38. Allen, *East Texas Lumber Workers*, 128–132, 142–143.

39. The South Carolina Fibre Company in 1884 produced kraft paper from pine using a sulphate process (Clark, *Greening of the South*, 52). The first sawmill west of the Allegheny Mountains was operating in 1825 near Parkersburg, West Virginia (then Virginia) (Cowdrey, *This Land*, 91). A hardwood flooring machine for tongue-and-groove production, mostly of maple, was in use by about 1880 (Cox et al., *This Well-wooded Land*). The first furniture factory in High Point, North Carolina, began operation in 1888. Ten years later the National Hardwood Lumber Association was formed.

40. C. Van Duyne and W. L. Byers, "Soil Survey of Harrison County, Texas," in *Field Operations of the Bureau of Soils, 1912* (Washington, D.C.: Government Printing Office, 1915).

41. And to trees funny things did happen, as people with unusual ideas expressed themselves. An oak in the city of Athens, Georgia, was made, by a judge's pronouncement, the owner of itself and the land on which it grew. To this day the deed to the land on which the tree stands remains inviolate. Even eminent domain is precluded: a public road divides to go around the tree.

42. Clark, *Greening of the South*, 60.

43. Cowdrey, *This Land*, 136.

44. Clark, *Greening of the South*, 62.

45. Ibid.

46. Ashe, *Forest Fires.*

47. Clark, *Greening of the South,* 49.

48. J. Witherspoon, *Southern Lumberman* (15 December 1948), and L. C. Walker, "The Nation's Oldest Forest Plantation," *Journal of Forestry* 62, no. 4 (1964):269. While this historic forest, with trees spaced at twenty-by-twenty feet, was probably established from wildlings without distinguishing between the species, seeds may have been collected and seedlings grown in a hothouse on the property, as such a facility did exist. Some loblolly pines occur naturally in the area in a small virgin tract about three hundred yards from the plantation. But shortleaf pine is notably scarce, and most of the coniferous virgin timber on these Fall Line Sandhills was longleaf pine. The fine sandy soil, the upper three inches of which is a gray layer, contains about 5 percent organic matter. No evidence of a plow sole exists, though the site was almost certainly cultivated prior to the planting of these trees, three-fourths of which were loblolly pine. Diameters averaged eighteen inches for loblolly pine and seventeen inches for shortleaf pine in 1962. Heights for both species were about the same: eighty-five feet. Basal area approximated 120 square feet per acre. Site index—if I might use a term technically reserved for pure natural stands—was about 75 for loblolly pine and 66 for shortleaf pine. There is neither pine reproduction nor rough, the grassy ground cover of a longleaf pine forest; however, a dense understory of Carolina cherry, sometimes called cherry laurel, had encroached during the thirty years prior to the 1962 tally. Before that time, goats and hogs grazed the woodlot. Fire probably never has been an important influence.

49. F. E. Abernethy, ed., *Tales from the Big Thicket* (Austin: University of Texas Press, 1966), 136. Bear seasons are again scheduled in some southern states.

50. Ibid.

51. C. A. Schenck, *Birth of Forestry in America* (Santa Cruz, Ca.: Forest History Society, 1974), 31. See Schenck, too, for seldom-noted references to Pinchot's Calvinist persuasion. As a member of the Society of St. Andrew, the forester was to lead at least one person to Christ each year. "Of all my friends," Schenck wrote long after he and Pinchot had professionally disagreed publicly, "Gifford Pinchot was the most religious and the most abstinent" (p. 31). Schenck also recalls Pinchot's sabbath preaching to mountain people "in the humble substitutes for churches in Pisgah Forest" (p. 31).

52. This Sunday color comic strip I well recall, but I am unable to document it.

53. Clark, *Greening of the South,* 30.

54. Special trains carried potential land buyers from the North for public land sales in the South. Over two-thirds of such sales 1881–1882 were to northern lumbermen. In that year, 5.5 million acres of public domain land were sold in five states of the region (Cowdrey, *This Land,* 112).

55. Maxwell and Baker, *Sawdust Empire,* 208.

4. The Boat Builders' Forest

1. T. D. Clark, "Ships to Nowhere: The Southern Yellow Pine Fleet of World War I," *Journal of Forest History* 30, no. 1 (1986):4–16. The United States entered World War I in April 1917.

2. Francis P. Porcher, *Resources of the Southern Forest* (1863; reprinted, New York: Arno Press and the New York Times, 1970).

3. J. J. Malone, *Pine Trees and Politics* (Seattle: University of Washington Press, 1964), 34–35; Gerry Reed, "Saving the Naval Stores Industry," *Journal of Forest History* 26, no. 4 (1982):168–175; and John Lord Sheffield, *Observations on the Commerce of the American States with Europe and the West Indies: Including the Several Articles of Import and Export* (London: Robert Bell, 1784; Chicago: Library Resources, 1970, microfiche).

4. Thomas R. Cox, Robert S. Maxwell, Phillip D. Thomas, and Joseph J. Malone, *This Well-wooded Land* (Lincoln: University of Nebraska Press, 1985), 45.

5. Quoted in G. M. Herndon, "Forest Products of Colonial Georgia," *Journal of Forest History* 23, no. 3 (1979):134.

6. Thomas D. Clark, *The Greening of the South* (Lexington: The University Press of Kentucky, 1984), 21.

7. P. Perry, "Naval Stores," in *Encyclopedia of American Forest and Conservation History* (New York: Macmillan, 1983), 475.

8. Clark, *Greening of the South*, 22.

9. Virginia Steel Wood, *Live Oaking* (Boston: Northeastern University Press, 1981), 9, 25, 54.

10. L. C. Walker, *Trees* (Englewood Cliffs, N.J.: Prentice-Hall, 1984), 252.

11. Quoted in Wood, *Live Oaking*, 108.

12. J. A. Lawson, *New Voyage to North Carolina, 1709* (London: J. Knapton, 1708–1710) cited in Wood, *Live Oaking*, 10.

13. Wood, *Live Oaking*, 28, 47.

14. Whether animals assisted in pit sawing is speculative.

15. Wood, *Live Oaking*, 10.

16. Ibid., 35. See also Albert E. Cowdrey, *This Land, This South* (Lexington: The University Press of Kentucky, 1983), 90.

17. Acquisition of these islands set a precedent that would be useful when conservationists a century later lobbied for the purchase of lands for national forests.

18. Cowdrey, *This Land*, 90.

19. Sheffield, *Observations;* Thomas Barrow, *Trade and Empire: The British Customs Service in Colonial North America, 1660–1775* (Cambridge: Harvard University Press, 1967); and James Shepherd and Gary Walton, *Shipping, Maritime Trade, and the Economic Development of Colonial North America* (Cambridge: University Press, 1972).

20. C. F. Carrol, "Shipbuilding," in *Encyclopedia of American Forest and Conservation History* (New York: Macmillan, 1983), 602–603.

21. Clark, "Ships to Nowhere," 5.

22. Carrol, "Shipbuilding," 602.

23. Robert S. Maxwell and Robert D. Baker, *Sawdust Empire* (College Station: Texas A&M University Press, 1983), 187.

24. Clark, "Ships to Nowhere," 6–7.

25. Ibid.

26. Ibid., 12.

27. Ibid., 13.

28. Ibid.

29. Maxwell and Baker, *Sawdust Empire*, 192–193.

30. Ibid., 184.

31. Carrol, "Shipbuilding," 14. However, Maxwell and Baker, in *Sawdust Empire*, say Mrs. Wilson suggested the ship's name and Nina Cullinan, the daughter of a Texas industrialist, christened the vessel (p. 193).

32. Maxwell and Baker, *Sawdust Empire*, 193.

33. Carrol, "Shipbuilding," 602–603.

5. The Foresters' Forest

1. H. H. Barrows, J. V. Phillips, and J. E. Brantley, *Agricultural Drainage in Georgia* (Atlanta: Geological Survey of Georgia, Bulletin 32, 1917).

2. Editorial, *Life* (ca. 1948), p. 34.

3. Henry Clepper, *Crusade for Conservation* (Washington, D.C.: American Forestry Association, 1975), 24. Clepper notes that the House Committee on the Judiciary declared the federal government without power to acquire land within a state solely for forest reserves, but under its constitutional power over navigation might purchase forests, provided such lands conserve and improve river navigation. The Weeks bill, first proposed in 1908, was opposed by western interests. The measure also "was stubbornly opposed by a clique of old-fashioned states' righters" in the South (p. 24). The law set a precedent for the Southern Forest Fire Compact of 1956, a congressionally approved interstate covenant permitting fire fighters and machinery to aid in fire suppression beyond the boundaries of the residents' states. Because water was a concern, the U.S. Geological Survey teamed with the U.S. Forest Service in choosing lands for national forests.

4. L. C. Walker, "Forest Influences," in *Encyclopedia of American Forest and Conservation History*, ed. R. C. Davis (New York: Macmillan, 1983), 216. Marsh Hall at Syracuse University's College of Forestry and Environmental Science was named in honor of the ambassador.

5. Roy White, "Austin Cary, the Father of Southern Forestry," *Forest History* 5, no. 1 (1961):3, 4.

6. Robert S. Maxwell and Robert S. Baker, *Sawdust Empire* (College Station: Texas A&M University Press, 1983), 65–66.

7. Thomas Croker, *Longleaf Pine: A History of Man and a Forest* (Atlanta, Ga.: U.S. Department of Agriculture Forest Service, Report R8-FR7, 1987).

8. L. C. Walker, "An Oral History with Andy Anderson," *Texas Forestry* 26,

no. 2 (1985):10. Clepper in *Crusade for Conservation* includes the report that Ellen Call Long, a Floridian and a leader of the Southern Forestry Congress (which united with the American Forestry Association in 1888), recognized the value of early burning of longleaf pine woodlands to avoid takeover by deciduous species (p. 13).

9. L. C. Walker, "Oral History Interview with Joe McPherson," *Texas Forestry* 24, no. 4 (1983):6.

10. L. C. Walker, "Hursey, First Industry Forester in Texas," *Texas Forestry* 22, no. 4 (April 1981):8.

11. Stephen J. Pyne, *Fire in America: A Cultural History of Wildland and Rural Fire* (Princeton, N.J.: Princeton University Press, 1982), 158.

12. Walker, "Andy Anderson," 12.

13. George Vitas, "Forest Conservation in the Bible," *Southern Lumberman* (15 December 1948).

14. Rev. 22:2. The Authorized (King James) Version italicizes words that are implied.

15. L. C. Walker, "Andy Anderson Remembers," *Texas Forestry* 26, no. 4 (1985):12.

16. Croker, *Longleaf Pine.*

17. Possibly apocryphal, though presented as true, the story is told that Professor Chapman named the natural hybrid *Pinus taeda* × *P. palustris* in honor of Sonderegger. After so much professional recrimination between the two, Chapman, when asked why he so honored his long-time adversary, is said to have responded, "A hybrid is a bastard, is it not?"

18. L. C. Walker, "Don Young: First Ranger on Davy Crockett National Forest," *Texas Forestry* 23, no. 5 (June 1982):8. Young was unable to recall Red Jared's given name.

19. Herbert L. Stoddard, Sr., *Memoirs of a Naturalist.* (Norman: University of Oklahoma Press, 1969). *The Bobwhite Quail* was published in 1931. As Stoddard described the situation, "Young foresters fresh from school . . . poured into the region, arguing and pleading with the natives [to cease burning the woods]. To the natives, the new arrivals were as beings from another world. Chaos and bitterness were the inevitable results" (p. 245).

20. Walker, "Hursey," 8, 9.

21. L. C. Walker, "W. E. Merrem," *Texas Forestry* 24, no. 9 (1983):6. Reviewers of this chapter have been appalled that the South's early foresters allowed the woods to be logged so little differently from the ways of the migrating lumbermen.

22. Walker, "Hursey," 22.

23. Walker, "Don Young," 9.

24. Henry Clepper, *Professional Forestry in the United States* (Baltimore: Johns Hopkins Press, 1971), 235, 244.

25. Elwood R. Maunder, *Voices from the South* (Santa Cruz, Ca.: Forest History Society, 1977), 233.

26. Ibid.

27. Clepper, *Professional Forestry*, 35. See also Carl Alwin Schenck, *The Birth of Forestry in America* (Santa Cruz, Ca.: Forest History Society, 1974), 224, and S. T. Dana and E. W. Johnson, *Forestry Education in America* (Washington, D.C.: Society of American Foresters, 1963). Accrediting agencies had not yet been formed. For instance, Pennsylvania's Department of Forests and Waters controlled its Forest Academy, awarding bachelor degrees to its graduates.

28. Clepper, *Professional Forestry*, 238, 242. The Yale class of 1912 reported on conditions on the Crossett Forest.

29. L. C. Walker, "Foresters: How Many and What Kind," *Society of American Foresters Gulf States Section Newsletter*, 18, no. 2 (1976): 6.

30. L. C. Walker, "Technical/Professional Bugaboo," *Journal of Forestry* 69, no. 12 (1971):865.

31. Walker, "Andy Anderson Remembers," 12.

32. Oral communication (1981, 1982) with the industrialist, whom I prefer not to identify, and another who confirmed the story.

33. Walker, "Don Young," 7.

34. Ibid., 7, 8.

35. See William E. Shands and Robert G. Healy, *The Lands Nobody Wanted* (Washington, D.C.: Conservation Foundation, 1977) for the transition from timber production to recreational use of national forests.

36. Walker, "Hursey," 9.

37. "Charles Holmes Herty and the Birth of the Southern Newsprint Industry, 1927–1940," *Journal of Forest History* 21, no. 2 (April 1977):79.

38. Until 1937, the Emergency Conservation Work Corps (ECWC) did much of the work later assigned the CCC, which was created by statute in 1937. ECWC, unlike CCC, was not permitted to work on private lands. Both organizations enrolled rural and urban youths. Those from Washington, D.C., I recall, were assigned to Roosevelt Camp 1, located at old Civil War battlefields in Virginia's George Washington National Forest. Because the South had little public land until the national forests were created in the mid-1930s, the work of the Corps was at first greatly limited. By 1940, 342,000 men worked out of 424 camps in the South. See Clark, *Greening of the South*, 80–81.

39. Maunder, *Voices from the South*, 64.

40. Walker, "Andy Anderson Remembers," 12.

41. "Thirty Years Ago in East Texas Forestry," *Texas Forestry* (August 1972).

42. Walker, "Hursey," 9.

43. Clepper. *Crusade for Conservation*, 58, 59. Chief Watts was forced to soft-pedal regulation during the Second World War by a verbal understanding with the War Production Board. The board had contracts with the Forest Service that provided funds for the maintenance of much of the bureau. The board, tied closely with industry, let the chief know the contracts would be terminated if service people continued espousing regulation. Acting Chief Clapp, who followed Watts, perhaps never appointed chief over this issue, had written that the federal government should be authorized to enforce regulatory law, withholding aid provided to the states under Weeks and Clarke-McNary laws if necessary.

44. A. G. T. Moore, *Opportunities for Foresters in the Southern Lumber Industry* (Durham, N.C.: Duke University School of Forestry, Lecture no. 1, 1941), 15.

45. American Pulpwood Association, *Fifty Years of Service to the Pulpwood Industry*, condensed ver., (Washington, D.C.: American Pulpwood Association, 1984), 18.

46. All of the examples in this section are my personal experiences as a forestry school dean at the time. Discussions with other school heads indicated these attitudes were not limited to the school over which I presided. Reader, please note I am here serving as a reporter of the scene and not as defender of the attitudes expressed by many of my contemporaries.

47. Ralph Waldo Emerson, "Waldeinsamkeit" in *Selections from Ralph Waldo Emerson,* ed. Stephen E. Whicher (Boston: Houghton Mifflin, 1960), 454–455.

48. C. S. Lewis, *The Abolition of Man* (New York: Macmillan, 1975), 44.

49. Christopher Derrick, *The Delicate Creation* (Old Greenwich, Conn.: Devin-Adair, 1972), 14. For a fuller discussion of this subject, see my article, "Resource Managers and the Environmental Ethic" in the *Journal of the American Scientific Affiliation* 36, no. 2 (1986):96–102.

50. L. C. Walker, "Trees—for Business or Pleasure?" *American Forests* 73, no. 3 (1967):16, 58. In 1991, legislation was introduced in Congress to enlarge the preserve, partly by trading industry land for national forest, thereby reducing national forest multiple-use land acreage while enlarging a single-use set aside.

51. Stoddard, *Memoirs of a Naturalist,* 253. Stoddard also found quail nests destroyed by imported fire ants.

52. Ibid., 38–40. Stoddard observed three ivory-billed woodpeckers in the Southeast between 1954 and 1969, when he was "confident that the ivory-bill still has a chance to survive" (p. 282). A pair of ivory-bills was sighted by A. A. Allen, a Cornell University ornithologist, in northern Florida in 1924. Stoddard searched the Texas Neches River area in 1967 but failed to find the birds.

53. Ibid., 39–40.

54. Walker, "Hursey," 8.

55. Page in author's files; edition unknown.

56. The roles of politics, liability insurance, economics, regulation, and medicine in the environmental conflict that led to the cancellation of the use of "T" (trichlorophenoxyacetic acid) in any technique in forestry—even when injected in trees—but permitted its use in food-producing rice fields and pastures would make a fascinating story. During the thirty years of use of 2,4,5-T in forestry and utility rights-of-way maintenance in the South, I know of no serious undocumented or documented allegation of its danger to human health. With its withdrawal from the market, southern forest managers lost an inexpensive and useful tool.

57. L. C. Walker and R. Hicks, "America's Forest: An Energy Enterprise" in *Agriculture and Energy,* ed. by W. Lockertz (New York: Academic Press, 1977), 523–525.

58. Walker, "Andy Anderson Remembers," 13.

59. R. West, "The Petrified Forest," *Texas Monthly* (April 1978):106.

6. The Next Generation's Forest

1. A. Kirkland, "The Rise and Fall of Multiple-use Forest Management," *New Zealand Forestry* 33, no. 1 (1987):9–12.

2. Francis A. Hunt, "We Asked for It, or Did We?" *American Forests* 92, no. 10 (November–December 1986):20; L. W. Hill, "Policy Update," *Journal of Forestry* 89, no. 5 (1991):6.

3. Hunt, "We Asked for It, or Did We?" 21.

4. Ibid., 63.

5. Wildlife managers classify coastal wetlands into fourteen categories. Only coastal swamps, inland swamps, bottomland hardwoods, and other forested riparian wetlands influence and are influenced by forestry.

6. The interest alone on the federal debt totals almost $200 billion annually.

7. S. G. Boyce, E. C. Burkhardt, R. C. Kellison, and D. H. Van Lear, "Silviculture: The Next Thirty Years," *Journal of Forestry* 84, no. 6 (1986):46.

8. The reader will recall that "timber famine" has been a cry periodically heard throughout the land since the 1870s. Some claim that it was a ficticious complaint, serving to build better budgets for government forestry agencies. Others say the alerts prompted better management, the development of substitutes for wood, and more frugal wood consumption.

9. Donald Taylor, "Developing Competitive Industrial Forestry Programs," *Texas Forester* (October 1986).

10. Ibid.

11. Boyce et al., "Silviculture: The Next Thirty Years," 41.

12. Ibid., 46.

13. See David A. Tillman, *Wood as an Energy Resource* (New York: Academic Press, 1978) and C. L. Brown, "Forests as Energy Sources in the Year 2000: What Man Can Imagine, Man Can Do," *Journal of Forestry* 74, no. 1 (1976):7–12.

14. T. B. Reed and R. M. Lerner, *Science* 182 (1973):1299–1304.

15. R. L. McAlpine, C. K. Brown, A. M. Herrick, H. E. Ruark, "Silage Sycamore," *Forest Farmer* 36, no. 1 (1967):6–7.

16. R. R. Hicks, Jr., D. W. Jones, and R. C. Wendling, "Specific Gravity Variations of Young River Birch Trees," *Wood Science* 7 (1974):169–172.

17. L. C. Walker and R. R. Hicks, Jr., "America's Forests: An Energy Enterprise," in *Agriculture and Energy* (New York: Academic Press, 1977), 532–533.

18. W. R. Kaiser, *Texas Lignite: Near Surface and Deep Basin Resources*, Report of Investigations 79 (Austin: Bureau of Economic Geology, The University of Texas at Austin, 1974).

19. M. V. Bilan, "Growth of Loblolly Pine (*Pinus taeda* L.) on Lignite-mined and Undisturbed Land in Harrison County, East Texas," in *Proceedings: Reforestation of Disturbed Sites* (College Station: Texas Agricultural Extension Service, Texas A&M University, 1980).

20. Texas Industrial Commission, *Texas Giants: The New Breed* (Austin: Texas Industrial Commission, 1971). The quotation is attributed to Arthur Temple, Jr.

21. Boyce et al., "Silviculture: The Next Thirty Years," 44.

22. U.S. Forest Service, *An Analysis of the Timber Situation in the United States, 1952–2030,* Resource Report 23 (Washington, D.C.: U.S. Department of Agriculture Forest Service, 1982). A rule of thumb is that it requires one acre of forestland for each one ton of pulp produced by a mill, assuming the land is producing 1.5 cords per year and that 1.5 cords of wood produce one ton of pulp. (See R. J. Slinn, "The Impact of Industry Restructuring on Fiber Procurement," *Journal of Forestry* 87, no. 2 (1988):17–20. See, too, W. S. Bromley, "The Making of Forest Policy in Pulp and Paper Trade Associations, 1878–1986," *Journal of Forest History* 30, no. 4 (1986):192–196.

23. Neil Sampson, "At Issue," *American Forests* 92, nos. 11–12 (1986):10. Variance in the amount of forested lands of the South depends on the year the survey was made, the definition of forestland by the analysts, and the zone considered the South. The U.S. Forest Service includes Delaware, Maryland, and Kentucky in its Northeastern Region, though the forests are more typically those of the South.

24. News Note, *Journal of Forestry* 85, no. 5 (1987):9.

25. Boyce et al., "Silviculture: The Next Thirty Years."

26. H. A. Knight, "The Pine Decline," *Journal of Forestry* 85, no. 1 (1987): 25–28.

27. Roger Dennington, a U.S. Forest Service forester working in the regional forester's office in Atlanta, disagreed with this premise in a letter (12 March 1987), arguing that the internal rate of return is increased when initial investments are reduced, even if yield is also reduced.

28. S. E. McDonald and S. L. Krugman, "Worldwide Planting of Southern Pines," *Journal of Forestry* 84, no. 6 (1986):21–24.

29. Anonymous, "Pot Plot in National Forests," *American Forests* 92, no. 11 (November–December 1986):31.

30. Some writers include natural stands following the second complete cutting of a tract as the third forest.

31. Sampson, "At Issue."

32. Ibid.

33. U.S. Department of Agriculture Forest Service, *The South's Fourth Forest: Alternatives for the Future,* Resource Report 24 (Washington, D.C.: Government Printing Office, 1988.)

34. *Texas Forestry* (April 1987).

35. Cited by Thomas B. Wood in the *Journal of Forestry* 85, no. 6 (1987):15. The article originally appeared in Georgia's *Coffee County Progress* 26 January 1928. Italics are mine.

36. T. D. Clark. *The Greening of the South* (Lexington: The University Press of Kentucky, 1984), 139. A rule of thumb relating the wood-using industry to the South's economy reads like this: It takes a million dollars' worth of paper mill construction and land purchases to create a single job.

Afterword

1. See E. O. Wilson's *Biophilia* (Boston: Harvard University Press, 1984) for a thorough discussion of the subject.

2. My "Ecologic Concepts in Forest Management," *Journal of the American Scientific Affiliation* 32, no. 4 (1980):207–214, and "Resource Managers and the Environmental Ethic," *Journal of the American Scientific Affiliation* 38, no. 2 (1986):96–102, elaborate on the themes of this Afterword.

3. J. D. Hughes, *Ecology in Ancient Civilizations* (Albuquerque: New Mexico University Press, 1975), 96.

4. Loren Wilkinson, ed., *Earthkeeping* (Grand Rapids, Mich.: William B. Eerdmans, 1980), 131–132.

5. C. S. Lewis, *The Abolition of Man* (London: Geoffrey Bles, 1962), 47.

Index